Roger Baldwin

Roger Baldwin

☆ *Founder of the* ☆
American Civil Liberties Union

A PORTRAIT BY

PEGGY LAMSON

ILLUSTRATED WITH PHOTOGRAPHS

HOUGHTON MIFFLIN COMPANY BOSTON

1976

The author is grateful for permission to quote from the Roger Nash Baldwin Papers at the Firestone Library, Princeton University; from the Madeleine Doty papers in the Sophia Smith Collection at Smith College; and from The Reminiscences of Roger Baldwin, The Oral History Collection of Columbia University, copyright, 1972, by the Trustees of Columbia University in the City of New York.

Library of Congress Cataloging in Publication Data

Lamson, Peggy.
  Roger Baldwin, founder of the American Civil Liberties Union.

  Includes index.
  1. American Civil Liberties Union—History. 2. Civil rights—United States—History. 3. Baldwin, Roger Nash, 1884–
JC599.U5L28   323.4'092'4 [B]   76-25100
ISBN 0-395-24761-6

Printed in the United States of America

V 10 9 8 7 6 5 4 3 2 1

Acknowledgments

I ACKNOWLEDGE with gratitude the many persons who generously shared with me their thoughts and views of Roger Baldwin. Primarily I thank his family, in particular his brother Robert and his daughter Helen Mannoni, as well as his stepsons, Roger and Carl Baldwin, his brother Herbert and his sister Deborah Thomas.

Others who worked closely at one time or another with Roger and whose reminiscences were extremely helpful are Alan Reitman, Edward J. Ennis, Lucille B. Milner, Corliss Lamont, Osmond K. Fraenkel, Walter Gellhorn, Morris Ernst, Herman F. Reissig and Ida Netzer.

William J. Butler and Jane H. Butler, Margaret James, John L. Saltonstall, Jr., Robert Reinhart and Marjorie M. Bitker contributed valuable impressions.

I should like to thank Wanda Randall, Mardel Pacheco and Alexander Clark for their kindness in making the hours I spent at the Firestone Library in Princeton pleasant and fruitful, and for their untiring and cheerful responses to my many requests.

I owe a special debt of gratitude to my daughter-in-law Gay Lamson and to my friend Catherine A. Johnson, who has once again undertaken to lead me cheerfully through the morass of problems involved in preparing the index; in this endeavor I have also been greatly assisted by Barbara N. Parker.

Carol Hulsizer has, with her intelligence and experience, contributed immeasurably to the final product by reading and vastly improving each chapter as it came fresh and flawed off the typewriter.

My editor and friend Daphne A. Ehrlich has been warmly supportive and, by her own enthusiasm for this project, has been immensely encouraging to me.

Although I have run out of ways of adequately thanking my husband, Roy Lamson, I am grateful that he has not run out of ways of sustaining my efforts by his thoughtful and understanding counsel.

And finally my thanks must go to my subject not just for the obvious reason that without him this book would not be possible, but also because working with Roger Baldwin personally has been for me a refreshing, informative and memorable experience.

Preface

On a sparkling day in May of 1974 Roger Baldwin came from New York to Cambridge, Massachusetts, to begin the interviews that constitute the major part of this book.

Although he had not lived in the Boston area since he left it sixty-eight years earlier to take his first job in St. Louis, he was still, in a sense, coming home. Through all the ninety eventful years of his life Roger has remained exactly what he has always been — a proper Bostonian.

Put him, as he has indeed been put, behind bars in a New Jersey prison, in a Pennsylvania steel mill, in a dacha outside Moscow or an industrial farm in the Caucasus; put him in Geneva at the League of Nations, in New York at the United Nations; put him in London, Paris, Rome, Vienna; in Japan with General MacArthur, in St. Louis with Emma Goldman, in India with Jawaharlal Nehru; put him in mid-town Manhattan presiding over the destinies of the American Civil Liberties Union, or in New Jersey canoeing on the Ramapo River — still he emerges unmistakably and ever a Boston Brahmin.

His craggy narrow face with its sharp patrician features, his piercing eyes, his slightly weatherbeaten look, his hurried purposeful gait are all pure Yankee.

So too are his clothes — although if there were a singular of that word it would be more appropriate — which bespeak the shabby gentility that is a mark of the man.

When I picked him up at Harvard Square, he was wearing his one suit, a serviceable, shapeless nondescript gray-worsted with three buttons all buttoned, a brown fedora (in relatively good condition) and carrying a properly battered briefcase.

Since he was planning to spend two or three days in town visiting

his relatives — his brothers Bob and Herbert, his sister Deborah —
I inquired if that was all he had in the way of luggage.

Certainly that was all, he said. He had a clean shirt and his shav-
ing kit in the briefcase and what else could he possibly need.

No coat? I asked, for we had been having a typically damp New
England spring.

"No, it has rained enough," he said firmly, his tone suggesting that
God should kindly take notice.

When we arrived at my house he took off his hat and, indulging in
his one known vanity, immediately began combing his hair, carefully
arranging longish brown strands to cover his otherwise bald head.

As I watched him I remembered that about twenty-five years ago,
one of the first times I had ever met Roger, I had been swimming on
his beach on Martha's Vineyard — a beach once famous for its nude
bathers. But on this particular occasion, as I recall it, suits were
being worn. Or maybe they weren't. The only picture that sticks
in my mind is of Roger Baldwin wearing a brown rubber bathing
cap to protect the hair that protects his bald spot.

Since that distant summer I had often seen Roger casually — almost always on the Vineyard — but not until a few months ago had
we begun to meet to talk seriously of his biography.

The first of these discussions took place in New York on October
30, 1973. The date is significant because a few days earlier the
American Civil Liberties Union had run a full-page ad in the *New
York Times* advocating the impeachment of Richard Nixon. Although Roger no longer played an active role in running the ACLU,
the organization that he started in 1920 is still so closely associated
with him that it seemed natural for openers to commend him on the
ACLU's bold stand on the impeachment. His answer surprised me
as, I was soon to learn, would many of his responses.

"I don't like it," he said. "It's too hysterical."

"What do you mean 'hysterical'?"

"It's an unnecessarily emotional commitment for an organization
that's as legalistic as the ACLU. It's not in keeping with the Union's
way of behaving, which is to go into the courts."

Wasn't impeachment, in a sense, going into court?

In a sense, yes, but not in the ACLU sense. "Oh, I want Nixon
impeached, of course," he said. "But I don't think the grounds for
impeachment are so exclusively civil liberties to justify our taking the

lead. I think you can make a case for the ACLU's participation but not for doing it alone and not for taking full-page ads in the paper. I think we should have joined with other groups like the Bar Association and the Americans for Democratic Action and others who are just as interested as we are. And that's what I told our chairman."

In the months ahead Watergate and the Nixon impeachment were to be a tragicomic backdrop against which we would look at all the other dramas that had occurred during Roger's lifetime; it seemed appropriate that this was almost the first topic to occupy our attention at our first meeting.

We, of course, covered a wide range of subjects in our several preliminary talks, the result being our decision to go ahead with the plan to work on an account of his life. Roger agreed that he would cooperate fully, that he would submit to as many hours of interview as I thought necessary — a lot of hours, I rightly judged — and that he would exercise no veto power over the final product.

From the beginning, however, he insisted on one condition. "Everybody who has ever thought of doing a biography about me has wanted to go into my bedroom," he announced in his clarion voice as we were lunching in a restaurant. "And I don't want anybody in my bedroom."

He was so vociferous about it and repeated the statement so many times that I wondered if he had perhaps in his early or even in his later years been some sort of Bertrand Russell about whom one could not conceivably write a biography that rang true *without* going into the bedroom.

Accordingly I made some discreet inquiries. The results led me to conclude that Roger Baldwin had always had a quite ordinary bedroom, one that he shared — at appropriately spaced intervals — with two wives and, in all probability, with one or two transients. It therefore seemed to me that I could probably manage a reasonably lifelike portrait of the man without invading what he considered a sacrosanct precinct. I agreed to ask no indiscreet questions.

Since a portrait of a living subject is of necessity a joint venture, I was careful always to refer to "our" book. However, I had been warned by others — some with firsthand experience — that no matter what I called it, how I thought of it, or even how I wrote it, the final product would never be anything but Roger's book because no one could write a book about Roger Baldwin except Roger Baldwin.

But for many years he had resisted this opportunity despite incessant requests by publishers.

At the ACLU the reaction to my — our — project was favorable ("long overdue") but skeptical ("well I wish you luck"). Alan Reitman, now associate director and one of the luminaries of the Union, knows Roger well and is devoted to him; he was delighted with the idea of a book about him. But Reitman, who had been hired by Roger shortly before his retirement to be director of public relations, pointed out that he was the *fifteenth* director of public relations that Roger had engaged in *two* years — making the job expectancy under Baldwin less than three months. Why? Because Roger was impossible to work for. He was a frustrated editor; he never thought anything was written the way it should have been. Any time you gave him a piece of copy he would rewrite every word.

But, I wasn't going to give Roger a piece of copy. What I was planning to give him was a finished version of his biography. I have fulfilled that expectation and actually none of the dire predictions have come true.

Not that Roger has been shy about offering his ideas and suggestions, and for the most part I have welcomed them. There is much we have agreed on. From the beginning we were both certain that this was not to be an account of the ACLU, although of course the Union would, and indeed should, loom large. Second, we agreed that the history of Roger's public life, which is also the history of liberal thought during nearly three quarters of a century, should be the focus of this book. We also agreed that since Roger was alive, entirely clear-headed and sharp-witted, and since his memory was prodigious (though selective), his story could and probably should be told in his own words.

Roger did not, as he is sometimes wont to do, play the bashful hero on this score. It was he who suggested one day, "What it should be is my *auto*biography — you writing my autobiography with your commentaries running right along with it. You are the Greek chorus."

Although I have no profound grasp of the function of Greek choruses, I recognized that I would need more than just the on-stage character himself on which to base my "commentaries." Fortunately many talks with family, friends and former associates afforded me valuable insights. And the Roger Baldwin Papers in the Firestone

Library at Princeton University (which also houses acres of un-catalogued ACLU papers) provided a treasure trove of varied and il-luminating documentation of the man. In fact Roger's reaction to what I showed him or told him about his own papers was often as il-luminating as the documents themselves because it was sometimes difficult or even distasteful for him to reconcile the written record with what he remembered of it so many years later. "You know more about me than I know about myself," he kept saying ruefully.

Another aspect of my Greek chorus role, which at first made me uncomfortable, was the necessity it imposed on me to use the first person singular instead of the usual third person behind which writers of biography invariably assume a properly anonymous posi-tion. Accustomed as I was to all the well-known dodges designed to express the author's point of view without seeming to do so ("it is possible to conclude that — ," "some may suspect that — ," "one could mistakenly imagine that — "), I nervously faced the prospect of being out in the open, appearing in the book naked and unpro-tected, simply as the "I" who suspected, thought, doubted, knew or hoped.

But finally listening to Roger on the tapes persuaded me that his own words would do justice to his story better than any distillation of them was likely to do. And if he was going to talk on these pages, I would have to be there too to talk with him.

Inevitably as file drawers filled, as forty hours of taped interviews were transcribed and hundreds of questions were asked and an-swered, the moment arrived when a beginning had to be made.

When Roger called up from New York one day, I told him I thought I was about ready to start writing. I must have sounded as unconvincing as I felt, for promptly in the mail came "Memo to Peggy Lamson (with apologies)."

"What is the biography about?" it began briskly. "A 'Mr. Civil Liberties,' or a 'Mr. Universal Rights,' or a sort of Don Quixote look-ing for utopia?"

Bold words, I thought, except *he* doesn't have to write that open-ing paragraph.

"I would think," the memo continued, "that the material should be handled as entertainingly as possible, emphasizing the sense of ad-venture, the contradictions and the memorable events. After all, the drama of these whole sixty or seventy years has been so extraordinary. I couldn't have picked a better time to be born or a more dramatic time to live in the world."

I glanced at the rest of the memo — detailed, specific, even including suggested chapter titles. But (with apologies to Roger Baldwin) I have disregarded most of it.

His memo had, after all, set me on the right track. The beginning would have to be the beginning of those extraordinary years and the extraordinary way in which he chose to live them.

Contents

Illustrations
(following page 144)

Roger Baldwin at two.
The Baldwin children.
Roger Baldwin in St. Louis.
Adopted sons, Toto and Oral.
Emma Goldman.
Madeleine Doty.
Roger at the time of the founding of the ACLU.
Norman Thomas and Roger Baldwin.
Roger at an ACLU meeting.
Clarence Darrow and William Jennings Bryan at the "Monkey Trial."
Bartolomeo Vanzetti and Nicola Sacco arriving at the courthouse.
Morris Ernst and Arthur Garfield Hays, long-time counsels for the ACLU.
During the United Front days. Roger Baldwin with Herman Reissig and
    Evan Thomas, brother of Norman.
Roger with Evelyn Preston, shortly after their marriage.
Daughter Helen, Roger and Evelyn at Windy Gates, Martha's Vineyard.
Elizabeth Gurley Flynn.
General Douglas MacArthur.
Patrick Malin, new director of the ACLU, with Dr. John Haynes Holmes
    and Roger at the occasion of his retirement.
Bill Mauldin's tribute to Roger at the time of his retirement.
Roger in his beloved canoe.
Roger and René Cassin at the United Nations Human Rights Commission.
Roger and Nehru at the United Nations.
Roger at eighty-five.

Roger Baldwin

(1)

Very Respectable Heresy

THE TALL, GABLED VICTORIAN FRAME HOUSE still stands at the top of a hill on Maugus Avenue in Wellesley, the house where Roger Nash Baldwin was born on January 21, 1884. He was the first of six children of Lucy Cushing Nash and Frank Fenno Baldwin.

His parents, who were both born in Boston, had been neighbors in the city's then fashionable Union Park. Since each came of a large family — his mother was one of six, his father of nine — Roger recalls an endless succession of grandparents, aunts, uncles and cousins all over the Boston area.

The lines on both sides of his family go back to the Pilgrim fathers and to what Roger refers to as "the inescapable *Mayflower*." Possibly the Nashes, whose antecedents came from Scituate and around the South Shore, were a notch above the Baldwins. But in any case, neither parent was inclined toward stuffiness or social snobbery concerning background, and their attitude is reflected in Roger's complacent: "If I was conscious of the 'better people' it was only to know that I was one of them."

Frank Fenno Baldwin was a prosperous leather merchant who owned several manufacturing companies. In fact all Roger's forebears were "engaged in commerce and industry" with one exception. His grandfather, William H. Baldwin, who had started out in the conventional way as a dry goods merchant, gave up his business at the age of forty-two to devote his entire energies to the work of the Boston Young Men's Christian Union of which he had just been chosen president. This organization was founded in September of 1851 as the Biblical Literature Society. Three months later the Young Men's Christian *Association* was formed in Boston; from the beginning the YMCA frowned on Unitarians and excluded them from positions of responsibility and from many privileges. In protest, the Biblical Literature Society changed its name to the Young Men's Christian *Union* to emphasize the fact that they offered a union, free of any restrictions, to *all* religious denominations. As the moving force of this liberal organization William Henry Baldwin was welcomed into the fold of distinguished nonconformist Brahmins.

Not that the other relatives — those in commerce — were conformists. On the contrary they were all Unitarians, and Unitarianism after all was heresy. Very respectable heresy of course, Boston in those days being a place where dissent in any form was respectable. "We Unitarians knew we were very advanced people and that the other churches were backward," Roger told me matter-of-factly. "They believed things we Unitarians knew were not so. But" (with a little grin) "we were very tolerant. We never said so."

Roger's three sisters and two brothers were all born in the same spacious Wellesley house. "It was really country on our hill," he recalls. "Above us was a five-acre pasture and a pine forest where the crows nested. Below us was the barn with a kitchen garden and chicken yard. My father liked to farm; he had pigs, sheep, cows and horses on what must have been about fifteen acres in all. And he kept a coachman, a gardener, a cook, parlormaid, nurse, laundress and I don't know what else. I think there were seven or eight in help. Those were the surroundings we children grew up in."

Wanting for nothing, young Roger took full advantage of his privileged life. He had his pets — his rabbits, guinea pigs, pigeons, his dog, his aquarium filled with fish that he had netted from the ponds around the house. By the time he was twelve, his best friend Laurence Gross had interested him in birds; soon he became an enthusiastic bird watcher. "At first I scoffed at the idea of chasing around after birds with a pair of glasses, but I soon caught the infection. It was a good game full of speculation and excitement, and a good adventure, taking me far afield into surprising places I never would have gone otherwise."

In fact his first publication, at the age of sixteen, was *Bird and Flower Record,* a calendar listing the spring arrival times of birds such as bitterns, warblers, wood thrushes, and song sparrows and of the flowering times of plants such as holly, anemone, arbutus, and lupin, with a blank space to fill in when and where they were seen.

Once he became a birder Roger promptly gave up one of his "regrettable early errors" — removing birds' eggs from nests — a practice which he says is now happily banned by law. "But I had the collection bug strongly," he says, "for eggs, minerals, pressed flowers — anything I could get my hands on."

At the same time that he was gratifying a love of nature and the outdoors that he was never to lose, Roger was reaching out eagerly for the many cultural stimulations that the city of Boston — just twelve miles away — offered him. In his early teens he started going regularly to the Boston Symphony Friday afternoon concerts, and each year when the Metropolitan Opera came to Boston he went to every performance he could, hearing all the luminaries — Melba, Schumann-Heink, Calve, Emma Eames, Caruso. From his mother he had inherited a gift for the piano and at ten he began studying. His lessons "took"; he became and remains a better than average pianist.

In the Wellesley public schools he was always a good student, but reluctantly admits that in high school, "others were smarter — at any rate two of them were." Roger was third in his class of twenty-five. He recalls his reading as "varied and serious, mostly the classics, history and biography."

He also liked to draw and paint and especially enjoyed doing water colors of the wildflower preserve he had established around the Maugus Avenue house. For a year, while he was still in Wellesley High School, he went into Boston in the afternoons to attend classes at the School of Design in the Museum of Fine Arts.

However, despite his many and successfully realized interests, Roger was notably weak in the one area that habitually makes for youthful heroes. On the playing fields of Wellesley he was less than a star. "As an athlete I was a failure," he admits. Not only was he poorly coordinated but he was entirely noncompetitive. He hated any sort of physical struggle, never fought with other boys, and neither punched nor was punched.

His brother Bob, who is eleven years younger and who regards Roger with warm but amused affection, recalls that one year Roger was persuaded by his high-school classmates to at least come out and try for the football squad. Reluctantly he complied, taking his place warily in the line. At the first scrimmage he found himself, not in possession of the ball, but somehow at the bottom of a large pileup.

"Please get up," he asked his teammates politely. "You're hurting me."

Still, not all sports involve physical contact (although most involve adversaries). Roger played tennis, it is said by some who have seen him, as if he were catching butterflies. Perhaps he was basically so noncompetitive because he wanted to be the whole show himself, unhampered by any opponent. Alone in a canoe, for example, he has always been superb.

But for whatever reason, his lack of prowess in sports, coupled with his interest in music, art and nature, did set him slightly apart. He had his friends, boys and girls, he joined in the social life of the town, but he knew that he was regarded as "different" and that made him seek, very early in his life, unconventional, nonconformist avenues of expression.

He did not have far to look. "There was a reflection of Concord in our town," Roger has said in his Columbia Oral History. "I was aware of Emerson, Thoreau and the Alcotts about as soon as I was aware of any intellectual figures. They were household names."

Referring to this remark, I asked him whether that meant he had read Emerson and Thoreau as a young boy. "No," he answered. "When I said that in the Oral History I meant their *influence* came to me through the people in my own town and through my relatives. Now in the *Boston Transcript* for instance, which I, like all proper Bostonians, read daily, there was a column that appeared a couple of times a week written by the so-called Clerk of the Woods, who was a man in our town named Bradford Torrey. He had edited Thoreau's journals and was his literary executor. He was an old man, as old as my father and rather shy, but I used to take my bird identification problems to him and he would talk to me about Thoreau. I guess I was in my teens when I made my first trip to Walden Pond; the cabin site was marked by a pile of stones. I was intrigued by the idea of living alone by a pond, growing your own food and isolating yourself from society. It took me years to appreciate Thoreau's philosophy and wit, but from the beginning I knew he was a critic of everything around him. I liked him and kind of thought I belonged in his world."

I mentioned that someone had pointed out that while Thoreau made nature his vocation and civil liberties his hobby, Roger had simply reversed the process.

"Well, I couldn't go off and live by myself — even for a hobby. I mean I'm not that much of an individualist." Chuckling, he added, "Of course everything I heard about Thoreau wasn't so kind. I had an uncle — a great-uncle I guess — who lived in Lexington and who had known him. He called him 'that loafer.' And then James Russell Lowell said once that that man out on Walden Pond spent most of his time in Mrs. Emerson's kitchen, which was true. He was Emerson's hired man."

"Did anyone in your family know Emerson?"

"Yes. My aunts out in Lexington knew him and my mother heard him lecture once when his mind was failing and his daughter had to prompt him. Of course I was impressed by that too. He was a great name."

Suspecting that we would be talking about these New England literary giants, I had looked up the word "transcendentalism," and found it to mean, "a philosophy emphasizing the intuitive and spiritual over the empirical," which stressed the doctrine of individualism and self-reliance.

"Does the notion of instinctual self-reliance also apply to you?" I asked Roger.

"Yes, that part of it does, but Mr. Emerson, who after all was the chief transcendentalist around here, really looked upon it as a sort of justification for his own brand of heresy. He left the Congregational Church with its acceptance of the divinity of Jesus and all that sort of thing. And I think transcendentalism was for him a kind of substitute for revealed religion."

"Off the top of your head," I asked, "would you give me a definition of revealed religion?"

"It's something you accept because you believe that somebody had a very close contact with the Deity. Moses revealed religion with the Ten Commandments. And Jesus was supposed to have had some connection with headquarters. God gave his only son to redeem us for our sins. And it's possible that the Mormons who got their religion out of some brass plate left on a mountain by Mr. Smith — it's possible they had some tie-in too with God. Anyway they said they had."

"Don't they all *say* they have?"

"That's it, sure they do. That's how they get followers. Otherwise it wouldn't be revealed, I guess."

"But you and Mr. Emerson and Mr. Thoreau and most of the people who influenced you when you were growing up didn't believe in Jesus as the son of God sent to redeem you?"

"Oh, no, of course not, although there was quite a lot more of Jesus in the Unitarianism of my time than there is today. So I got to revere Jesus, not as a divine figure but for what he said. And I still think it's a great doctrine — impossible doctrine, but I think it's great stuff."

I told him that when his brother Bob had taken me out to Wellesley to see the Maugus Avenue house, he had pointed out the Unitarian Church — or rather where the Unitarian Church had been — just down at the bottom of the hill. "Did you go regularly?" I asked now.

"Oh, yes, I did. Very regularly. I helped teach Sunday school and I even listened to the preacher. In fact, as I look back I would say that social work began in my mind in the Unitarian Church when I was ten or twelve years old and I started to do things that I thought would help other people. You know, you absorbed an atmosphere in Boston when I was growing up. It influenced you without your knowing it. Around me it was an accepted assumption that you had to help the underdog — that you had a moral obligation to help the people on the bottom."

"The white man's burden?"

"No," he said tentatively. "No — . Well, yes maybe. There's a bit of white man's burden in all social work. You know there's a slight flavor of doing good — *your* way."

"Did you have a minister who encouraged you or did you think up ways of doing good — your way — all by yourself?"

"Well, I'll tell you. My grandmother's pastor was Dr. Edward Everett Hale, a gentleman who was distinguished in Boston annals. I knew him toward the end of his life. He had started a society called Lend a Hand to help people who couldn't help themselves, and a group of us children banded together at our Unitarian Church to join the Lend a Hand Society there. I took it all quite seriously."

"How about your brothers and sisters? Did they absorb the same assumptions you did about helping the underdog?"

"No, it's very strange. They didn't. I don't know why none of this rubbed off on them at all. Same church, same community, but they didn't get it."

"And your parents? Did they influence you?"

"Well, my mother was extraordinarily tolerant about all these things. She didn't push me. She didn't say, 'Now, my son, you ought to do so and so.' But she never objected. And she was very approving. The fundamental difference is whether you believe in change or you don't. And my mother believed in change."

"And your father?"

"Well, 'believe' would be a strong word for him, but my father did *accept* change. My brothers were satisfied with things the way they were, and my sisters took for granted what they found. None of them challenged. They didn't question. I was the only one that questioned things."

"Except, of course, your grandfather Baldwin. With his Young Men's Christian Union he must have been an influence."

"Oh, yes, of course," Roger said, sounding not quite convinced. He thought perhaps that unconsciously he was imitating grandfather Baldwin, yet he didn't remember that they had ever talked about social service as a way of life. His grandfather was not an intellectual, he was not a college graduate, he was not even always grammatical. But if Roger, as he admits, was not particularly impressed with him as a person, he was impressed with all the people his grandfather knew: Phillips Brooks, Thomas Wentworth Higginson, Edward Everett Hale, and William Ellery Channing, whose home on Mt. Vernon Street William H. Baldwin occupied for many years. Roger also liked to walk around the streets of Boston with the old gentleman because all his "constituents" from the Young Men's Christian Union knew him and were very respectful in greeting him. "I remember feeling that, well, this is quite a prominent person, this grandfather. And then I was very proud of him."

On the other hand Roger reacts very positively to the example set by his uncle, William H. Baldwin, Jr., the only one of his grandfather's six sons to merit the title of reformer. Although he was by vocation a capitalist — he was president of the Long Island Railroad — he was director of the National Child Labor Committee, chairman of the New York Committee of Fourteen, which dealt with prostitution, a staunch Democrat in a solid family phalanx of Republicans, and a trustee of the Negro Tuskegee College.

In the latter capacity he brought Tuskegee's president, Booker T. Washington, and his family to Wellesley to have dinner with his brother Frank and his family. The event made an indelible impression on Roger, but its significance seems to have become blown somewhat out of proportion over the years. Roger tends to refer rather airily to the social tolerance of his parents who entertained Negroes and Jews at dinner. He makes it sound like an ordinary occurrence when the evidence seems to be that the Negroes were represented almost exclusively by Mr. Washington and his family, and the Jews by an occasional business acquaintance of Frank Baldwin's. This is not to say that Roger's parents would not have been glad to have other Negroes and Jews in the Maugus Avenue house. But like so many upper-middle-class suburban families, they didn't know any to invite. In Wellesley, as Roger points out, "we didn't have any colored and we didn't have any Jewish."

The fact is underscored by one of Roger's early recollections. When he was in kindergarten a Negro was brought one day to visit the class. Since he was such an oddity, the children were warned not to stare and not to show too much surprise at his color. The gentleman spoke to the little ones for a few minutes and then asked if they had any questions. Up piped Roger, "Are you black all over?"

What they did have in Wellesley was a lot of Irish Catholics. And for all the tolerance of those enlightened Unitarians surrounding him, Roger concedes that they were just a trifle condescending toward Catholics. "Catholics were not really regarded as being quite as good as us," he says ruefully. This distinction was brought home to him very poignantly on one occasion.

"When I was in high school I had a sweetheart named Anastasia Kilmain. I loved Anastasia Kilmain, but she was Irish Catholic and my family said, 'Now Roger, I wouldn't ask a girl like that to come to the house to your birthday party.' "

"So you didn't ask her?"

"I was discouraged from doing so and I didn't, no."

"Did you understand why?"

"Yes, I think I understood." He spoke sardonically. "After all, it really wasn't quite the thing — the servants went to Catholic Church. But I've always had this little sentimental recollection about Anastasia Kilmain."

"Was she the only Irish Catholic girl you ever had?"

"No, there was another. Quite a few years later there was another — more serious. Much more serious. But all through college — well, I didn't have many girlfriends in college but the ones I had were all quite respectable — my social equals. Very, very proper."

Wondering if this was one of the places where I'd have to be careful not to "go into his bedroom," I asked rather tentatively, "Shall we talk about that other Catholic girl now?"

"We can," he answered agreeably. "Her name was Ann Drew. Or we can wait until we get to my St. Louis days."

"She was from St. Louis?"

"Yes, she was," he said, taking on a slightly faraway look. Then abruptly he added, "But right now I think we might talk a little about the older women in my life."

"Were there many of them?"

"Yes, there were. Let the psychiatrists figure out why. But out of all of them as far as influence goes, my Aunt Ruth — she was my Uncle Will's wife — was the most important one."

Ruth Standish Bowles came by her liberal viewpoint more naturally than did her husband, William H. Baldwin, Jr. She was the daughter of Samuel Bowles, who was the editor of the *Springfield Republican,* always a more progressive newspaper than many of its more stodgy Boston competitors. After her husband's death (at the age of forty-one), Ruth Baldwin, although already an invalid, devoted herself to public causes, supporting many pioneer labor movements, and serving on numerous boards of experimental, innovative agencies. She was a founder of the National Urban League, a trustee of Smith College, and a member of the Socialist party.

Says Roger, "My almost saintly Aunt Ruth was an endless source of comfort and inspiration to me. She was wise, selfless, and sensitive. She shared my radicalism, but in her own more respectable way."

Later she would also share his pacifism, although on that score she once wrote him, "I may not agree with you in every detail and thought, but I know I applaud your spirit. It is great, Roger, and I thank God there is another Baldwin ahead of his time."

Charlotte M. Ryman, variously referred to as Ma Ryman or Grossmutter, was another of Roger's "older women." They had met in 1897 at the Sea View Inn in North Scituate where both the Baldwins and the Rymans were spending part of the summer. Mrs. Ryman had a husband and two daughters (both older than Roger) but no son, which perhaps explains the tremendous fuss she made over the thirteen-year-old boy.

Soon after they separated at the end of the summer, a fervid correspondence began between the doting forty-nine-year-old Grossmutter in Wilkes Barre, Pennsylvania, and the romantic "Ritterino" in Wellesley Hills. Parts of this correspondence, largely the early portions of it between 1898 and 1900, are preserved. Roger emerges from his letters as a precocious, lively, alert, often pretentious (and sometimes downright silly) adolescent, but nonetheless appealing.

Salutations by both correspondents tended to be in Italian or German or, on Roger's side, a mixture of both ("Mein carissima," or "Mia Liberissima kleine tante"). His letters were peppered with unnecessary quotation marks and endless sallies into French (often misspelled). He complained of the lined note paper on which he was writing — "Est si disgustin" — adding, "I write *lots* of things in French when I mean English." And again, on December 21, 1898, "The Symphony this week was le plus excellent de tous les symphonies dans cet an. That's in French not to 'show off' — honestly now — but because English can't express it."

Occasional touches of a youthful snobbery, hardly consonant with the Roger Baldwin image, crept into his letters. In response, for instance, to the possibility that Mrs. Ryman's "dotter" (*sic* both spelling and quotation marks) Roselys might go to Wellesley College, Roger responded that "although it may not be the best in the world in the social line, I guess she'll get her share of the social if I am here."

To "Mia Donna — Mia Zia — Mia Carissima" he wrote from the Sea View Inn where they had met two years earlier, "The people here are very interesting, but they aren't the very best, I imagine. There is a little Jewish girl from New York who is 'perfectly killing.' She says her father is a German Jew but she is only the *German* percent!"

And in an otherwise very amusing letter describing his boat trip from Norfolk to Boston, he referred not once, but twice, to the "niggers who lounged about" and "the niggers who accosted me to carry my bags." (When I pointed this usage out to Roger recently he said, "Impossible! I must have put the word in quotes." But no. With all the "awfullys," the "galores," "ship shapes" and the "cold shoulders," this word that should have been in quotes — if it had to be there at all — was not.)

A different and more engaging boy described his surprise birthday party ("most completely overwhelming"), his fine lark exploring Boston with Laurence Gross ("I showed him some of 'our' good points"), his dancing class ("a gay affair, lots of scholars, lots of fun"), and his excitement over a winning Harvard football team ("we 'well nigh' burst").

A touching youth responded to a lugubrious letter from Mrs. Ryman written six months after her husband's death in which she spoke with envy of those who had "finished the fight . . . Who can see the look of blessed peace that always comes to the faces of the dead and not find that they are enviable and certainly have the best of it . . . Do you laugh at this mood?"

Roger did not. "That unfortunate letter cut me as much as it could . . . I am just beginning a little life and I don't like to think when I am so young that anyone wants to get out of this beautiful place."

In August 1899, when he was fifteen years old, he wrote one of his most thoughtful and least affected letters (it began simply "Dearest Grosmamma"). "I think I have grown more — mentally — in the last six months than ever before . . . I can see much further into things. It seems I can't think enough. I always used to wonder what good it was to have this life unless one were going to become a President or a Prince or other noted 'bug.' But I think it is all clear now. Now with all this 'thinking' I don't want to get 'grown up' yet . . . I don't want to be a dignified person — I find the true way to fun is to let oneself go and be free . . . It just came upon me last week that I had grown tall, but when I think of some things as I used to see them, it makes me laugh. I cried one night because I couldn't see what I was ever made for, and how far 'space' went and such things. I can't say that the extent of space is at all clear, but what's the use of thinking of it — it never stops. Those days of thinking's crying have gone. I laugh over the cry."

Finally, just before his sixteenth birthday, he wrote Mrs. Ryman a letter which, as it turned out, was not very prophetic. "Sometimes I wonder if I will ever do anything in the world. There isn't a thing a boy could meddle in very much except athletics that I haven't tried. Music, drawing, swimming, driving, writing essays for fun and a thousand and one things. And in every one I have begun with a most earnest spirit and in almost every one I have attained practically nothing. I feel disgusted with myself . . . I can't keep at any one thing. It means certain failure if I keep on. I can become editor of some Yellow Journal perhaps — there's enough variety there, if that's what I need. Perhaps I'm too young to judge myself . . . only I don't like the beginning."

Unprophetic yes, but still there was a grain of truth in his early introspections and doubts. In his later years Roger would refer on many occasions to the "unclassified occupation" that marked his whole public life.

Later we would talk about a different friendship with yet another of his older women. I again commented on how many such relationships he had had.

"Yes, I had a good many. Very affectionate they were, but sexless." He grinned. "And you know the Freudian implications of all that." I nodded knowingly, but could only speculate.

To be sure, homosexuality came to mind, but there is no evidence to support that particular Freudian implication. Nor is it the only, or even a probable explanation, given Roger's relations with his parents. The most plausible thesis seems to be that Roger never "related" to his bombastic, domineering father and because he had a fear of being like him, he was strongly drawn to his tender, yielding mother. Thus, since he was reluctant to give up the rewarding mother-son affinity, he may have sought other mother figures to reinforce that relationship.

Interestingly enough, the women to whom he was sexually attracted were quite the reverse of his mother; both his wives were dominant, self-willed and staunchly independent. Neither, for example, took his name.

Roger's own words about his parents, who were separated just about the time he finished college, are quite revealing.

"My mother was gentle and nonresistant; she was so little assertive that she seemed almost self-effacing, especially in comparison to my father. It was supposed to have been a Nash trait to be so bashful and shy, but even if Mother never made much of a fuss, she usually got what she wanted. She didn't influence me directly by advice or guidance but by what she was herself. She liked good music, good solid books — no trash around our house — and good talk about things that mattered. I never saw her angry or bitter or hardly ever irritated, the way Father often was."

I asked, "Were you children afraid of your father?"

"Well, he was certainly more formidable than mother. But he was kind and considerate to us and I think all of his children respected and admired him. He had a very positive manner about everything and he was not shy about expressing his opinion on men and events. It wasn't profitable to contradict him either. You'd get the same answer all over again."

"Did he have a sense of humor?"

"Yes, he always enjoyed a good laugh but not at himself. Once I gave him Clarence Day's *Life with Father* to read. I was a little afraid he would see a picture of himself in it and resent it. But not at all. When I asked him how he liked it, he slapped his knee and said, 'By God, that's just like your grandfather.'"

It occurs to me that if Roger's daughter Helen were to hand him a book about a cheerful, voluble, opinionated egoist, she might wonder if her father would see something of himself in the character. But probably he wouldn't. He too might slap his knee (although he's not really a knee-slapper) and point out that it was certainly a perfect picture of her grandfather.

(2)

Inescapably Boston

"I DON'T SUPPOSE THERE WAS EVER ANY QUESTION about your going to Harvard, was there, Roger?"

"None whatsoever. Harvard was quite inevitable."

"But you liked it just the same?"

"Oh, yes, I was very satisfied with Harvard College. More than satisfied, really — I was very much in love with it; it was an adventure and it was exciting. I was curious about it all; I liked my friends and my roommates."

Roger lived alone his freshman year in Weld Hall in the Harvard Yard. He had a sitting room, a tiny bedroom and no plumbing or heat. The janitor kept up a coal grate fire in winter and brought a pitcher of water daily to his washstand. Much of the space in these somewhat spartan quarters was taken up with Roger's piano, which he carried with him when he moved from the Yard in his sophomore year to team up with his double cousin, Herbert Nash, Jr.,* and live in a private dormitory off of Harvard Square. His dwelling place for his last two years was almost as "inevitable" as Harvard itself for a Boston boy. He and his cousin joined another Brahmin, Francis P. Sears, Jr., and moved to Westmorly Court, the grandest and most exclusive of Harvard's living quarters.

Westmorly Court, which stands unchanged today, is a solid handsome structure of brick and stone, elaborately leaded glass windows and an unmistakable look of Gothic elegance. It has spacious rooms and a swimming pool in the basement (Ann Pennington was reputed to have taken a daring nude plunge there in the twenties); it is in the heart of what was known in Roger's time and for years afterward as

* Nash's mother was Roger's father's sister. Nash's father was Roger's mother's brother.

the Gold Coast — the ultimate in privileged living. Roger, some-what defensively, says that since all the boys — almost all New Eng-landers — he knew moved to the Gold Coast he had no choice but to go along too.

I refrained from pointing out that I had never thought of him as such a sheeplike follower, but said instead that it seemed to me his living arrangements were about as unshakably Boston as he was.

"Yes," he conceded, "it was all quite Bostonian, which made it very secure. But certainly not snobbish. If you're secure you're not a snob."

I said he sounded like a most secure young man.

"I was. I never really felt I had to bow down to anybody. I had no real frustrations or disappointments either in college work or in my social relationships and activities."

A small proportion of Harvard's elite always have belonged to what are known as Final Clubs. Roger, who doubtless would have qualified socially, did not join one of these exclusive groups.

"I suppose I would have joined them if they'd asked me," he ad-mits. "But they probably didn't ask me because I didn't care for their style. They really *were* snobs."

"But still you think you would have joined them if they'd asked you?" (Both his brothers, incidentally, would belong to Final Clubs when they came to Harvard.)

"I don't know what I would have done. I just know what I did do. I got together with a bunch of the more democratically minded fellows and we plebians put up a slate of class officers to run against the club boys — the patricians."

"In other words," I suggested, "if you can't join them, lick them."

Roger did not respond to the bait. "We licked them all right," he said gleefully. "Our candidate for class president was a Kansas farm boy — he had, however, gone to an eastern finishing school, Hotchkiss — and he was elected overwhelmingly. But it was very ironic too, because after college he married one of the Boston pa-tricians."

I wondered if Roger had considered being one of the plebian can-didates himself.

"No, I would have been embarrassed to be asked to be a can-didate. To tell the truth, in spite of the fact that I've been in so many exposed positions in my life, I'm shy about that sort of thing.

I'm much more comfortable behind the scenes than I am on the stage. I guess the reason is that I'm likely to be on the dissenting side whatever the situation is. I don't think I'd feel at home with the majority. My tendency is to look at the minority viewpoint."

"Would you say that Harvard more or less reinforced your non-conformist Unitarian upbringing?"

"Oh, yes, certainly, although none of my teachers were social radicals. I wasn't looking for that kind of heresy when I was in college."

In his Oral History Roger has described his reactions to the eminent professors who flourished in his day.

> My admirations among the Harvard professors were for the independent and odd characters I had learned to admire at home in person or through their writings. Harvard was full of them at the time, but I would know only a few; Santayana, whom I saw only casually and who did not appeal to me; Josiah Royce, who seemed remote; Muensterberg, forbidding and Prussian; George Herbert Palmer, a distant figure of great repute as a teacher; Nathaniel Southgate Shaler, whom I so admired that I took every course he gave in geology, which turned out to be philosophy, history, and social science combined; Charles Townsend Copeland, who brought literature to life and whose tart remarks were common student currency; Barrett Wendell, an earthy gentleman whose sagacious wit enlivened what passed for English literature; and A. Lawrence Lowell, the most forceful lecturer of them all.

A few days after Roger entered the freshman class at Harvard, President McKinley was shot and killed at a Pan American Exposition in Buffalo by a half-crazy (so it is said) anarchist, and on September 14, 1901, Theodore Roosevelt became President of the United States. Roger had been a great T.R. admirer for reasons which would later be alien to his pacifist views. "When I was fourteen years old the Spanish War broke out and I became a patriot at once. I rejoiced in Teddy and his Rough Riders. I went to hear him lecture as soon as the war was over — shortly after anyway — and I was full of hero worship."

When Roosevelt became President, Roger still admired him, but was perhaps more stirred by other dynamic movements that were afoot in the country. At the turn of the century social reform was becoming more and more widespread, covering a far greater range of activities than ever before. Muckraking (the phrase made famous by Lincoln Steffens) laid bare the iniquities of municipal corruption.

Protests over long hours and low wages and attacks on Wall Street had been issues in William Jennings Bryan's 1898 Democratic party campaign for the presidency. "Evils were on trial," says Roger. "And social work was taking form as a profession."

However, Roger had not yet seriously considered it as such. At Harvard he simply continued the Lend-a-Hand, help-the-underdog instincts that by then seemed second nature to him, and gravitated naturally to Phillips Brooks House, which was and is the center for those concerned with helping others. He began going to the teas at Phillips Brooks House and was quickly enlisted in good works, agreeing to take on some classes for working people in the night school of the Cambridge Social Union on Brattle Street, an adult education center run by Harvard professors and staffed by able, motivated Harvard students. Roger started out giving piano lessons one night a week on an ancient square grand, and the other night teaching a hundred and fifty middle-aged men and women (mostly women attracted by the Cambridge Union's ads in the newspapers) what little he knew or was learning as fast as he could about social science.

The following year he was put in charge of recruiting student teachers for the center. "I got a fine bunch of bright boys," he says, "who thought it was a lark. They taught what they had been taught; it was warmed-over Harvard — the gospel once removed. I taught the same way. We teachers also put on a variety show at the Brattle Theatre to make money for the Union and we did too. At the end of my senior year the students and teachers at the Social Union presented me with a handsome set of the works of Herbert Spencer for which I was so grateful that I left it in Cambridge for somebody else to read."

"But even without Herbert Spencer you must have gotten a good deal out of that teaching experience."

"Oh I did, I certainly did. It gave me great satisfaction and I learned a lot that was not included in the Harvard catalogue."

As for what *was* in the Harvard catalogue, the curious young student seems to have taken a little bit of everything — "everything that interested me," he says, "and that was quite a lot. Languages that were of no use, literature, art, history, geology, botany."

"What about social sciences?"

"You know, it's a strange thing, I don't think I had a single course in political or social science as an undergraduate. I did take one in government that A. Lawrence Lowell taught; but, for instance, I should have taken social ethics with Professor Francis Peabody, and I don't know why I didn't. I wonder now how I could have omitted those subjects which obviously interested me then and have since, but I guess it was because no teacher attracted me."

I asked him if he had been a good student in college, although I assumed he probably had been. Yes, he was a good student, he told me. Good enough to have done his undergraduate work in three years and to have taken a master's degree in the fourth year. By that time he had discovered anthropology (which *was* a social science) and he coupled work in that field with a course in philosophy given by the famous Ralph Barton Perry.

In 1905 he received both an A.B. and an M.A. along with an honorary Harvard scholarship given, he says, to students with consistent A's.

"It has been very useful. After all the Harvard label never hurt anybody and the M.A. sounds as if you know something."

I made the expected rejoinder.

"Well, yes, I guess I really did know a little something. But the fact is that I was not then and have never since been an intellectual concerned with thoughts, study or originality."

This time I made no rejoinder; none, I felt, was called for.

"What I was, was an activist."

"What you *are* is an activist."

"Yes, exactly. I've always been a doer."

"But in college you weren't just a do-good doer, were you, Roger?"

"Oh no, certainly not. *Certainly* not. I joined the clubs of my interests, the Musical Society and the Natural History Club, where I found the most congenial friends. I got into the freshman glee club, which was an undistinguished assortment, though the few audiences we had seemed to tolerate it."

"Did you keep up your interest in birds?"

"Yes, of course, always. I joined the Nuttall Ornithological Club and went to their meetings regularly for a couple of years at William Brewster's museum on Brattle Street. In fact I was one of the few student members among mostly elderly professors, but at the time I thought of the Nuttall Club as the very heart of what I recognized as

Harvard culture — restrained, sophisticated and so, so genteel." He gave a mischievous little grin, and then went on. "In our sophomore year I remember there was a great deal of speculation about who was going to be elected to the Institute of 1770, which was an ancient honorary society that took ten groups of ten each year from the sophomore class. It was a sort of mark of social acceptability — the right kind of guy — "

"Which you wanted to be thought of as?"

"I guess I did. But I tell you I just made it by the skin of my teeth. I was the last man in the last group of ten that they picked. Still the Institute was not all honor; it had a clubhouse, very conveniently located with first-rate home luncheons served by an English butler whose wife cooked them. I ate there regularly for two years. Then in my senior year I transferred interests to the Hasty Pudding Club."

"I know about that," I said, "because I looked you up in your yearbook and saw a picture of you dressed as a courtier, or something of the sort, in a Pudding show called — " I groped for the title.

" 'Machiavelli,' " Roger supplied, remembering after seventy years what I had managed to forget in a week. "And I wasn't a courtier, I was a ghost. That was a better than average Pudding show," he continued. "The music for it was written by Leland Hall, who was my closest friend in college. He later became a professor of music and literature at Smith. The Pudding was very important to me, and I still like to go and see the shows. Besides, it was the scene of my graduation spread. In those days you used to give luncheon affairs to which you invited your family and your lady friends."

"Speaking of which — "

"Oh, I had a few. No one special."

"You were certainly very good looking in your class picture."

"Well, yes, maybe. I was nice enough looking, I guess."

Women, from all I have heard, have always tended to chase after Roger; I wondered if this had been true in college. He of course gallantly denied that it had ever been true at all. "I had a social life of sorts," he said. "I went to the Brattle Hall dances for the season — proper affairs they were for the best people, and also I'd go to an occasional ball at the Somerset in Boston, but girls really had nothing to do with life at Harvard. They were for outside. Connections with Radcliffe were not regarded favorably. The girls were not the popular types and they were carefully guarded anyway as vestal virgins."

"Did you talk much about sex with your roommates or other friends?"

"No, as a matter of fact I don't recall that we did." He chuckled. "But I do remember one discussion when our bunch tried to estimate what percentage of our contemporaries were still virgins when they left college."

"And?"

"We figured on almost half. Things are different now, I hear."

I agreed that they were quite different and asked him whether as a student he'd spent much time in Boston or whether he'd stuck pretty close to Cambridge.

Boston was for fun, he said. They would take the trolley (in Cambridge he walked everywhere) in to the theater and maybe stop afterward at the Hotel Touraine for a nightcap. Did he ever take girls out for such an evening? Not often he said. It was too expensive. Since he had mentioned it, this seemed to me as good a time as any to digress and give a little attention to the notorious Roger Baldwin parsimony.

"Were you on an allowance in college?" I asked by way of a lead in.

"Yes, indeed I was. My father gave me a thousand dollars to pay all of my expenses. Room, board, tuition — tuition in those days was a hundred and fifty dollars."

"So really you should have had enough money to spend on frivolities?"

"Well, I suppose I did have enough, but somehow the New England tradition of stretching dollars got into me very early."

"But you didn't come by that honestly did you? I mean I don't have the impression that your father was in the least miserly."

"On the contrary, my father liked to live in style. He even got the title of the Grand Duke among his relatives. I think he enjoyed playing the role of a suburban country squire whom the neighbors looked up to."

"And he was generous to you?"

"Very. For instance when I was about fourteen Father bought a large farm — some four hundred acres — about twenty-five miles away from Wellesley in Hopkinton. At the time I never thought to ask, or even to wonder why he bought it. But when he saw that I enjoyed being out there in the country he built me a camp of my own — a shingled cabin in a pine wood with a stone wall around it and a shingled privy. All during college it was a sort of retreat for me. I took friends there for weekends, riding farm horses over dirt roads, swimming in ponds and cooking the most monstrous dishes over the camp stove."

"But not spending money?"

"No, of course there wasn't anything to spend it on there, but you're right. The fact is I have always been very conscious of *not* spending money. I'll always take a bus or a subway instead of a taxi. I don't want to get the habit of taxis. I shop in basement stores; the stuff is good enough. I never had the taste of expensive things if the cheap stuff would serve the purpose. I look at prices. I read menus from right to left. I'll pay what convention requires but I don't waste money on the superfluous. I enjoy giving money away if it doesn't cost too much. So there's no question about it — I have the vice of frugality."

"Does that annoy people do you think?"

"It either annoys them or makes them laugh at me. People always used to smile because for years I carried in my pocket a little black book to record my cash expenses."

"Every penny of them, I've heard."

"That's right. That was the whole point. I decided to record every penny when I found there were so many expenditures I couldn't account for."

"But Roger — " I began.

He held up his hand. "I know, I know. The fact is I don't approve of my monetary habits either. I think they're inconsistent and a little ridiculous."

I considered that a handsome concession and told him so.

"I rarely think about money, or talk about it," he said, not, it seemed to me, quite truthfully. "When I was growing up there were three subjects we never discussed: age, money and sex. I never knew how old people were — even my mother and father. Birthdays were ageless. Money was too vulgar to be mentioned and sex was certainly not a conversation piece."

It may not have been a conversation piece but Roger's father's activity in that area, although not discussed or, for many years even acknowledged, did lead to a radical disruption of the family. Just after Roger graduated from college, his parents separated.

Frank Baldwin had for a number of years prior to the separation "befriended" a widow — her husband had been killed in a railroad accident — named Mrs. Balch. According to Roger's brother Bob, Frank Baldwin first installed Mrs. Balch in a cottage near the Maugus Avenue house; when he bought the farm in Hopkinton he moved her (and her three children) in there and subsequently lived with her on a more or less permanent basis.

Roger had no knowledge of this liaison, he says, at the time his parents separated. "You wouldn't believe how goddamn innocent I was, I thought my father was just being a good neighbor and taking in a widow lady and her three children, giving her a house up at the farm and helping to support them. I thought this was just so kind of him. But, of course there was more to the relationship than I realized."

Not only was Roger innocent, he also appears to have been somewhat ostrich-like about the relationship between his parents. Although he must have realized that there was discord, he does not seem to have taken in the reality of the family situation.

In part, his haziness about his parents was due to preoccupation, during his senior year at Harvard, with the fast deterioration in health of his favorite Uncle Will, who was dying of cancer at the age of forty-one. Uncle Will's wife, Roger's beloved Aunt Ruth, came to depend very much on Roger during the last months of her husband's illness; he was often with her in Long Island during those agonizing days. (When William Baldwin died, Roger played the organ at his funeral at the Mount Auburn Cemetery in Cambridge. He ended the service with *Fair Harvard*.)

By the time he graduated from college, Roger knew that his father was going to sell the Maugus Avenue house and buy a new one in West Newton. He knew that as he was finishing college two of his sisters were also finishing high school, and that with a change of residence in the offing, a year in Europe for the entire family seemed suitable. He knew his father was not going abroad with them (although Frank Baldwin did join them for a month in Florence) and, if he asked himself why, he told himself it was because his father had to "stay home and pay the bills." He also knew, without question, that as the oldest son, he was in charge of "the whole shebang": his mother, his sisters Margaret, Ruth and Deb, his brothers Herbert and Bobby (who was ten years old), his mother's sister Aunt Emma, and later Aunt Ruth.

Roger's attitude today about his position, at the age of twenty-one, as tour manager and surrogate head of the family is extremely off-hand. To hear him talk about it one would suppose that he was simply another member of a large and rather cumbersome party that spent a year living and traveling in Italy.

Indeed it was not until Bob Baldwin referred on one occasion to "the year that Roger took us to Europe" that I had any idea of just how extensive his responsibilities had been or with what verve and resourcefulness he had carried them out.

"He had to do it, of course," says Bob. "Our sweet gentle mother would not have had the remotest idea how to buy so much as a railway ticket." And even brother Herbert, who is often less than enthusiastic about Roger's activities, admits that he managed the whole year with great style.

They all set sail in the summer of 1905 on the S.S. *Bohemia.* They were barely out of sight of land when Roger gathered the entire clan and most of the other passengers around him on deck and produced a crate of carrier pigeons he had brought on board (along with God knows how many pieces of "hold" luggage and "wanted in state-room" luggage which he had to look after for his "shebang" of eight people). Family and strangers cheered as Roger opened the crate, and the released pigeons, which belonged to some cousins in Welles-ley, circled the boat and then took off on a beeline — presumably back to Wellesley.

After some grand-touring in the British Isles and the Netherlands, the family went to Florence where they expected to spend the win-ter. Roger installed his charges in a *pensione,* while he set off to find a suitable place to establish them permanently.

Fortunately the redoubtable and ever devoted Ma Ryman (Gross-mutter) was living in a villa in Florence with her daughters and a niece (perhaps that was one of the reasons why Roger chose Florence) and with her assistance he soon came upon the Villa I Cedri seven miles up the river Arno at Bagno a Ripoli. Roger was enchanted by the medieval elegance of the forty-room palazzo, by the fact that it had once been occupied by the Duke of Connaught and by the rent of one hundred dollars per month. He leased the place forthwith. The superintendent was Adolfo Bertini,* his wife was the cook; there was also a second cook and five other servants; The Bertinis made wine and olive oil from vineyards and orchards on the villa property.

As soon as Roger got his brood installed he hired a series of tutors to come out and teach his brothers and sisters Italian (he himself picked it up very quickly) and to keep the younger children up on their mathematics and other school subjects. He personally took care of their historical and artistic education. He would pile them all into the *diligentsia* (four-wheel carriage) and take them to galleries, cathedrals, gardens, circuses, theaters and operas. "We had a gorgeous time," says Bob. "Roger really made a lot of things come alive for us. I remember he took us — I think it must have been four nights in a row but maybe it was only two — to see Puccini's *La Bohème*. We really knew that opera and what impressed us the most was that when we got home Roger would sit down at the piano and pick out the tunes."

But the Baldwins' life under Roger's aegis was not entirely devoted to widening cultural horizons. Numerous classmates of Roger's were "bumming around" in Europe at the time and many of them dropped in at the Villa I Cedri to enliven the already spirited household.

Roger himself enjoyed the company of a number of young ladies. Notably, during the fall of 1905, he concentrated his attentions on Mrs. Ryman's niece, Marjorie Rose, with whom he "kept up a romance" until she saw that he was "too young to be serious as a prospect for marriage," so she went home, married her childhood sweetheart and in due course named her first child Roger.

Christmas was an especially gay time. Frank Baldwin came over to join his family for the holidays, and marital discords were temporarily buried. On Christmas Eve, Bob recalls, Roger arranged to have a donkey cart laden with presents drive right into the two-storied living room of the Villa I Cedri while small gifts were distributed to the thirty or so workers who lived on the adjacent lands.

If such a noblesse oblige attitude toward the "peasants" seems more in line with Frank Baldwin's lord of the manor instincts than it does with Roger's empathy with the underdog, it should be pointed out

---

* Fifty-eight years later Roger and his daughter Helen returned to Bagno a Ripoli to find the Villa I Cedri the same but somewhat modernized under a rich man's ownership, and the Bertinis' daughter running a beauty shop in town.

that Roger was not unaware of the plight of the Italian poor. Bob says that he often expressed feelings of compassion for the oppressed, but at that early date did not yet know how to implement his concerns.

Unfortunately Christmas was also the end of the Baldwins' tenancy at Bagno a Ripoli, for by that time the cold and the inadequacies of the heating at the villa drove them out; on January 3, Roger moved the family to Rome and installed them at the Hotel d'Inghilterra.

By chance a diary of Roger's exists for the months from January 1, 1906, until August of that year. Roger found the tattered, unbound pages not long ago in a box of old letters, the only diary of any period of his life that is preserved (actually he says he was not prone to keeping diaries anyway, and only did so at sporadic intervals), and this small bonanza provides a refreshing insight into the young man who became twenty-two on January 21, 1906. "I feel actually now just *one* year *old*," he wrote on that date, "for twenty-one was the culminating year of youth and I now climb the long road to manhood's forty — the next goal post."

The day was not marked, however, by only lofty thoughts. After "heaps" of presents and a birthday cake in his room, Roger and his friend Johnny Montgomery went to the Grand Hotel where they settled down for "a long evening over drinks" with an American Embassy attaché named Santini, a nameless (in the diary) Italian and an American named Porter. Eventually they all went on to some café where they were joined by a "very drunken Princeton grad and a professional lady named Jesus or Jesu." At this point, Roger wrote in his diary, they got a private room and "had a rough house à la Romaine," which ended with Johnny and Roger taking the lady to her door in a cab and "footing the little bill!" The meaning of that last line with its use of the word "little" is obscure; the rest of the entry less so.

After a few weeks in Rome the family all went to Naples, then to Capri, with side trips along the way to Ravello, Sorrento, Pozzuoli (where Roger haggled with the guards about the price charged to ferry his party across the river Styx).

There were times when his burden must have been tedious. "Family plans, family packing, family disagreement, all family," he wrote in disgust on February 28. But for the most part his good spirits, his curiosity and his joie de vivre prevailed.

Early in March, after sending his mother and sisters Margaret and Deb and young Bobby back to Rome, Roger took off with his sister Ruth (a family favorite and probably the most spirited of the three girls) and his brother Herbert for a month-and-a-half tour of the classical antiquities of Sicily and Greece.

The weather was mostly awful, the seas rough, but the three Baldwins were undeterred. Roger read history ("got simply broiling over the Punic Wars and the fate of poor Carthage"), studied and slavishly followed his Baedeker (probably the most celebrated guide books ever written), took lessons in modern Greek, looked up and recorded every strange bird he saw, and complained, in the manner of most well-traveled Americans, about the regrettable habits of American tourists. ("I hate to own them as countrymen.")

The last two days were spent in Olympia and Corfu: In the first, Roger wrote in his diary, the "Hermes of Praxiteles claimed our chief attention. The statue has faults, long nose, strained pose and effeminate muscle treatment, but I think it is about as satisfactory as any naked being that I have yet seen." In Corfu his admiration was equally aroused by a living beauty. "Herb and I walked down to the town well and en route met *the handsomest woman that ever could have been* [italics Roger's]. No exaggeration." So impressive was the vision of this native girl with the jug of water on her head that Roger still remembered her as one of the standouts of the voyage when he wrote about it sixty years later (and before he had found his diary to remind him).

The family was re-united in Florence where they spent another month in a *pensione* (not a "ne plus ultra" one, Roger noted) before sailing for home on May 18, on the S.S. *Romanic*.

Reality faced Roger on his return; no longer could he hide from the disunity between his parents. On May 31, the day they landed in Boston and were met by Frank Baldwin, Roger reported in his diary that his father seemed "nervous, tired and irritable," and a few days later he faced what seemed to him a very dismal future. He wrote, "Mother and I were left alone. I have spent the entire afternoon just thinking and worrying over the family, I haven't been so miserable since Venice * and haven't come as near the tears of despair for many months."

* When I asked him, Roger could not remember at all why he had been so miserable in Venice which is, after all, quite characteristic; he is always likely to forget a dreary time and remember a happy one.

Without question Roger took his mother's side and grew more and more resentful of his father, until ultimately there was a complete rift between them, during which they did not speak to each other at all, lasting four or five years.

"Did you have to take sides?" I asked.

"Oh, yes, I did. My mother depended on her oldest son to sympathize with her. When she lost her husband's love, it broke her up. Of course it never did come to divorce, but it was a permanent separation. But that summer when we got back from Europe and found out what was going on I got real mad at my father and told him what I thought of him and said you're disgraceful and so forth."

Reading his diary it is a little hard to picture Roger being quite so outspoken and disrespectful to his father, although on August 2 (in almost the last entry) he did report: "Went in town to see father, who just returned this A.M. from a week in Maine, and delivered an ultimatum which has cost me hours! There seemed no cause for anxiety, as it appears father understands everything O.K."

The diary indicates, however, that despite family problems, there was much else to occupy the time and thoughts of a handsome, energetic young man: There were dozens of meetings with friends whom he hadn't seen for a year, visits to the farm, lively evenings in Brookline and Cambridge, bird walks, picnics and Harvard Class Day. Surprisingly what there was not, at least during the first weeks of their return from Europe, was any apparent thought on Roger's part about his future profession or means of livelihood.

But finally on June 23 he records, "Learned of a business offer in philanthropic line in St. Louis." Apparently the idea stirred him, for later that same day he "went to the Hotel Bellevue in Boston to see the man about the St. Louis job, but he wasn't in." Two days later, however, he had breakfast with Mr. E. M. Grossman (Harvard 1896) "when the St. Louis project began to look very real and very possible." Afterward "to father's office where I was surprised to find he highly approved. He had met Grossman also. Uncle George was called in for consultation and grew enthusiastic. So I decided to go to St. Louis next Sunday with Grossman and look over the field."

The job in question was really two jobs: first to be director of a neighborhood settlement house, rather grandly called Self Culture Hall (it had been founded by Ethical Culturists); and second to create a department and give the first course in sociology at Washington University.

Roger's recollection is that he was recommended to Mr. Grossman (although his diary makes no mention of this) by Professor Francis Peabody of Harvard whose course in social ethics Roger had *not* taken. How, in that case, did Professor Peabody know about him I wondered?

"Oh I was fairly well known when I was in college. I was often mentioned in *The Crimson* for various activities and I guess also Professor Peabody knew about me from some of my classmates who had taken his course."

At any rate, without ever having studied social ethics, Roger went off to St. Louis to be looked over for the job of teaching it.* His mode of transportation to the Midwest was characteristically Bostonian.

On June 30, after dining at the Hotel Lenox on Exeter Street with his boyhood friend Jack Remick (Harvard 1906), he took a train to Fall River (sixty miles away) and from there caught the night boat to New York. After breakfast at the Waldorf he spent the morning "perusing a new Baedeker of the United States" (presumably boning up on St. Louis), then went to the Harvard Club for lunch and caught the four P.M. train to St. Louis ("a beautifully equipped train . . . we made sixty-five miles steadily").

Roger liked the city right away, and indeed he should have been pleased, for he was received with the utmost cordiality, was wined and dined extensively and, in the course of four days, met all the people of "social conscience who were involved with philanthropic institutions and with civic and educational movements in the city." The setup both at Self Culture Hall and at Washington University struck him as full of possibilities.

Not the least of his satisfactions was a canoe trip upcountry to the Meramec River that Grossman had thoughtfully arranged for Roger, himself and three other men. "That alone could have sold me," Roger notes.

The day after he came back from St. Louis Roger beat a quick path to Cambridge and registered for a Harvard summer school course in sociology, so there seems not the slightest question that he

---

* It will be remembered from his Cambridge Union days that Roger had rather a predilection for teaching subjects he had not himself studied.

returned fully determined to accept the position offered him and was bent only on learning enough sociology during the summer to keep one jump ahead of his prospective students.

Roger's recollections of how and when he made up his mind include an additional fillip not recorded in 1906. He invariably manages to mention that after his return from St. Louis he went to his father's lawyer, Louis Brandeis, to ask for advice as to whether or not he should take the job. Brandeis urged him by all means to go to St. Louis; he needed to get away from Boston where he was too confined by family commitments, and where, in a career of public service, he would be too much his uncle's nephew and his grandfather's grandson.

Brandeis at that time was prominent only locally as a liberal lawyer and especially as a people's advocate against trusts. It seems perfectly natural that Roger, though already resolved to go to St. Louis, should have discussed his future with a man whom he obviously admired. At the time, however, his talk with Brandeis did not seem remarkable enough to be so much as noted in his diary. But through the years, as Louis Brandeis became one of the country's most eminent Supreme Court justices, his advice on that summer's day somehow has, in Roger's mind, become the decisive factor in a young man's decision to go west.

(3)

The Boy Reformer

W HEN R OGER TOOK HIS LEAVE OF B OSTON in the fall of 1906, his sense of relief and release was palpable. Family problems and family connections were behind him; he arrived in St. Louis "full of confidence and ignorance," ready to flex his muscles as an independent.

"What I felt was a certain democratic enlightenment, a tremendous sense of freedom, a feeling that a man was himself. The caste system which I grew up with was entirely absent. You could move from one group to another without any feeling of restriction. It was all very exhilarating. I sailed into both my jobs.

"My hosts in the Ethical Culture Society and Washington University made me feel at home. I lived right in the settlement house which was in the eastern part of the city — that is east of the Mississippi River — which is the way the flat rectangular checkerboard pattern of the city was divided. In fact I lived all my years in St. Louis in the eastern part while most of my friends lived west in the fashionable district. We got around by streetcars in those days. There were few autos and poor roads.

"The neighborhood house was right in a slum district on a dirty unpaved street. The house itself was a converted tenement three stories high with a backyard playground. It was managed by a resident janitor and his wife. The neighborhood was crowded, full of activity and, as I soon learned, of hostilities between Irish Catholics, who were the first comers, and the later-arrived immigrant Poles and Russian Jews."

"And Washington University? Was that anywhere near?"

"Nowhere near. It was six or seven miles west — forty minutes by trolley, standing up on a slope full of Tudor dignity. Actually it was an impressive group of stone buildings mostly left over from the

World's Fair. I taught my course in sociology at the university with a discussion of topical issues. I had a lively bunch of students — Fannie Hurst and Zoë Akins were among them — who became friends. Together we explored the darker sides of city life — red light district, gambling and opium dens, police courts, institutions for feeble-minded and mentally ill poor. It was as new an experience for me as it was for them. I learned as I taught — quite the right way it seems to me."

"What about the lighter side of the city though — I mean what was St. Louis really like when you got there?"

"Well, let me say that if you judge a city by its newspapers, it had a very high and civilized standing because the *Post Dispatch* was a paper that was like the *New York Times;* it was a very cultivated newspaper. And then there were about a half a dozen other papers; there were two papers in German, a weekly in French, and there was also a literary paper called Reedy's *Mirror,* which was edited and written by a fellow named William Marion Reedy who was a friend of all the avant-garde writers in the Middle West — he was sort of spokesman for them. Vachel Lindsay and Sara Teasdale, for instance, were first published in Reedy's *Mirror.* So there was quite an atmosphere, when I went there, of an intellectual elite, a cosmopolitan elite as well. There was this trace of old French influence — you remember that St. Louis was once a French city in the old days of the Louisiana Purchase — 1804 I think it was — and the Catholic Church was very strong. As I've said, to be Catholic in Boston was not to be of the best upper classes, but St. Louis society was very lively and conditioned by Catholic influences."

"French Catholic, that is?"

"Yes, mostly French Catholic. And then in south St. Louis, there was a solid German population."

"Lots of Jews there, weren't there?"

"No, not so many. Of course there were two kinds: the very successful, very wealthy Jews who ran the big businesses and had a Jewish society of their own, with their own Jewish clubs, and then the very poor Jews, the immigrants who had just come over from Europe in 1905 and 1906 when immigration was open in the United States and there were no restrictions. We had a lot of Jews around where I lived at the settlement house. There was always trouble with the Irish boys and the Jewish boys being in battle against each other. The Jewish community center was only about three blocks away from me. We worked together down there."

I was trying to get a grasp of St. Louis and of his first year or so there, knowing that, more than Harvard, which had mostly extended the sights he already had, and Europe, which had been a cultural romp, St. Louis was the time and place of Roger Baldwin's real emergence. Almost everything he was to achieve in his public life stemmed from his initial plunge into those particular waters of reform and I wondered aloud just how soon he had taken his first bold stroke.

He understood exactly what I was getting at. "Well, I didn't do anything notable right away," he said. "I was pretty well committed to the university and the neighborhood house in the beginning and I didn't get very far away from those bases. However, I was quite well aware of what was going on all around me and it wasn't too long before I organized what I called a Social Service Conference, which brought together all the people in social reform to discuss the problems of the town. It had never been done before. It began very small, then it got bigger and bigger. We used to get luncheon audiences of anywhere from fifty to two hundred people."

Watching him as he talked, I thought about how many such organizations Roger had created or revitalized by his own initiative; how many groups of like-minded persons — reformers, idealists, progressives, liberals — he had brought together by the force of his own enthusiasm, energy and vision.

"But perhaps more importantly for my future in St. Louis," Roger was saying, "was the fact that after I had been there just a little over a year I was offered the position of chief probation officer of the juvenile court."

"How on earth did that come about?" I asked, adding that he must have already had his hands full with his jobs at the university and the settlement house.

It was the most natural outgrowth of the settlement house, Roger explained. Any neighborhood house in a slum district swarms with lively youngsters who get into trouble, mostly fighting and stealing, as kids are pretty well bound to do in the streets. Jewish and Irish kids would fight each other, get picked up by the police and Roger would find himself following them to the courts. He was intrigued by what he found there. Special courts for juvenile offenders were still in their infancy. The original juvenile court in Chicago was only two years old and in Denver Judge Ben Lindsey was pioneering to create a public consciousness about the fate of young malefactors. In St. Louis, Judge George H. Williams, a member of the circuit court (he was later a senator from Missouri), had been assigned a six months' tour of duty on the juvenile court to try to deal with the problems of delinquent and neglected children in a faster and more imaginative way.

In due course Judge Williams spotted Roger following his brood into the court, arguing for their rights, pleading for probation instead of detention for them. Forthwith he offered him the job of chief probation officer. "The judge got the okay from his colleagues on my appointment," says Roger, "although I was only twenty-three at the time and innocent of the law. But the politicians thought the job belonged to them because it carried fairly good pay, a staff and quite a lot of authority. So the next year they engineered a bill through the legislature making twenty-five the minimum age for the job of probation officer. But the bill passed in April 1909, which was four months after my twenty-fifth birthday. Fortunately they had not verified the date. But it did hit one of my best assistants and I had to pass the hat — my own included — to pay him until he reached twenty-five."

In response to this political gambit Roger soon proposed to the judges that a civil service system be instituted for parole and protection officers of the juvenile court. It would be the only one in the city at the time. Examiners were appointed; Roger and his staff took the written tests along with quite a few competitors, and naturally, since they knew the answers from experience and the others did not, they easily rated high enough to keep their jobs. "I was learning politics at first hand," Roger says, "and in extremely practical terms."

On-the-job training being rather a specialty of his, Roger was also learning a great deal — and quickly — about how to translate idealistic reforms, in this era when reforms were in the air, into practical realities.

Some of his early innovations in the court were quite straightforward. No longer were the police allowed to grab children off the street, put them in the paddy wagon and haul them into court; first they had to have a summons. Roger and his staff were bent on giving every child brought into court anonymity: Roger himself went to see the editors of every newspaper, urging that the youngsters' names be kept out of the press to avoid giving them bad names in their neighborhoods. The probation officers also managed to get a law passed, aimed at keeping the very young off the street and prohibiting boys of under fourteen from selling newspapers.*

Most important, however, then, as now, was the effort of all juvenile court reformers to keep juveniles out of detention and away from the evils of institutionalized reform schools. It was during those early years, as Roger describes it, that the entire idea of the juvenile court as a *criminal* court gave way to the concept of the court acting in loco parentis.

Under this principle of the state as parent, the burdens of the juvenile courts would ideally be shared by community agencies — schools, churches, recreational and health groups — working to keep the children out of court altogether. Those errant children who did come to the juvenile court, particularly those whose misbehavior stemmed from their deprived environment — and they constituted the largest percentage — were to be cared for by a nonpunitive program of probation of which the keynote was education and friendship.

"Looking back now," I asked, "do you think it was naive to hope that the schools and other institutions would really take up the slack?"

"Kind of naive, yes. It was kind of naive to think that this preventative work would keep children out of court, because there were too many 'bad' boys and girls whom you couldn't reach. Still there were some great successes. The personification of loco parentis was Ben Lindsey. I visited him in the Denver Court and liked all I heard and saw. It was so personal a relationship — personal with the kids, with his staff, with the public, that it could not be duplicated. He did more than any other man to create public sympathy toward erring kids and to elevate the behavior of other judges."

I broke in to quote to Roger from a review he had written in 1931 of Ben Lindsey's book *The Dangerous Life,* an account of his early years on the bench.

I recollect that in my own days in the juvenile court I looked with a critical eye on the Denver Court's haphazard system, on his (Lindsey's)

* There was no federal child labor law at the time.

preponderance of personal influence, his lack of organized probation. But I have come to see — and this book states the case convincingly — that above all method and system rises the power of a personality which understands children, trusts them and fights for them.

"Well of course Ben and I didn't always agree," he said. "I differed with him quite regularly when I would see him in later years on his New York visits and thought some of his projects were a bit off base. He was a pioneer more daring than wise sometimes."

I asked him what he had thought of what must surely have been considered one of Judge Lindsey's more daring projects — his advocacy of trial marriage as expounded in his 1927 book *Companionate Marriage.*

"I think he advocated that as a very genuine recognition of reality," Roger answered succinctly. "Ben was not what people call 'sound,' meaning predictable. Well, I'm not either and I have never wanted to be thought of as dull or unimaginative."

I assured him he had not the slightest worry on that score and went on to ask him how he had first come to know Lindsey. Had he simply gone out to Denver and presented himself at his court?

"Exactly. I went out to Denver and sat in his court. But then I got to know him better when I organized a Probation Officers Association. The movement was developing rapidly and when all of us court officers got together, it turned into the National Probation Association, which is today called the National Council on Crime and Delinquency."

"And you created the first such organization?"

"Well," Roger said off-handedly, "it wasn't such big stuff." Then more naturally, "But it was what might be called a good initiative."

Once the Probation Association became national, Roger's contacts in the juvenile field quickly proliferated. Outstanding among his new acquaintants was Bernard Flexner, an eminent Louisville lawyer, a bachelor, drawn more to the juvenile court system by its compelling legal problems than by any personal relations with the children themselves. His interests in this new area thus complemented Roger's very neatly, and perhaps for this reason, the two men conceived the idea of compiling a handbook of standards and procedures then in practice in various juvenile courts around the country.

The book was based on answers to a detailed questionnaire that was sent to all the activists in the juvenile field, a list that included in addition to Ben Lindsey such well-known judges and leaders as Harvey H. Baker, Julian W. Mack, Homer Folk, Henry S. Hulbert and, interestingly enough, Roger's old childhood acquaintance, Booker T. Washington. (But Washington addressed his answer to "My dear Mr. Baldwin," so perhaps he did not connect Roger, the juvenile court expert, with the young boy he had known in Wellesley.)

The questions that Roger and Bernard Flexner asked were aimed mostly at trying to discover the sort of disposition that the various courts made of a wide range of juvenile offenses. What were considered the most effective treatments for false fire alarm cases, cutting cases (boys using knives), sex offenses — usually involving mature boys with little girls and boys — auto thefts, manslaughter and even murder? In the more serious cases, did one commit to an institution regardless of mitigating social circumstances? Were fines helpful? Was a jury trial for a juvenile ever desirable?

After many months of correspondence between St. Louis and Louisville, Roger and Flexner eventually produced a draft and a few years later the final version of *Juvenile Courts and Probation,* with an introduction signed by Lindsey, Baker, Mack and all the other authorities who had contributed to the work.

"It was a pioneering effort," Roger says, "but actually it was the authoritative book in its field for quite a time. Still, I don't think it was nearly as good as we could have made it, because we weren't writers or authors and we didn't sense the need for more human interest and illustrative materials to back up our commentary. I guess all you can say is that it served its purpose. But it has long ago been superseded by much better books."

At the time that Roger was first appointed probation officer, he realized that even he, with his boundless energy, could not manage three jobs at once. He therefore decided to continue his teaching at the university for another year but to drop his position at Self Culture Hall, move out of the settlement house and give what time he could there on a volunteer basis.

Thus he had to find a place to live and, ever resourceful, he soon joined with a Mrs. Atlanta Heckler, who was the mother of one of his Harvard classmates, a widow, and teacher in a reform school, to lease a house at 3018 Pine Street large enough to take in a number of boys as boarders. They hired a cook, who served the meals and made a pleasant home for the seven or eight young men who lived there.

Roger made such an arrangement because he needed a home, not only for himself but also for a young charge for whom he had become legal guardian — assigned so by the judge in the juvenile court. "His name was Otto Stoltz, but one day he was monkeying around with the typewriter and he turned his name around and got Toto, and Toto he remained."

"How old was he when you took him?"

"I think he was eleven. No, I guess actually when I first got him, which was before I even left the neighborhood house, he was just ten. You see there was a sloppy situation at the juvenile court that Judge Williams was trying to clean up. A number of boys were in the so-called House of Refuge — a reform school — who had just been left there. They were abandoned kids taken in without a court order or record. Among these was a shy silent little boy whose mother, they said, had brought him there some time ago, left him and run out crying. Judge Williams tried to find her but couldn't, so he asked me if I could look after him temporarily at the neighborhood house."

"But temporary became permanent?"

"Yes, but at the time I certainly didn't think it would be because Toto was a silent sullen little boy. He never seemed interested in what was going on around him, and I certainly wasn't going to take on any little boy in such a glum listless state. So I told Judge Williams, but he urged me to hang on just a little longer. It was summer, I remember, and the neighborhood house had a camp — a tent camp — out in the suburbs where some of the kids and their parents could go. I spent a few weekends there with Toto in a tent, and one moonlight night when I was swimming in the pond with a crowd, I looked toward the bank and there was Toto standing waiting for me with a lighted candle in his hand to help me see the path back to the tent. It was his first gesture of friendship and when we got to the tent he sat on my cot and put his arms around me. I knew then that he would not leave and that I had to keep him. I told the judge I would do the best I could."

"But didn't you have misgivings — a bachelor of — how old were you then?"

"Nineteen-o-seven that was. I was twenty-three. Yes, certainly I had misgivings, taking the responsibility for raising a youngster all alone."

"For instance, what did he call you?" In later years Roger's two stepsons, his grandchildren and oftentimes his second wife called him Bunkle and I wondered if this affectionate variation of uncle had begun with Toto, who was but the first, although the most constant, of Roger's adopted boys.

"He always called me Mr. Baldwin," Roger answered. "And I never urged him to change."

"Why not? Wasn't that awfully formal?"

"Yes, it was. And I regret it now. I regret that I didn't make him feel more intimately related. He knew that I was his legal guardian but even so a 'Mr.' relationship seemed appropriate to him I guess. He was very dignified and aloof and withdrawn."

I asked Roger if he thought he had done all he could to bring the boy closer.

"He was always with me. For ten years his home was where I lived. He always sat right beside me at the table — "

I said I meant emotionally closer.

"Yes, I think I could have done more for him that way."

"How?"

"Well, he used to ask me who his parents were. He even ran away when he first came to me to try to find his mother. Of course he was an illegitimate child and his mother had put him away because she didn't want him around. So what I should have done is given him an artificial mother and father."

"How do you mean?"

"I mean I should have made up the names of his parents — fictitious people. It would have satisfied so many instincts in him. Because he wouldn't have always had to write 'parents unknown' when he filled out forms and got his passport and things. And I would have told him the truth. I would have said, 'Now don't tell anybody but for the record, these are your parents.'"

I stared at him wondering if he really thought that such a patently superficial remedy could possible have made up for the emptiness of a little boy who had no one of his own — a void that Roger himself might have filled had he been able to feel something more than pity for Toto and treated him with a warmth more enveloping than simple kindness.

Shortly after Toto was installed, Oral James, also eleven years old, came into Roger's life, also via the juvenile court. He was a very different sort of boy — bright, eager, responsive and his circumstance, while superficially similar to Toto's, varied markedly. Oral was considered a neglected child; he had been put in the House of Refuge to get him away from his foster mother, Mrs. James, who was a dissolute drunk. But Oral liked his foster mother and he kept running away from reform school to go back to her. Roger was finally persuaded to let the boy stay with her when he realized that she was, as he puts it, "a devoted drunk who cared more for motherhood than her other pleasures." Still he kept a close eye on Oral, who had greatly impressed him (as Roger says Oral clearly tried very hard to do) with his apparent desire to learn and to pull himself out of his sordid surroundings.

More and more Oral looked to Roger as a father figure, although there was only twelve years' difference in their ages. "He imitated me in many ways," says Roger with obvious pride. "My friends would refer to him as my carbon copy or as little Roger." And indeed as the years went on, Oral James imitated Roger in more than superficial ways.

Although Oral did not live in Roger's household (nor did Roger actually support him financially) until he was sixteen or seventeen years old, Roger says he handled the two boys as a team. Understandably he was more responsive to the outgoing Oral. "Our relations were closer; we read together and played dominoes evenings as Toto and I did not. A sense of identity had grown up between us. Even my father remarked on it. [By that time Roger and his father were again on speaking terms.] When he visited St. Louis now and again on business, he would invite all three of us out to dinner and he took a shine to Oral, as he did not to my withdrawn Toto."

The house Roger had rented with Mrs. Heckler did not work out financially because in the depression of 1908–1909 most of their young boarders lost their jobs and the project had to be abandoned. So Roger and Toto moved from 3018 Pine Street to what Roger refers to as "a really elegant pension" at 3739 Winsor Place where the company was lively and intellectual. There were about thirty guests. Roger lived there for the rest of his eleven years in St. Louis with a series of roommates, mostly Harvard friends and classmates. ("Joe Plumb, Harvard 1906; Joe White, my class; Clairborne Garrett,

1907; James Hudson, 1908 — " Roger reeled off their names seventy years later as if he'd had lunch with them the day before.)

Despite his parental obligations and the multiplicity of his jobs, his social life was extremely active and varied.

On many an evening he would hurry to his room after dinner, change to black tie — or on some occasions white tie and tails — don his top hat and set off for a debutante party, a dashing, eligible young bachelor, speedily transformed from social reformer to social butterfly. And he loved it.

"It was a crowd that I was thrown into by my background; I liked the parties and I liked the people. Their conversation was very pleasant. It certainly wasn't consistent with anything I was doing. I mean they weren't people who were interested in civic or social reform — they were rich people who had beautiful homes and gave nice dances and I enjoyed it all very much."

I said I was glad to hear about his frivolous side, and since our conversation had veered to the private sector of his life, I suggested that this might be the moment to follow up his earlier reference to Ann Drew, the young Catholic girl who played such an important role in his St. Louis years.

I had noticed that when Roger, in responding to a question, began by calling me by name, it usually presaged an emphatic or a deeply felt sentiment.

"Peggy, I guess I'd have to say that Ann Drew was the real love of my life," he said. "We had an idyllic relationship. No spring was ever so fresh and beautiful as it was when I saw it with her. None has ever been so since."

I waited.

"As you know, most of the women I came close to marrying and the two I did marry were very high-powered and independent. But Ann Drew was just the opposite. She was petite and demure and lovely and graceful. Yet she was not self-effacing. She was one of the officers of the Woman's Trade Union League, and she was active in Catholic public work. She was the daughter of a man of considerable prominence — president of a local bank. They lived in a great big house and she had seven or eight brothers and sisters. Ann was so beautiful and charming that she had men after her all the time, but her family was very strict. When I went to call on her, I had to wear a dinner coat. And a butler in a white coat would meet me at the door and introduce me into the drawing room and she would be there in a long evening gown. That was the way we courted each other. For three or four years we kept company. Some evenings we even read poetry together. I guess we both kind of assumed that we were going to get married sometime, but she insisted — or rather her family did — that I should sign some Catholic pledge about raising the children in the Catholic faith and that we should have a wedding in a Roman Catholic Church with a priest. And I demurred at that. I was very hesitant about it — it kind of troubled me to commit myself to that sort of thing because I didn't believe in it. Meanwhile Ann was being pursued by a fellow that she really didn't love, but because he knew about me and why I was hesitating, he took the vows in the church and became a Catholic convert and presented himself as her suitor and asked her to marry him. At first she refused, but then when I came east to Philadelphia one time to visit some friends I got a telegram saying she was going to marry the other fellow. I called her on the telephone and tried to undo it but it was too late. The other man was so determined to get her to the altar that he had already announced the engagement to the press. And she said she felt caught by it. After she was married she refused for months to live with her husband. Her whole marriage would take a novel to explain."

"But did you continue to see her?"

"Somehow I was involved in all the drama. I saw her on and off up till the day she died. When she first left her husband she came to me in New York, but I was married by then and she was clearly becoming an alcoholic. I got her a room in a hotel up on East 52nd Street. But her husband followed her and begged her to come back and she went back, finally hoping it would help her stop drinking. But it didn't. In the end she had to cure herself. She committed herself to a hospital in St. Louis and took no drink. Then she joined the AA and became a counselor for them, and she cured many people after that. I don't think she ever lived with her husband — I mean as man and wife — again. And then when he was on a business trip to New York, he was found dead in his bed at the Waldorf Astoria. Every time I went to St. Louis after that I saw Ann. She had a stroke when she was seventy or so and had to live in a hospital for the rest of her life. But she was beautiful still and very saintly looking. She was close to eighty when she died, but right to the end she was a delicate understanding spirit. And all our lives, time and again, both of us cherished thoughts of a might-have-been."

Roger's normally booming voice had become very quiet.

"Poor, poor Ann. She was a lovely, lovely person."

As I listened to the end of this moving recital I suddenly thought of a line from Dwight Macdonald's well-written, perceptive, but acerbic profile of Roger in *The New Yorker*.* "Roger Baldwin," he wrote, "is so excessively public a figure that to imagine him having a private life is as difficult as to visualize the interior of Grant's Tomb furnished with scatter rugs, easy chairs and bridge lamps."

"Of course I was also formally engaged to another girl in the St. Louis years," Roger offered, quickly resuming his cheerfully vociferous tone.

"Before or after Ann Drew?"

"Before. Anna Louise Strong came to St. Louis around 1910, I guess it was, to arrange a child welfare exhibit. She was a social worker and a Ph.D.; she was beautiful and she intrigued and fascinated me."

"In other words, one of your standard powerful women."

"Exactly. Masterful — too masterful as it turned out. But we fell in love — there was a strong physical attraction. I told my family we were going to get married; I went to Oregon to meet hers. But pretty soon conflicts developed over my way of life. She was a minister's daughter and very strictly brought up and she expected me to behave myself in accordance with the Protestant raising she'd had. No smoking, no drinking, no card playing. Self-indulgence to her was a sin. I remember my Aunt Belle, the wife of my father's brother Dick who lived in St. Louis, saying to me after she met Anna Louise, 'Roger, do you see that crack on the floor? The line you will be walking on will be narrower than that if you marry her.' "

"So you didn't?"

"No. But in the end it was she, not I, who decided to call it off after tears and entreaties for me to mend my ways."

"Your wicked, wicked ways."

"Of course it was ridiculous. I did smoke about a pack a day of Turkish cigarettes, which I didn't inhale. And I kept a collection of pipes and when sometimes I felt like sitting down and reading a

* July 11, 18, 1953.

book and being calm and philosophical, I liked to have a pipe for consolation. And if they passed cigars after dinner I would take one. In St. Louis I remember I used to have a favorite, a little cigar called a Bok Panatella that I always got at the University Club."

Knowing that he enjoyed a glass or two of sherry but never took anything stronger, I asked him what his drinking habits had been at that time.

"I never liked to drink until I got dizzy. If it would have given me pleasure, I would have drunk more, but it didn't. As soon as I got even a little out of control with my words, then I would stop."

"But still you wouldn't give up these 'vices' for Miss Strong?"

"No, certainly not. The domination would have been complete if I had. I loved her, but I loved my independence more."

I asked what had become of her and Roger said that she went on to be a very prominent radical. She had gone to Moscow, become editor of the English language newspaper there, married a Russian Communist, and after many books, lectures and much international publicity, was finally repudiated by Stalin and left Russia. Then, as Roger puts it, "The Chinese Revolution claimed her to the true faith and she went off to live in Peking where she stayed until she died at the age of eighty-five.

"We saw each other sometimes; she came to a couple of my lectures and I to hers. We never mentioned the days of our endearments, our little passions and our tearful debates on Christian conduct. But I'm sure we never forgot them."

"I wonder, Roger, did you *like* being in love?"

"No, I didn't like it. I hate being possessed and being in love doesn't let you think of anything else. In each case I recovered as fast as I could."

(4)

Guardian of Public Virtue

IT WAS NOT LONG BEFORE ROGER'S REPUTATION as a comer, a young man to watch, began to spread beyond the confines of St. Louis. In 1910, a bare two years after his arrival, he received his first offer of a job elsewhere and by coincidence the elsewhere was Boston. Actually it was not a firm offer but a look-over for the post of chief of the department of public affairs for "Boston 1915," a municipal plan aimed at ridding the city of its widespread corruption by building up a new organization to replace the existing political machine. The plan was conceived by Lincoln Steffens and was to be implemented by him working with a committee headed by Edward A. Filene, the merchant philanthropist and reformer (whose department store still bears his name and is known far and wide for its famous automatic bargain basement). The year 1915 was the target date when this cleansing was to be completed.

Steffens devotes considerable space in his autobiography to "Boston 1915," explaining his basic concept, which was that the leading grafters and other crooked politicians should themselves become leaders of the proposed reform movement. His rationale was that the best men had tried and, all through Boston's history, had failed. Therefore, the good should give way to the strong even if the strong were bad, since the bad were natural leaders who liked hard, challenging jobs and who loved a fight. "Indeed," wrote Steffens, "it was the fighting which might convert these bad men to carry on where good men commonly lay down."

Understandably, the "good men" were shocked at Steffens' proposed method and Roger Baldwin didn't think much of it either. When he came East to consider and be considered for the job, he said he did not hesitate to tell both Filene and Steffens that he thought "Boston 1915" was nothing more than a romantic notion. "I was not impressed by Steffens. He was a public relations man. Just his physical appearance put me off. He had a big flowing necktie and a beard and kind of longish hair, and he looked like an old type of newspaperman, you know, a very careless rumpled-up fellow. Not the kind I wanted to work with. He was an awful glib talker. I'm always scared of glib talkers. They talk more than they think. Steff was selling a bill of goods; he was trying to sell me one too. I think Filene was a good man; I always liked him, but he was a bit of a romantic too. And I thought of myself as a pretty solid citizen and I liked the practical work I was doing in St. Louis. I didn't regard things in 'Boston 1915' as very practical. It looked quite nebulous to me."

And indeed it so turned out. "Boston 1915" failed because, according to Steffens, it fell into the hands of the ward heelers rather than what he called the "principals," the politicians with clout who were in decision-making positions.

Roger often saw Lincoln Steffens after that first meeting in Boston and while he continued to look on him as a romantic — particularly about Russia — he came to regard him as a pretty good fellow with a wonderful sense of humor. And he considered the *Autobiography* to be "great stuff."

From 1908 on, feelers and job offers came to Roger at regular intervals; three among them were tempting. The North American Civic League for Immigrants — a new organization in which his aunt, Ruth Baldwin, was interested and which had a distinguished board of directors — wanted him to be their secretary general. But ultimately he declined on the advice of Homer Folk, then state probation commissioner of New York, who suggested that this was a private organization taking on matters that properly belonged to public bodies.

The National Consumers' League offered him a job as secretary of the Minimum Wage Commission in Washington. His name was submitted by Florence Kelley, the well-known social worker and associate of Jane Addams at Hull House in Chicago. In her letter recommending him (and written unbeknownst to Roger), she spoke of his brilliant career in St. Louis and went on to describe him as ". . . a Harvard graduate and a man of unusual ability and power to conciliate and persuade people of many different kinds and dispositions."

Roger rejected that offer because at the time he did not feel he could leave St. Louis.

The Association for Improving the Condition of the Poor (AICP) applied a great deal of pressure to get him to come to New York as their general agent at a salary of $6,000 per year (far more than he was making at the juvenile court). Roger apparently did give very serious consideration to this offer. There was considerable correspondence between him and a Mr. R. Fulton Cutting, whom Roger finally went to New York to see. He was impressed by Cutting as an "old and courtly aristocrat," but, as he says now, "the name of the organization alone should have scared me off. Association for Improving the Condition of the Poor! The whole attitude was wrong — very noblesse oblige and I didn't like it. So I turned it down and the man who eventually did get the job was Harry Hopkins, President Roosevelt's closest adviser and friend."

On July 16, 1910, just four days after Roger finally wired the AICP in New York saying a polite no (and while various board members were still urging him to reconsider), he received a letter from Edward C. Eliot offering him a job right in St. Louis as secretary of the Civic League. His response was immediately favorable. Ever since his arrival in St. Louis he had been a member of the Civic League, which had been established just after the turn of the century during the great muckraking years. He liked the organization's broad sweep of activity that took in every phase of municipal government: "There was nothing you couldn't touch in the civic reform movement, where in the juvenile court you were dealing only with children. And so I liked the bigger opportunity."

"So you moved to civic reform. Did that mean you left social work behind you?"

"More or less, yes, although civic reform was a larger framework into which social work fitted. But in effect, yes. I did put social work behind me, except that people tell me I'm still a social worker at heart."

"Are you?"

"Maybe. Except there's an element in it that I recoil from."

"A condescension perhaps?"

"Yes, a condescension and a do-goodiness. A cult of smugness. Or what someone once called the sterilized milk of human kindness."

I asked if the Civic League had met the six-thousand-dollar salary of the New York offer, and he said no; that the salary as he remembers it was four thousand five hundred dollars, but that the Civic League had agreed he might do some work on the side to make up the difference.

"Still," he added, "New York was supposed to be the chosen land and a job there was not to be turned down."

"But hadn't you found another chosen land by then?"

"Of course. Exactly. I had. That's why I did turn it down. I liked the Midwest with its freer ways. I had roots by then in St. Louis. It was a solid town with a strong democratic base in the trade unions, with courageous newspapers and a fringe of liberals who were opposed to what was known as the Big Cinch."

"Meaning the establishment?"

He nodded. "And more than anything, the Civic League gave me a chance to experiment with changes in the democratic basis of government. In fact, I take satisfaction in feeling that in the history of St. Louis there remains one page where my name may be written."

Every now and again Roger would utter such an uncharacteristically sentential statement; usually it led up to a description of an outstanding accomplishment to be followed then by one of his modest disclaimers.

"One of the major achievements of my activities with the Civic League was a new charter for the city."

Indeed, I said, that seemed to merit a page in history.

"Well, perhaps I shouldn't claim credit for what others had been working on for years, but, as it turned out, I seem to have been in a position to play a key background role."

At the heart of the new charter were three provisions known as initiative, referendum and recall, which were basic instruments of people's participatory government and which Roger and his Civic League colleagues considered vital good government safeguards. The first, initiative petition, provided that a percentage of the voters (five per cent in this case) could initiate any law and if the council failed to pass it, could bring it to the people for a vote. The second allowed a sufficient number of citizens (two per cent) who objected to an existing ordinance to introduce a referendum on the measure to kill it. The third permitted five per cent of the citizens to recall undesirable public officials in the midst of their terms by special election.

To Roger the new charter, which also included a single small council of aldermen (as opposed to a previous bicameral municipal assembly), was the "perfection of democracy." To the ward heelers, to members of the Big Cinch and interestingly enough to a good many labor elements, the worthy reforms were anathema, regarded with degrees of distaste varying from jaundiced eye to downright antagonism and determination to defeat.

Soon Roger became acutely aware that his image as "the boy reformer" was hurting the cause, that it was better for him to stay in the background and, while plotting strategy, to hide behind the facade of such Civic League luminaries as Charles Stix, president of the city's largest department store; Frederick N. Judson, a scholarly lawyer and member of the Yale Corporation; Luther Ely Smith, also a lawyer and champion of public welfare; Mrs. Philip North Moore, president of the General Federation of Women's Clubs; Dwight Davis, of Davis Cup fame and perhaps less well known for having been later secretary of war in the Coolidge Cabinet; and numerous other distinguished men and women.

Ultimately, in his efforts to implement the charter Roger negotiated a sort of three-way deal with a Civic League member, a crusading real estate man, who was owed a favor by the chairman of the Republican City Committee, who in turn had influence and used it on a German-American "tough guy," a member of the House of Delegates who was blocking the charter in the lower body of the bicameral municipal system. The maneuver proved successful; the day after the charter was passed the *St. Louis Post Dispatch*, which had been strongly pro–new charter, reported (to Roger's embarrassment, he insists) that due to Roger Baldwin's "single-handed efforts" St. Louis would now have an enlightened municipal government.

The charter fight permitted Roger to engage in the kind of backstage string-pulling that he loved and, throughout his life, excelled in, although on numerous occasions and in many quarters his machinations led him to be regarded as an operator — a characterization, incidentally, to which he has never greatly objected.

For seven years the Civic League was the chief instrument for change in the city and Roger delighted in each fight to achieve each innovation. Through his efforts the city's agencies dealing with children were reorganized; campaigns against billboards and pollution (simply called smoke in 1910) succeeded; civil service, which he had once instituted in the juvenile court, became accepted throughout all municipal agencies.

Meanwhile he had organized the St. Louis City Club, a luncheon club that was a focal point for discussions of good government activities and aspirations. Eminent (and unpaid) speakers presented all sides of public questions. Roger remembers: "Woodrow Wilson spoke there, so did Teddy Roosevelt and Taft and a dozen senators, governors and mayors. I got in some heretics too. An IWW strike leader, a socialist mayor of Milwaukee, a leftist British leader, and Sylvia Pankhurst, the militant British suffragette."

In addition to the wide range of speakers presented, Roger took great pride in the City Club's membership of 2,000 — all male. "I was for woman's suffrage and equality," he added, "but not in our clubs. We wanted privacy and privacy meant no women." Then a touch ruefully, "Equality is a more difficult right to concede than freedom, I'm afraid."

In his Oral History Roger has said that he found it difficult to appraise the impression he made on others, or had of himself during this St. Louis period. "I knew that I was part of a movement of hopeful reform and useful social work. My backing was 'respectable' and assured; the best people and the press were with me. I belonged to the right clubs and associated with the right people. I was not regarded as a busybody, as I might have been. Indeed I was flattered by being listed in the press around 1915, as a result of some poll, as one of the ten most influential citizens of St. Louis."

His influence, however, did not come from staying close to his job and minding his last. In the years after he took the Civic League position, Roger was involved in all sorts of diverse pursuits; many were straws in the wind, signaling actions that would one day bring him widespread fame. But at the same time the diversity of his endeavors (some of which seemed slightly amateurish even though they usually brought forth good results) harked back to the sixteen-year-old boy who once wrote to Ma Ryman: "Sometimes I wonder if I will ever do anything in the world. There isn't a thing a boy could meddle in very much except athletics that I haven't tried . . . I feel disgusted with myself . . . I can't keep at any one thing . . . I can become editor of some Yellow Journal perhaps — there's enough variety there, if that's what I need."

Fortunately for the world and for Roger Baldwin, he did not have

to resort to yellow journalism to achieve the variety his spirit seemed
to require.

Race relations in St. Louis were poor, and Roger soon jumped into
that breach. Early in his Washington University days Roger had run
into an unexpectedly virulent prejudice when he invited two black
high-school principals to visit his class in social relations and give his
students a firsthand insight into the denial of rights that Negroes
suffered in the border state of Missouri. The students reacted with
warm sympathy and indignation. The press, for all its supposed
enlightenment, also reacted, but with a different sort of indignation,
playing up the story with large headlines proclaiming, "University
Professor Invites Negroes to Address White Women."

"I learned no lesson at all from that experience," Roger says, "except caution! I went right ahead and mixed up Negroes and whites
on a Joint Committee for Social Service among Colored People."

Spurred by the effectiveness of this group of ten whites and ten
blacks, and in particular by the expressed desire of the blacks to try
to mitigate some of the multitudinous problems facing the 45,000
members of their race in the city, Roger proposed to David H.
Houston, chancellor of Washington University, that blacks be admitted to some of the courses in the School of Social Economy.

In a letter dated August 4, 1911, Roger qualified his proposal,
demonstrating that he had indeed learned caution, by specifying
that the classes open to blacks be "special [obviously suggesting sep-
arate], so that no embarrassing questions would arise as to the presence of colored people in the same class as white."

Dr. Houston replied that, since such a proposal would "create
complications and stir up opposition" if the classes were held in university buildings, he thought it better that they be held in one of the
Negro school buildings.

With such a degree of unenlightenment by the chancellor of the
university as a precedent, it is not surprising that a year or so later
other "leading citizens" proposed that a Negro ordinance be
adopted that would segregate housing by race.* The ordinance that
declared itself for "preserving peace and preventing conflict and ill

* David Houston, who was never a favorite of Roger's at best, went on to become a
member of President Wilson's wartime Cabinet, in which capacity he and Roger again
crossed swords at a later date.

feelings between the white and colored races" provided that "separate blocks for residences, churches and schools be allocated to white and to colored people." A perfectly fair arrangement, they claimed, since whites could not invade the Negro areas any more than the blacks could cross over to the white districts.

Fortunately the St. Louis City Council thought differently about the fairness of residential segregation and refused to pass the ordinance. At this point Roger was hoist by his own petard because the proponents of the Negro ordinance now took recourse in his cherished progressive new charter and used the initiative petition to get their segregationist ordinance on the ballot where it was passed by an overwhelming number of white voters.

Roger was bitterly disillusioned by this ironic twist. "In cases where minority rights are concerned," he says, "you can't trust the majority."

But, as it happened, a similar ordinance had also just been adopted in Louisville, so the two cities jointly took their cases to the Supreme Court, which ruled that property ownership could not be thus restricted. After this, Roger says, "I placed my faith in the courts. It was my first conversion to judicial supremacy and it has stayed there ever since."

For his efforts on behalf of the Negroes in St. Louis Roger received another "Dear Mr. Baldwin" letter of commendation from Booker T. Washington. It should be noted that Roger, for all his honest indignation about the Negro ordinance, tended to accept the separate-but-equal doctrine that Booker T. Washington had espoused in the Atlanta Compromise of 1895. Since that date Washington's increasingly conciliatory attitude had been repeatedly challenged by Negro leaders. In particular he was repudiated by the famous black scholar W. E. B. Du Bois, one of the founders in 1909 of the NAACP, who was a far more progressive and militant leader.

Roger, however, came down strongly on the side of his old friend, Booker T., who he says was "nearer right than Du Bois." His loyalty to Washington was severely tested in 1914 at an early NAACP meeting which he attended in Chicago (there was as yet no branch in St. Louis). After hearing "the Booker Washington myth" bitterly attacked by the majority of the membership, Roger wrote a forceful letter of protest to Oswald Garrison Villard, then chairman of the NAACP board of directors.

Villard responded politely, regretting, as Roger had, the mud-slinging and the time wasted over internal struggles, but stating that it was hard for the Association not to comment on the "pitiful position in which Booker Washington finds himself . . . His name is getting to be anathema among the educated colored people in the country and he is drifting further and further in the rear as a real leader."

Roger answered — equally politely — saying, "The real error in this matter seems to me the assumption that Mr. Washington is a leader of his race, and that the race needs a leader. I do not subscribe to either proposition. Mr. Washington to me is a very effective educator, but his work does not touch the great and important field of contact between white and colored people. It is in the working out of our democratic principles that the big issues lie. The work is so entirely different that I do not see how it encourages comparison. I think Mr. Washington may properly confine himself to the educational and economic field."

As the decade progressed Roger began to chafe just a bit at a St. Louis that he found was too solidly self-sufficient to breed experimenters and reformers who had more than wholly local reputations. His instinctive penchant for progressives of national note led him to Chicago, which was full of what he called "big-name disturbers of the peace."

"It was to them I turned, taking trips to Chicago just to get inspiration. It was a sort of flowering of reformers, like the New England generation before mine."

"Who would you say was the central figure in Chicago — or was there one?"

"Yes, there was, and I would say without question it was Jane Addams."

I asked how he had gotten to know her.

"Well, I first met her when she came to St. Louis shortly after I arrived there. We dined with friends. I found her a quiet, almost self-effacing middle-aged lady, remote from small talk, who spoke only when questioned and then so modestly. But there was a firm conviction under the sweetness. One could see she was a force, like the Quaker she was. She was always resolute in her championship of rights for the underdog and she was often vilified for some of her disreputable associations by a press that could not understand how she could defend anarchists without being suspect as one herself.

"From that first meeting over all the years until her death in 1935 I saw J.A. — as her friends knew her — frequently at Hull House where I stayed when I went to Chicago."

"Who were some of the other great names in that group?"

"Oh, let me see — there was Graham Taylor, and Julia Lathrop, who was the first head of the Federal Children's Bureau, there was Mary MacDowell, and the Abbott sisters and Sophonisba Breckenridge. There were a couple of sociologists at the University of Chicago, and there was Judge Julian Mack of the juvenile court and there was Clarence Darrow and Harold Ickes and Walter Fisher and Julius Rosenwald."

"Do you think all those riches in Chicago made you restless in St. Louis?"

"Well, I'll tell you, Peggy, I don't call it restlessness. I call it search and as far as I'm concerned all life is a search. I like new ideas and new people and new experiences. That sense of restlessness is not a sense of dissatisfaction, but of discovery. And I have always had a sense of discovery and curiosity about anything new and different."

Many of Roger's new and different discoveries were, nevertheless, made right in St. Louis. There was, for example, Dr. William Preston Hill's campaign to bring before the voters a referendum advocating the single-tax, a campaign that Roger plunged into, perhaps heedlessly, but with his characteristic vigor.

The single-tax was first expounded by Henry George in his famous 1879 book *Progress and Poverty;* the doctrine provided that taxation of land be the sole means of support of the government. In other words the state would get all but a very small proportion of rent derived from land and this would be its *only* source of revenue. After the publication of his book Henry George ran for mayor of New York and, according to Roger, almost won. Single-tax clubs sprang up all over the country, all based on the conviction that a single-tax on land was the only remedy for social ills.

"There was a passionate group in St. Louis advocating it," said Roger, "and I identified myself with them. We had a big campaign, we got the issue on the ballot, but, of course, we got licked by the farmers who misunderstood the implications and by the real estate speculators. Later I came to look at the single-tax as an impractical reform, but at the time I was right with it."

I asked how the Civic League, which, though good government–oriented, was basically quite conventional, had reacted to his participation in such a far-out venture.

"Oh, I didn't bring the Civic League into this experiment. They would never endorse a thing like that. But as a matter of fact, my board of directors didn't object to my doing it."

Roger's participation in outside groups while he was employed by the Civic League began a pattern that was to persist all during his working years. "I never allowed myself to be monopolized by one organization." Later, as director of the American Civil Liberties Union, he involved himself with scores of outside associations and committees and publicly espoused dozens of causes, acting always as an individual rather than as a representative of the ACLU.

Causes, it seems, had a way of moving headlong into Roger's orbit, or perhaps more explicitly, vice versa. For example, along about 1915, Roger remembers reading one day in the newspaper that Margaret Sanger, the celebrated advocate of birth control, had been denied the use of a hall in St. Louis for a scheduled and widely advertised discussion of her subject.

"Being a guardian of civic virtue, of course, I had to intervene," Roger said with a little grin.

"Had you ever met Mrs. Sanger?"

"No, I never had."

"So what did you do?"

"I simply got in touch with her and her sponsors and told them that we would have a protest meeting in front of the hall where she had been supposed to speak. A bunch of her followers went along and of course the building was locked and there were lots of police all over the place. I held a little informal meeting on the steps of this building; I said a few words and introduced her. She said something about how important her subject was and how she regretted that the police would not allow her to speak. All in all it took about three minutes. Then we dismissed the crowd."

"Do you suppose Mrs. Sanger was impressed to have you suddenly appear out of the blue and champion her cause?"

"Not at all. I think Margaret expected people like me to do just that."

"And did you get to know her then?"

"Oh very well. She was always in the liberal crowd in New York that I was in when I got there. At any kind of meeting against wars or any other liberal thing, Margaret Sanger was usually there. Also I often saw her socially. She was a frail, beautiful, unassuming woman. She never thought of herself as important, even on the public platform, but she always had a quiet insistence on the rightness of what she was doing. I saw her on and off for the rest of her life, and when she was dying of what they used to call consumption in those days, I went out to see her in Arizona."

His contacts with the IWW men in St. Louis came about in much the same fashion. These International Workers of the World came to town in winter to hole up until farm work opened up in the spring. But they soon ran out of funds and there were no public facilities for them. So, they slept in public places and ate in restaurants, blithely telling the cashiers to charge it to the mayor. Of course they were arrested, sent to court and landed in the workhouse. "I felt I had to find a solution," says Roger, "and I did. I created the first municipal lodging house in the city and the first free food. The IWW's reputation for radical violence alienated a lot of my colleagues, but these peaceful, determined men won what was only their right. I used to attend their meetings in a hall they managed to rent, and I came to respect them very much. They were serious and clean and fraternal — completely in the tradition of the American frontier independence. Most of them didn't marry; they were too migratory to settle down with a family. Bill Haywood, their general secretary, used to say that a 'married rebel is a dead rebel.' "

The more Roger talked about St. Louis, the more I had the impression that although he was not, as he says, a busybody, he was a very busy bee, who was into everything.

With all this activity he was an eminently suitable bachelor (in between two serious romantic episodes). Mothers of young society girls cast covetous glances at such a well-mannered, enterprising young man from such a good family; Roger continued to be sought after and to enjoy the company of nice girls. "I didn't know any other kind," he says.

Weekends were invariably devoted to the country — usually to canoeing on the Meramec River which was accessible in those days by the Frisco Railroad. Roger and his companions — usually Harvard men — would load their canoes onto the freight or baggage cars; the trains ran close enough to the river, and engineers were obliging enough to stop at convenient points along a hundred-mile stretch for them to unload the canoes and portage to the river. Roger took one of his more memorable trips with his brother Herbert in 1913, clocking 108 miles from Steelville to Moselle in twenty-three hours, which he figures was four and two-thirds miles per hour, or one mile every thirteen minutes. (The river ran at three miles an hour.)

Roger says he was entranced by the "swift down-stream paddles on clear jade green river which bent and turned around high limestone cliffs and had varieties of wildlife unknown to me on eastern waters. Camping on sandbars was a ritual: getting out duffel bags, cooking an edible dinner, sitting around the campfire and talking after the meal, then wrapping up in blankets, dousing with citronella and sleeping under the stars.

"I figured if all else failed me, the Meramec would not; it had been there so long, it was my refuge and my delight."

There were urban delights as well. There was the University Club where Roger most often lunched, the St. Louis Club where most of the society balls were held, the Public Question Club consisting of a group of young "pseudo-intellectuals" who met twice a month to discuss public issues ("their pretensions were greater than their knowledge"). There was also another "super supper club — a gilt-edged, high-brow establishment where you dressed for the monthly dinners." In addition to these clubs Roger was a member of the Artists Guild, which he describes as "a collection of odd and more or less creative personalities." The fifty or sixty members had monthly dinners that Roger attended regularly. "I liked the informality, the kidding, the wit and good fellowship, but I functioned very little. I guess I was too self-conscious to perform or speak up in such an atmosphere."

Still with all his exposure to new ideas it does not appear that at the time Roger had a very sharp awareness of the larger world around him. When I asked him, "Do you remember if you were thinking at all in global terms in those days," he answered, "Now that's quite a question."

Ultimately when I got around it another way he said no, what he was in those days was a social worker and reformer with little understanding of the realities of universal thought and experience.

Fortunately the slightly self-satisfied pattern of his life was disrupted one day when he accepted a dare by a fellow social worker who looked on him as an overprotected Harvard man dabbling around in good works, and thought he needed to have his limited horizons widened.

The name of the social worker is so extraordinary that it must be recorded here: she was Cynthalia Isgrig Knaffler. The dare was that Roger go with her to hear a lecture by Emma Goldman, the "Red Queen of Anarchy."

At the very least it was the most significant dare that Roger ever accepted; his meeting with Emma Goldman ripened into a friendship that changed the course of his life.

(5)

The Red Queen of Anarchy

ONE OF THE MOST TITILLATING FEATURES of the initial Roger Baldwin–Emma Goldman encounter is that each has remembered and recorded the event and each has misremembered it. The facts as borne out by their own correspondence clearly indicate that both have lumped what was in reality at least three separate meetings taking place over a period of three years into one single meeting, although their memories differ as to *which* single meeting. Also fascinating is the disparity of the impressions each made on the other.

Here is what Roger has to say about what *he* looks on as their first meeting, which was at the lecture to which Cynthalia Isgrig Knaffler took him. "Emma was on tour around the country talking to her working-class followers in obscure halls, raising funds for her magazine *Mother Earth*. Even with my friend at my side I felt a little uncomfortable in such a crowd of unfamiliar faces in a smoky little hall. But when Emma arrived, walking between the rows to the platform amid excited applause, I was surprised to see a quite ordinary woman, modestly dressed in dark colors, with a face distinguished by thick eyeglasses and piercing blue eyes. Not beautiful, not ugly, but arresting. When she spoke I was more surprised. Her English was impressive; she had hardly any accent and her flow of words was as eloquent as her plain good sense. I was quite overcome by the range and depth of her speech. I had expected fireworks, denunciations and anger. I got reason, sense and sympathy."

Afterward Roger approached Miss Goldman and asked if he might call on her. She was "politely willing," and he went off, he said, determined to correct the false image among his friends of Emma Goldman, the dangerous revolutionary.

"I gave quite a party for Emma — at the Planter Hotel. I remember very well where it was. I had the intellectual elite there to meet her — social workers, lawyers, editors — some twenty of them.

She was a bit uneasy with such strange company, but she hit it off with charm, wit and such subdued good sense in answering their questions that the 'Red Queen of Anarchy' was nowhere to be seen or heard. Of course it was front-page copy but the auspices were too respectable to make it a sensation for attack.

"Then I got my lady friends to hold an evening for her at the Wednesday Club, which was the swankiest women's club in town. She talked on Ibsen. What an eye opener that was for me into a whole new world of literature. Ibsen, of course, and Strindberg, Kropotkin, Tolstoi, Dostoevski. Nowhere was there a word of violence and hardly a mention of revolution though it was implicit in everything she championed. From that first visit I became a friend for life."

Now here is what Emma Goldman has to say in her autobiography *Living My Life* about what *she* believed to be their first meeting. "On this visit I made the acquaintance of Roger Baldwin, Robert Minor, and Zoë Akins. Baldwin was helpful in arranging a luncheon at one of the large hotels, where I met a group of social workers and reformers. He had also been instrumental in securing the Women's Wednesday Club for two drama lectures. He was a very pleasant person though not very vital, rather a social lion surrounded by society girls, whose interest in the attractive young man was apparently greater than in his uplift work." *

Emma Goldman has placed this visit in 1911 (as does her biographer Richard Drinnon in describing it), which would have been the third of her trips to St. Louis in as many years. Roger thinks that the great meeting took place during Emma Goldman's first trip to St. Louis, which he recalls was sometime in 1909. Actually it was early 1908 so Roger is more nearly correct. He is not correct, however, about how quickly the friendship flourished. On the other hand it did move a little faster than Miss Goldman recalls.

Emma Goldman, while saying she met Roger in 1911, did in fact first write to him on September 10, 1909: "Dear Mr. Baldwin, Your letter of the 7th was forwarded to me as I have been touring Massachusetts and Rhode Island during the last month. Your subscription [obviously a reference to Roger's subscription to her magazine *Mother Earth*] has been credited to you and our magazine forwarded. I contemplate being in St. Louis sometime in November. Do you

* Emma Goldman, *Living My Life* (Garden City: Garden City Publishing Co., 1931), p. 477.

think I could get the hall of the Self Culture Society [the neighborhood house where Roger had first lived and worked] for a series
of lectures. If yes, will you let me know soon its seating capacity and
price. Very truly yours."

Roger replied on September 20, 1909, saying he was glad she
would be in St. Louis, and he noted her request for use of the Self
Culture Hall. "But," he went on, "we are all slaves to public opinion,
and in the world of our membership I hardly think that the board
would consent to its use for such subjects as you would desire to
speak on, although many of us personally are very interested. A
number of persons active in social work wish to meet you privately
when you come and I should be obliged if you will let me know in
advance."

Whether or not she did so, whether Roger did have friends in to
meet her socially on that trip is unknown, but unlikely; there is
no further reference in their correspondence to the proposed November 1909 visit. However, in *Living My Life* Emma Goldman
writes that "The man who now steered me through the shoals of society luncheons and would be Bohemian dinners was William
Marion Reedy, the brilliant editor of the *St. Louis Mirror*. [A man
whom Roger greatly admired.] His suave manner could smuggle
the most dangerous contraband into the enemy camp. There were
many questions hurled at me at my first luncheon with the 'nice'
people of St. Louis where plenty of water was served with little spirit.
The one enlivening element at the affair was Bill Reedy . . ." No
mention here of Baldwin, nor of him in connection with her appearance on that visit at the Artists Guild, of which, it will be recalled,
Roger was a member. "The majority of Guilders," wrote Miss Goldman, "impressed me as people to whom Bohemianism was a sort
of narcotic to help them endure the boredom of their lives." This
chilly assessment is followed by more panegyrics about the charms,
breadth of vision and tolerance of Bill Reedy.*

Still, somewhere along the way (despite Emma Goldman's contention that she had not yet met him) Roger must have made an impression on her and also on her anarchist friend Harry Kelly. For
on December 7, 1910, she wrote him a rather arch letter: "My dear
Mr. Baldwin: What have you done to my friend Harry Kelly? You

* *Ibid.,* pp. 463–464.

must have hypnotized him, he is so taken with you. I can not really blame him. I would be myself if I did not fear to shock you."

The rest of her letter is concerned principally with asking Roger's help in securing Memorial Hall at Washington University for her forthcoming visit to St. Louis in March (1911). Roger did indeed make a vigorous effort in her behalf but was rebuffed by Chancellor Houston. Meanwhile he responded to her reference to Harry Kelly. "Really I did not hypnotize Mr. Kelly. He has quite captured me. I should place him as Exhibit A in the group of Sane, Male Anarchists." And then with the first hint of disdain for the St. Louis work that, up to the moment of his meeting with "E.G.," had apparently satisfied him, he ended the letter with: "Thank you for your kind wishes. I manage to survive even the mediocrity of such conservative work as the 'new civics.' "

Back shot Miss Goldman's answer to My dear Mr. Baldwin. "You seem to have been unfortunate with the male anarchists you have met. Were they really all crazy if you rejoice so in meeting Harry Kelly? We are very proud of Harry, but not for the same reason that you like him. Maybe we believe that sane ideals are very poor ideals." And then on to more about another possible hall (Hibernian) and a request that Roger let her have a list of names and addresses that she could use for mailing circulars prior to her March lecture.

At this point, although Roger does not remember it today, either Miss G's condescending tone or her continued request for his time and effort on her behalf may have slightly put him off, for he responded saying that he was turning her over to a Miss Alice Martin who would handle all further arrangements. But he did add, "Do not think for a moment that I am side-stepping a service which I offer you gladly. I think Miss Martin can do it more efficiently. I will guarantee the results. If you do not get them I will constitute myself a complaint department and you refer your troubles to me."

However, a letter written at the same time to the anarchist Harry Kelly, whom he had so greatly impressed, is more decidedly distant. After explaining about Miss Martin, Roger adds, "I am too busy to take on anything myself further than seeing that other people help Miss Goldman out. I am sure that Mr. Reedy will attend to publicity and the sale of tickets."

If there was some pique on Roger's part, it did not last long under

Emma Goldman's skillful re-wooing. "If I have not written you in all this time," she wrote on February 11, 1911, after a lapse of three weeks, "it is because you have turned me over to two grand managers, Miss Martin and Billy Reedy . . . However, I know that Miss Martin tells you all the secrets of our conspiracy. I also know that you are somewhat the commander of the stratagem. But what you probably do not know is that I appreciate greatly your interest and the grand people with whom you have placed my fate."

It is impossible to imagine any words more calculated to soothe Roger's ego. E.G.'s letter, after confirming her arrival date, ended, "And so I am to face the *ladies*. [Clearly a reference to the elite Wednesday Club.] Do you think I will survive it? I might not be so nervous with you and Reedy on each side. But all alone never!!! Au revoir."

But in *Living My Life* Emma Goldman gives Roger no credit whatsoever even for his Miss Martin. "*William Marion Reedy's* [emphasis mine] efforts in my behalf this year," she wrote, "brought even greater results than the previous occasions in St. Louis. Thanks to *him* and *his* [emphasis mine] friend, Alice Martin, who was at the head of a dancing school, I was enabled to speak in the Odeon Recital Hall . . . The lectures to the Women's Wednesday Club on 'Tolstoy' and 'Galsworthy's *Justice*' proved rather strong food for the delicate palates of the St. Louis society ladies. On this visit I made the acquaintance of Roger Baldwin, Robert Minor and Zoë Akins — " *

Miss Goldman's biographer has pointed out that "Baldwin made numerous acknowledgements of his great intellectual and moral debt to Emma Goldman. He wrote in one of his letters to her, for instance, 'you always remain one of the chief inspirations of my life, for you aroused in me a sense of what freedom really means.' " †

Drinnon also suggests that if Emma Goldman had "done nothing else than set Baldwin off on his career, her role as the woman behind the man behind the organization of the American Civil Liberties Union would have made her fights for free speech an outstanding success."

Of course Emma Goldman did more — a great deal more. Nor was Roger's career entirely molded by her, although certainly he was set on a new path by his meeting with her.

---

* *Ibid.,* p. 477.
† Richard Drinnon, *Rebel in Paradise* (Chicago: University of Chicago Press, 1961), p. 140.

Today while he enjoys remembering how "it didn't take me long to make Emma quite respectable in St. Louis," he also recalls, "Emma Goldman opened up not only an entirely new literature to me but new people as well, some of whom called themselves anarchists, some libertarians, some freedom lovers and some had no label — like me. They ranged far and wide in time and place, bound together by one principle — freedom from coercion. The State, since it was the supreme form of coercion, was their prime target philosophically. Most anarchists I read or knew accepted nonviolence; they were in fact and thought philosophical anarchists."

"Did that apply to that sane male anarchist of yours — Harry Kelly?"

"Yes indeed it did. In fact Harry Kelly was the most unlikely anarchist you could ever find — a middle-aged businessman who belonged to our City Club with all the other business and professional men. We had what we used to call a Crank's Table there — it held maybe ten or twelve men. Anybody could sit there that wanted to. I used to sit there because I thought they were the most entertaining men and so did Harry. Of course they were all slightly nutty."

"In other words," I laughed, "a slightly nutty sane male anarchist."

We moved on then to Kropotkin — Prince Peter Alexevich Kropotkin, the noted Russian author, scientist and revolutionary whom Roger regarded as his "solid base in anarchist literature." Despite his noble heritage, Kropotkin early in his life in the 1870's came under the influence of the new liberal-revolutionary literature, which led to his great concern for the condition of the Russian peasantry. During a year spent in Geneva he joined the International Workingmen's Association but soon found the organization too conservative for his views. His espousal of anarchism was based on his belief that true cooperation between human beings would make government rule superfluous. His utopia would come into being, he believed, when neither private property, nor the church nor the state exercised control over the individual spontaneity of men.

Kropotkin, who was widely regarded as a gentle and affectionate personality, was Emma Goldman's "true teacher and inspiration . . . who spoke to what was deepest in her." * It was natural, therefore,

* *Ibid.,* pp. 36–37.

that as Roger came under Emma's influence he tended to adopt the philosophy of her mentor.

But even without Emma Goldman as an ideological middleman, Roger was instinctively attracted to Kropotkin's anarchist ideas by his recognition in them of the New England tradition of freedom, individualism and resistance to tyranny. And anarchists, of course, derived inspiration from the philosophies, among many others, of Emerson and Thoreau, whom Roger practically claims as his kin.

In addition the Russian Prince and the Boston Brahmin had certain inherent patterns of habit and thought in common. Both, for instance, had deviated from their upper-class origins to espouse the cause of the less fortunate, yet neither — certainly not Roger — had renounced his own background. Neither was truly egalitarian: Both were able to translate essentially simplistic creeds into effective and far-reaching accomplishments.

Today Roger puts it this way: "I believe, generally speaking, that the human race is fundamentally good in the sense that people want to get along with each other. And if you think that people are good and can live by the Golden Rule, and you have faith in them as I do, then you believe that social relations are perfectible. Therefore, you can have a government that works without conflict and a society that is not bent on self-destruction. Now when you cast it on a world scale — you believe in the same thing — the capacity of people of all nations and colors and races to get along with each other and to create a world order."

Before arriving at this generalized overview, Roger would make ideological way stops at various "isms" that he today eschews: socialism, which he says he never seriously considered because he could not accept the all-powerful State ownership of industry (although he saw its practical need), Marxism and communism, which definitely did attract him.

All along this route Emma Goldman remained a friend, a force and a component in his thinking. Sometimes she was a burr in his side as she chided him for superficiality or inconsistency; sometimes she depended on his support. Sometimes, as their continued correspondence will reveal, she laughed at him; other times she was proudly admiring.

As for Kropotkin, Roger's esteem continued undiminished to the extent that he ultimately pulled together all he could find of the Russian anarchist's scattered pamphlets and tracts written in English,

French and Russian and published them in a book which he titled *Revolutionary Pamphlets*.

"It was not a scholarly job," Roger admits, "and according to my later examination, not too accurate, but at least the material was available in one place as it had not been before. In the second edition I changed the title to *Freedom Pamphlets*."

"Why was that?"

"Because they weren't what 'revolutionary' implies; they dealt with freedom from all forms of coercion, which is basically what anarchism is all about."

"Yet, Roger, for all your belief in the Golden Rule maxim of anarchism, you never called yourself or even considered yourself an anarchist, did you?"

"No. I left that to others to do. Because really I never accepted anarchism as anything more than *one* desirable social tendency among many others. And I don't think that Emma or any of the others ever really looked on me as a member of the fraternity. Of course there was nothing to join — no creed to support. So I never used the label, except when Norman Thomas used to kid me in public by referring to me as a 'Harvard anarchist'!"

"I would think," Roger said one day after we had been talking about Emma Goldman, "that I had two distinct periods in those years between 1907 and 1917. One was before Emma came and introduced me to the larger world of thought and experience and the other was later when the war came."

"They were distinct, not interrelated?"

"I would say so, yes. I don't think even after I'd met Emma, I'd ever heard the word 'conscientious objector.' At least I don't remember it. I think that when the war came in 1914 and I read in the *St. Louis Post Dispatch* about the English conscientious objectors, that was the first time I'd heard the word."

"And you reacted to it?"

"Yes, I did. I said to myself, why these are the kind of people I belong to. Still, you know those things don't come overnight like the creation in Genesis. They come gradually. In the first place I wasn't aware that the world was likely to have a war until it happened. Then when the World War struck us in 1914, I looked at it from the United States and I had a great feeling of alienation. It was something I just couldn't think of participating in. And I began to know that it was all wrong, and that this World War had explanations like economic situations and power struggles that weren't apparent on the surface. And then I read about those high-minded young Englishmen going off to jail and refusing military service and making very good arguments, Christian arguments, Old Testament and humanitarian arguments — the Sermon on the Mount — "

I interrupted him to ask if he remembered a letter that he'd written to a man named Roy Wallace concerning his own feelings about the Sermon on the Mount. He said he didn't remember, so I showed him a copy of the letter. Before reading it he explained that Roy Wallace was a Harvard man, a bustling executive social worker, a good friend professionally, very patriotic and rather a Boy Scout. Apparently Wallace wanted Roger to protest the pacifist stance of Jane Addams and to endorse the actions of President Wilson. Roger replied on March 9, 1917:

> Dear Roy, I would fall in line with almost anything in the world that you proposed, but your letter of March 7 is an exception. I am thoroughly with Miss Addams and the pacifists now and all the time. I am unfortunately one of those who take the Sermon on the Mount pretty seriously, which does not square with the current conception of patriotism. I am enough of a democrat to really put the interest of all the people of the world before some of the people; that means the world comes before my country. So, you will have to excuse me from being patriotic and standing behind the President. No doubt there are plenty of patriots out here in social work and I shall be glad to discover one of them and turn your letter over to him if you like. Always sincerely.

Roger shook his head. "What a letter," he said ruefully, his tone suggesting that he thought he had sounded pretty bumptious. But then with some pride he added: "Still, I didn't know I was quite so positive at the time."

But when I pointed out to him the date of his letter, he at once remembered just how positive he had in fact been at the time. For one month later he had made his total commitment to pacifism. On April 2, 1917, Roger Baldwin left St. Louis for good and went to New York to donate his services to the American Union against Militarism.

(6)

Anti-militant Peaceful People

"It was a wrench to leave the city where I had first tested my-self, where I had first learned the sociology I taught and where I had so many friends and associates. It was also a dramatic uproot-ing for me to move from a single municipal community to the big theater of a world war. From a domestic reformer I became almost an instant internationalist, concerned with the fate of the universe."

The grandiloquent sweep of Roger's statement left me momen-tarily hesitant to ask the more mundane questions about his move East. How did he happen to be asked to join the American Union against Militarism (AUAM), what were his duties to be, where was he to live, who were his associates?

"I was not and still am not awed by big reputations," Roger began, "but I must say it was reassuring to find the people who invited me so well known in public life."

The committee of the AUAM was indeed distinguished. Three social workers — Lillian Wald, of the famous Henry Street Settle-ment, Jane Addams and Paul Kellogg, editor of *The Survey,* the mag-azine that was the social workers' Bible — were the original founders. In 1914 they had informally organized the Henry Street Group, which expanded in November 1915 to counter President Wilson's demands for a larger army and for more active war preparedness into the Anti-Preparedness Group, which in turn joined with other peace movements to become the American Union against Militarism.

"Was it more or less assumed," I asked, "that social workers would be pacifists?"

"Certainly," Roger said without hesitation. "Social workers at that time were interested in human lives. They were all good anti-mili-tant, peaceful people."

"You say 'at that time.' Does that mean you don't think that applies to today's social workers?"

"No. They have a very different outlook. We've become a welfare state and that means that today's social workers are all — or mostly all — government employees."

I wasn't sure that entirely answered my question, but nonetheless I turned back to 1917 and to the other AUAM committee members whom Roger had met and been reassured by on his first visit to their New York office. Among them were Oswald Garrison Villard, editor of the *Nation;* Owen Lovejoy of the National Child Labor Committee; John Lovejoy Elliott of the Ethical Society; John Haynes Holmes, minister of the Unitarian Church; Emily Balch, who later won the Nobel Peace Prize; Norman Thomas, a young Presbyterian clergyman who had just resigned his pulpit; Agnes Brown Leach and L. Hollingsworth Wood, both prominent Quakers; Harry Weinberger, a fiery lawyer determined to have the war declared unconstitutional; Max Eastman, editor of *The Masses;* and his sister Crystal Eastman Fuller. And it was because Crystal Eastman, the dynamic young woman who was executive secretary of the organization, had become ill and was unable to devote as much time to it as she previously had, that Roger had been importuned by Miss Wald and Mr. Villard to come to New York and take her place.

The New York office of the AUAM was at 70 Fifth Avenue in a building largely occupied by reformers and church groups. The union also had a Washington office where work was done on a day-to-day basis with members of Congress and with the administration and here Roger was to begin, sharing the load with the head of the Washington office, a dedicated crusading newspaperman named Charles Hallinan.

"I was to commute weekly between New York and Washington, attending board meetings in New York and doing my work in the capital. I had a room in Washington and took sleepers two nights a week, living all the time out of a suitcase. I agreed to work only for expenses. I had some old Puritan notion that I should not make anything out of war service, so I settled for one hundred twenty-five dollars a month. I had no family obligations and could afford the luxury of a conscience."

Roger and Hallinan arranged to divide the assignments in the Washington office. "I don't think Hallinan ever quite approved of me," said Roger, "but he was gentleman enough not to say so out loud. All our associations were harmonious. I was a good enough manager — some say operator — to keep the peace. I think it was tact. I suppose my critics would call it compromise. But I never compromised with principles. Never!"

At any rate, according to their modus operandi in Washington, Hallinan was to handle the press and government officials, organizing teams of constituents to wait upon senators and congressmen; Roger was to take care of the correspondence with AUAM's far-reaching members and representatives (he himself had been their representative for a time in St. Louis) and to answer calls for help from pacifists suffering repression as a result of "an excess of patriotic fervor" on the part of others.

But Roger barely had time to settle into this new routine when on April 6, 1917, America declared war on Germany. "I was amazed at the way that declaration changed everything. Apparently I was very naive, but I couldn't believe it would instantly produce such savage attitudes. People were mobbed and persecuted — even their mail was stopped. A sudden sort of hysteria happened very quickly."

Equally quickly the thrust of Roger's own endeavors changed. He had joined the AUAM because he was wholeheartedly in agreement with the organization's long-range effort to develop a negotiated peace in Europe that would ultimately lead to world federation. But with America's entrance into the war it became evident to him that his primary objective would be to protect the rights of people to speak out and oppose the war as their consciences dictated. In other words, the AUAM would, in his opinion, have to become involved almost wholly in defending opponents of the war who were being prosecuted by their government.

From the moment of his arrival in New York and Washington, Roger had been actively engaged in fighting the conscription bill then before the Congress. But after the declaration of war, the AUAM realized that they could not realistically continue to oppose the draft. "We knew then," Roger explained, "that the only thing we could do was to try to get a decent law for conscientious objectors and reasonable provisions in regard to restrictions in wartime. The people in the AUAM were so much more prominent than those in any other peace organization. There was no comparison between them. Our people had such high standing they could go right in to see Wilson. So when the negotiations began in April 1917 to try to get provisions for conscientious objectors, Jane Addams came from

Chicago and she and Lillian Wald and Emily Balch went together to see Wilson. Norman Thomas went with them."

"What about you?"

"They wouldn't let me go with them. I remember I had lunch at the Raleigh Hotel with those girls, but I guess they thought I was too green and too young to go. Not that I wanted to go," he added defiantly. "I had a diffidence which has often inhibited me in putting myself forward." (I would hazard a guess that if a hundred of Roger Baldwin's legion of friends chosen at random were asked to characterize him with a single word, not a one would choose "diffident.") "My temperament," Roger continued, "is to act on my convictions, not to express them." And indeed it was not long before he had an opportunity in the spring of 1917 to do just that.

On May 18 a Selective Service Act was finally passed by the Congress and the very next day Roger organized within the AUAM the Bureau for Conscientious Objectors. The bureau's function was at least threefold: to try to enlist lawyers to help C.O.'s, to lobby for new laws and to negotiate for favorable ruling under the existing laws, and to urge all conscientious objectors to register and make their stands known.

The terms of the Selective Service Act were a great disappointment to the AUAM. They had been hopeful that the legislation would be liberal in dealing with conscientious objectors, because Secretary of War Newton D. Baker was considered sympathetic to the anti-militarists. He had, through Norman Thomas, even asked for a memorandum — which Roger promptly supplied him — on the AUAM's point of view. The memorandum urged exemption from combat service of political or nonreligious objectors whose convictions Roger considered just as legitimate as those of a Quaker or a Mennonite.

According to Donald Johnson in his excellent book *Challenge to American Freedom,* which deals with World War I and the rise of the American Civil Liberties Union, Newton Baker, while agreeing to refer the AUAM proposals to Congress, refused to endorse them himself. Wholesale exemptions, he said, were out of the question. And in a letter to President Wilson, he wrote, "So many kinds of people have asked for class exemptions that our only safety seems to be in making none." *

* As quoted in Donald Johnson, *The Challenge to American Freedom* (For the Mississippi Valley Historical Association: University of Kentucky Press, 1960), p. 17.

Johnson further points out that after the conscription bill had passed both houses and had gone to a conference committee, Roger asked for a hearing. "He sent the committee a copy of some recent British legislation that recognized political objectors and pointed out that the administration bill failed to 'recognize the individual conscience. Conscience is nothing if it is not individual.' But the conference committee was not inclined to change any important provision in the administration bill. The final Selective Service Act of May 18 left the rather vague exemption clauses unaltered. The consequence was to be many bitter and exasperating experiences for Roger Baldwin . . ." *

Parenthetically I take slight issue with that last sentence of Johnson's. I believe Roger no more capable of bitterness than of, say, diffidence. And the consequences of the conscription act quickly moved him into a position of power and conflict, neither of which condition has ever appeared to exasperate him.

Roger had recognized the moment he organized the Bureau for Conscientious Objectors that it represented a departure from the main objectives to which the AUAM was dedicated. As he put it, "The AUAM was using all the powers at its command to urge the administration to make a settlement of the war — a negotiated peace. Meanwhile the bureau was defending the people whom the administration was prosecuting."

In other words, since the AUAM was tactfully urging and the Bureau for Conscientious Objectors was bluntly attacking the administration, it was impossible to reconcile the two positions within the same organization. A considerable tug of war resulted. The three founding members, Jane Addams, Lillian Wald and Paul Kellogg, plus Miss Alice Lewisohn, vigorously disapproved of the bureau and even threatened resignation. "We cannot combine an aggressive policy against prosecution of the war with an aggressive policy for settling it through negotiation . . ." Paul Kellogg insisted. Roger for his part argued that the bureau had "an obligation to the work we have already started. Having created conscientious objectors to war, we ought to stand by them." †

Surprisingly, considering the distinction and prestige of those opposed to Roger, the full board of directors upheld him. Crystal Eastman, by then restored in health, plunged into the middle of the

* *Ibid.*, p. 18.
† As quoted in *Ibid.*, p. 20.

controversy by suggesting that perhaps the name of the new bureau be changed to something slightly less inflammatory. So Roger came up with Civil Liberties Bureau, which sounded more universal and less damaging to the AUAM's long-range hopes for world peace and democracy.

"Was the term 'civil liberties' at all current at the time or did you just make it up or what?" I asked.

"I don't think anyone had ever called anything civil liberties in the United States before we did. But the British had used it. In fact it's an old phrase that goes back for several centuries in British history, but it wasn't used as the name of an organization until the British used it in the first World War. And then we took it over because it seemed to fit."

But the name change did not seem to calm troubled waters within the AUAM or, for that matter, outside the organization. The *New York Times* bitterly denounced the new agency on July 4, 1917, pointing out that its leaders were "antagonizing the settled policies of our government . . . resisting the execution of its deliberately formed plans . . . gaining for themselves immunity from the application of laws to which good citizens willingly submit . . ." *

Lillian Wald was especially uneasy and in a letter to Jane Addams she complained of the impulsiveness of the board members and said in so many words that while Norman Thomas had judgment, Crystal Eastman and Roger, much as she liked them, were more than she could manage single-handed.

"I'm sure she would say that," Roger responded affably when I mentioned Miss Wald's reaction to him. "She was a lovely, cautious, gentle lady in the social worker tradition, in which she depended on a great many rich friends of hers in New York to support her projects. Her temperament was very conciliatory and cautious and sweet. And Crystal and I were the type of people she could hardly abide because both of us were activists and radicals."

"Impulsive radicals?"

"Yes, impulsive radicals. Both of us were just that. Still — I'm not sure impulsive is quite the right word. Because impulsive implies that you do something you regret afterward and I don't think Crystal or I were impulsive in that sense. I think what we did was to act quickly, without enough reflection."

* As quoted in *Ibid.,* p. 21.

"Why do you suppose Miss Wald would approve more of Norman Thomas?"

"Because Norman would never have been called impulsive. He was almost always reasonable. He was a clergyman after all, and he never got over being a clergyman. He always saw the other side, often much more fairly than I did. He and I were close friends and partners right up to his death."

Even though Norman Thomas himself was not one of the impulsive radicals, he belonged to another peace organization that Miss Wald considered made up of many hotheads. While the People's Council (PC) was, according to Thomas, a working-class organization and the AUAM was middle class, their aims, he said, were identical. Miss Wald disagreed; the AUAM was a far more reflective and temperate organization.

Roger, who was a member of the People's Council, says: "The socialists were the most daring of the anti-war crowd; they dominated the People's Council; it was not officially socialist but the party furnished most of the steam. I joined its board, headed by my friend Scott Nearing, one of the most eloquent spokesmen of the anti-war forces."

Besides Roger and Norman Thomas, several other members of the AUAM board — Crystal Eastman, Emily Balch and Rabbi Judah Magnes — belonged to the PC, so when that organization asked the AUAM to join them in a peace conference, the board voted to accept. Once again Lillian Wald, Paul Kellogg, Amos Pinchot and a few of those who were looked upon as the social workers of the AUAM board objected — this time so strenuously that Miss Wald, at least, threatened to resign.

Since she was in effect the lynchpin of the whole AUAM, this was considered unthinkable by all, so to avert a crisis and to try to heal the breach that had been incipient ever since Roger had first formed the Bureau for Conscientious Objectors, the AUAM board decided that the moment had come to cast the offspring Civil Liberties Bureau adrift from the mother organization.

Nothing could have pleased Roger more. He was delighted when on October 1, 1917, the Civil Liberties Bureau became the National Civil Liberties Bureau with him as director. He was now liberated and completely on his own, even though the rebellious infant was, as he puts it, "cozily housed right next to its parent at 70 Fifth Avenue, and with the most active of the AUAM's board on its directing committee."

Those "most active" ones were L. Hollingsworth Wood, the Quaker lawyer who was chairman of the new organization's directing committee, and Norman Thomas, vice chairman; others from the AUAM board included Crystal Eastman, John Lovejoy Elliott, John Haynes Holmes, Agnes Brown Leach and Judah Magnes. Helen Phelps Stokes also joined the new board.

Two staff members added greatly to the harmony and efficiency of the new office. Albert de Silver, who became associate director, was an affluent young New York lawyer who gave up his practice to work full-time for the Civil Liberties Bureau. "Albert was the most helpful and generous colleague I had," Roger recalls fondly. "He was wise and jolly and fat. He had inherited wealth and a sharp legal mind; he had a conscience and a Quaker wife. But he himself was not a Quaker or even a pacifist; he was simply stirred by the attacks on freedom of speech and press and conscience. I relied always on his good solid judgment — it was a lot better than mine. He had a great ability to see ahead to the results of a decision. And he figured them right — events proved it."

The other member who joined the Bureau as staff counsel was Walter Nelles, a classmate of Roger's at Harvard who worked effectively with Albert de Silver, whom he greatly admired, as well as with Roger.

"We three made a team that was never afterward equaled in the Civil Liberties Union," Roger said in his Oral History. "De Silver contributed the quick, unerring judgment, with a gay and easy approach to tough problems; Nelles, the reflective opinions of a studious lawyer, sometimes aroused by hot indignation; and I, the techniques of a social case worker, an organizer and a publicity man for such limited publicity as was open to us."

Actually Roger in this instance places a rather too low valuation on himself and his contributions. What he brought to the Civil Liberties Bureau, which he had created, was a driving leadership based on his own deeply felt belief in the rightness of his cause.

In his words: "Compared to my work in St. Louis, this wartime job was high tension, perpetual pressure. And I took to it almost with a feeling of elation. I was doing what my deepest convictions demanded and working with people who shared them."

Walter Nelles, one of the sharers, wrote a book about Albert de Silver, who died in a tragic accident at the age of thirty-six, in which he corroborates Roger's feeling about the unity that prevailed at the Civil Liberties Bureau. Of Roger's contribution he says, "No organization ever had a more harmonious board of directors or a more efficient executive than Roger Baldwin, operating with one stenographer, occasional part-time volunteer assistants and a little low-speed help from me as counsel. He worked at a high speed always without flagging, with scrupulous care to keep everything done in the Bureau's name within the object and law-abiding limits of our complete agreement . . . Whatever the value of its accomplishment for its object, it is hard to see how it could have been made greater than Roger Baldwin made it." *

In an earlier passage, Nelles also refers to Roger (along with Helen Phelps Stokes) as "the only radical among us," adding rather puzzlingly that "Roger Baldwin held views with which none of the rest of us agreed; Thoreau was his intellectual hero." Somehow Thoreau seems a hero unlikely to have been so widely disagreed with, except that, of course, he once took a position in favor of John Brown, which may have lost him his standing as a pacifist.

When the Bureau came into its own, Roger, instead of living in Washington and commuting weekly to New York, reversed the process and moved to New York to run the office while commuting to Washington weekly to confer with, badger and sometimes bargain with administration officials.

"I always had entrée to the departments in Washington with whom we dealt. At the War Department we started out on a cordial basis with Newton Baker and even more so with his assistant, Frederick Keppel, who was a former dean at Columbia," Roger said, "and my recollection is that Keppel was entirely cooperative until the time that Military Intelligence put pressure on him. Military Intelligence maintained that we were *creating* conscientious objectors, not defending them."

"Wasn't the word 'slackers' used?"

"Oh yes, all the time. The Military Intelligence called all conscientious objectors slackers and they persuaded Keppel that we were encouraging slackers. Actually I insisted that we be scrupulous in not

* Walter Nelles, *A Liberal in Wartime* (New York: W. W. Norton, 1940), pp. 123–124.

appearing to encourage refusal of military service. To encourage
disobedience to the draft was a crime, and we of course had been
very careful not to advise any man to resist."

"But if a man had already made up his mind to resist, you told
him what to do?"

"Theoretically, yes. The fellows would come to us and say: 'Look,
we're against the war, what do we do?' And we said if you do thus
and so you'll go to jail, and if you do something else you may get a
furlough from the army and so forth. We told them what the alter-
natives were and in the course of a conversation like that, it was very
difficult to appear not to be encouraging them. But the important
thing was we didn't ever try to change any man's conscience. But
even so, Keppel broke off all relations with us. I couldn't see him
and he would not answer letters."

This break was particularly serious because it hampered the
Bureau's efforts to try to soften the savage treatment that many conscientious objectors were receiving at the hands of the military who,
of course, despised them. Those who resisted *before* they were
drafted (as Roger himself was to do) were far better off than those
who waited until they were drafted, when technically they became
soldiers and were thrown into military prisons. This evil resulted in
gross inequities and even brutalities; prisoners were manacled and
given impossibly long sentences by the courts-martial who were determined to make examples of all "slackers."

Since the law recognized only members of religious sects histori-
cally opposed to war and forced even these men to render some service, the greatest sufferers were the so-called absolutists, who were
bound by no particular religious scruple and who still refused to
perform any service whatsoever. About four hundred and fifty of
these men were sent to Fort Leavenworth, which was one of the
most stringent of the military camps, although according to Roger it
had a superintendent named Colonel Sedgwick Rice, a comparatively
reasonable man who believed that, whatever he himself thought of
conscientious objectors, they did not belong in a military prison.
When Roger went to Fort Leavenworth — before the break with
Keppel — to see conditions at first hand, he stayed with Colonel
Rice. "He did not suspect my iniquity," said Roger in his Oral History, "and treated me as a VIP house guest. Later, following a prisoners' strike by objectors, he urged clemency for the men by cutting

the preposterous sentences, a procedure gradually followed and one which I and the Bureau had constantly put up to the War Department."

As it happened, one of the prisoners who helped implement this particular strike — prisoner number 16122 to be exact — was Oral James, who it will be remembered was one of the two boys Roger adopted in St. Louis, the one who was closer to Roger and who had always tended to copy him.

"When Colonel Rice addressed the assembled prisoners and asked them, 'What do you want, what are your grievances?' it was Oral who spoke up to voice the prisoners' complaints," Roger said; "it was all reported in the *Times*."

"Didn't the *Times* also report that you had something to do with Oral's speech — in fact that you wrote it?"

"They reported that, yes, but it wasn't true. I didn't even know Oral was going to do it. But I was proud of him. It took guts and the result was a complete shakeup in the system of handling releases on parole and segregation of the die-hard C.O.'s. Of course Oral was no die-hard, but he had not convinced the review board of his sincerity, so he was committed."

"Had he convinced you?"

"No, I think he paid his penalty for following me instead of his own conscience. Borrowed consciences are weak and I never thought his was really his own."

This seemed to me a rather harsh judgment, but since I had no way of knowing whether or not it was unfair, I let it go and asked only about his other adopted boy, Toto, and his war record.

"Toto was drafted and went to France. He hated the war and everything about it, but he did his duty in a battalion repairing communications wire under fire and was one of ten or so who survived."

"How did he feel about your being a conscientious objector?"

"He showed a complete detachment. When I went to jail, he wrote me with sympathy for my position. He had done his duty; he took no political stands. What his views were, he never said and I never asked. I now think it was my error. I should have drawn him out, but I had great respect for his privacy. In any case he never asked my views either. He knew them, of course, because I always talked freely but he showed no desire to follow up. Quite the opposite from Oral who was always discussing or inquiring. As I look back it seems strange that the two boys so attached to me could be so different in attitude and relationship. Oral went to prison as I did; he had taken most of his cues from me from boyhood. Toto had always gone his own way."

In addition to conscientious objectors who were perhaps their greatest concern, the Bureau also took up the cudgels for the thousand citizens who suffered repression from free speech as a result of the 1917 Espionage Act. In particular Roger acted in behalf of the IWW men who were being prosecuted by the government for calling strikes in order to obstruct the war effort.

"This Espionage Act gave us more trouble than anything else," Roger recalled. "There were over one thousand prosecutions — one thousand and seventy-three I think it was — under that one law during a very short period of the war."

"What actually did the law say?"

"Well for one thing it said in effect that anything that interfered with recruiting and enlistment in the Armed Forces was sedition — criminal offense. So they prosecuted people for making speeches that were held to obstruct recruiting and enlistment. I remember one very prominent woman — Anson Phelps Stokes's wife, Rose Pastor Stokes. She said in a speech in Kansas City at an anti-war meeting that 'the government is for profiteers and I am for the people.' She was indicted of course and convicted and sentenced to *ten* years in prison. It was a terrible time. Every district attorney enforced the Espionage Act as he wished. It wasn't until toward the end of the war that the Department of Justice established a central control, which was a step we had long urged. Then they appointed two assistant attorneys general who were in a sense friends of ours — John Lord O'Brian and Alfred Bettman — and those two men put the lid on most of the free-speech prosecutions.

I mentioned then that Donald Johnson had reported in *Challenge to American Freedom* on a meeting Roger had had with Colonel Edward M. House, who was President Wilson's closest adviser, during which Roger had told Colonel House flatly that radical groups like the IWW and the Socialist party would be a little more helpful about the war effort if the administration would stop badgering them. Rather to my surprise Roger responded vaguely with, "Maybe that's what I saw House about. I've forgotten."

Since his forgetting so significant a meeting with so important a figure seemed to me most uncharacteristic, I checked back later in the Johnson book to make sure I had not misread the passage. I had not. But apparently I had failed to notice the accompanying footnote — which I suspect Roger had not failed to do. "One has the impression," it said, "in reading the diary of Edward M. House (unpublished manuscripts, Yale University Library) that House did not take Baldwin or his friends too seriously; in fact, he rarely mentions their visits in his diary." *

This is not to suggest that Roger only remembered the meetings in Washington that went well. Indeed he recalled several for me that had gone badly and accomplished nothing. Censorship of mail — banning any publication that contained anti-war articles — was clearly a problem that the Civil Liberties Bureau felt strongly called upon to protest. And on one occasion Clarence Darrow happened to be in town and the Bureau figured he would be a pretty able ambassador to wait upon Postmaster General Albert Burleson and talk about the mail censorship problem. Here is how Roger describes that meeting. "Darrow was not an anti-war person. In his cynical way he accepted the war as something you couldn't do anything about, but he didn't accept the idea of surrendering liberties to win it. I had never met him before, and I don't know how it happened that just he and I went to the postmaster general. Of course it was really just Darrow. I went along as company and said hardly a word. I have always known when to keep quiet, and indeed prefer it if any big shot is along.

"Postmaster General Burleson was a political figure of patronage weight, sitting behind a big desk with no papers on it. He didn't get up when we came in. If Darrow was a national figure Burleson treated him as casually as the next visitor and me he barely included in his 'What can I do for you gentlemen?' Darrow went right to the point and argued in his folksy way against mail censorship, pointing out that driving protest underground would do more harm than good and that tolerance of dissent was in line with our democracy. When Darrow was through Burleson began to tell us some irrelevant stories about Texas politics that added up to his telling us he knew best how to handle the opposition. Darrow looked baffled. But he saw it was no use talking more and we left. Though the Bureau

* Johnson, p. 68.

kept trying to get the President to ease up on censorship we never did succeed in modifying the war policy adopted not only by the postmaster general and the attorney general, but by the Bureau of Public Information as well.

"Then another time I remember John Graham Brooks, a very prominent industrial conciliator and who, by the way, had been my Uncle William Baldwin's biographer, arranged a meeting for us with David Houston, who was a member of Wilson's cabinet."

"David Houston. Is that the same Houston who was chancellor of Washington University when you were there?"

"That's right. The same — my old boss. He was secretary of agriculture. And Francis G. Caffrey, U.S. district attorney [with whom Roger was to have other significant dealings], was there at the lunch too — it was at the Century Club in New York, and our purpose was to try to get to the President through Houston and tell him to lay off prosecuting the IWW if they wanted the war industry to prosper. Again I didn't say much. Mr. Brooks carried the conversation, but I spoke up once as a civil libertarian, pointing out the rights of the IWW people and suggesting what would happen if they were suppressed and what kind of strike they might pull."

"No success?"

"None. Houston was cold — very cold to me. He was a cold man anyhow. And Caffrey just said that the IWW people had to be suppressed and so nothing came of the meeting and the policy continued and the IWW men — a hundred and sixty-three of them — were indicted and the great Chicago trial took place."

I said I remembered reading that syndicalism was what was charged against the IWW in that trial, but I had to confess I was not entirely sure just what that meant.

"Oh syndicalism was a very misconstrued word. It meant the advocacy of destruction of property by a federation of industrial workers. And since slowing down on the job was taken to mean destruction of property, why slowing down on the job was a crime under the criminal syndicalist laws."

"You mean there actually were syndicalist laws?"

"Oh yes. The states had them. Not the federal government, but the states. But as far as the IWW was concerned, syndicalism was just so much bluff. They talked and they talked, you know, and they frightened their employers because they talked very revolutionary. They would say, 'The working class has nothing in common with the employing class. We're against them. And we will use whatever method we can to gain our end short of violence.' They didn't use violence."

"But if they weren't violent why was everyone so afraid of them?"

"Well there were three or four reasons. For one thing they were highly mobile. They didn't have wives and children so they could summon men from all over the country — thousands of them would come together very quickly to hold a huge meeting on freedom of speech for example. And a lot of angry unemployed men, all massed together in one place, scared people to death. And it scared people at a logging camp in the Northwest, where the food was so bad and the lodging so filthy that the men burned all their lousy blankets in one enormous bonfire. You can imagine what that did to people."

Although the IWW took no official stand on the war, virtually all of the men were openly opposed to it. Roger recalls one Wobbly saying, "How the hell do you expect us to be patriotic? What have we got to defend? A lousy bed in a bunkhouse, food not fit for a dog, wages you can't hardly live on and the toughest work in the world. So don't ask me to be patriotic." "Why should we stand up and be shot for thirteen dollars a month?" asked another.

Roger of course had admired the IWW men since the St. Louis days when he found winter lodging in the city for the migratory workers. He felt as they did: He was both opposed to the war and opposed to capitalism.

"That's right," he said. "I was very sympathetic with those boys."

"And when they were prosecuted?"

"We defended them. I went myself to the Chicago trial, which lasted for months, and got to know some of the defendants and their lawyers."

"Their lawyers? So when you say you defended the IWW men you don't mean that you provided them with counsel."

"No, that would have bankrupted us. But our lawyers did take a look at the indictment and what the government proposed to prove against them. Most of it ran quite contrary to our ideas of free speech and the press. But there was the troublesome charge of 'sabotage' — I use the word in quotes — that did look in some cases like an *incitement* to sabotage. So we decided to hold off full support until we saw what the trial evidence produced.

"But in any case we were fully committed to a fair trial and so we

defended the IWW boys by public support of their position, by raising money for their defense. We got distinguished liberals to sign,
even some pro-war people who risked their reputations, possibly
their jobs, in backing the defense of so hated an organization. We
gave the IWW's eastern fund-raising agent — a quiet, gentlemanly
young man named Chet Chumley — a desk in our New York office,
which attracted the attention of the FBI as we later found out."

What also attracted the attention, not only of the Justice Department but of Military Intelligence and the Post Office, was the publication by the Civil Liberties Bureau of a pamphlet entitled *The Truth
About the IWW*. According to Donald Johnson the pamphlet stated
unequivocally that "the IWW had not obstructed the war, nor advocated violence, disloyalty, treason or pro-Germanism. It had
always been a legitimate labor organization whose objectives were
economic not political, and the government therefore had no legal
right to prosecute it." *

Not surprisingly the pamphlet was at once declared unmailable by
the Post Office Department. Rather more surprisingly Roger does
not mention it in his Oral History, nor could he be persuaded to say
very much about the pamphlet to me. "I wrote it and the Post Office banned it, and that's all you need to say about it."

This would not be the only time that I would run into an uncharacteristic reticence on Roger's part concerning a *written* apologia
for a far left (and therefore usually unpopular) cause. Radical sentiments committed to paper obviously had a greater capability of returning to haunt him in later years than mere spoken words —
however extremist.

By late summer of 1918, not only was the Civil Liberties Bureau
regarded with suspicion and hostility by government agencies and by
private patriotic associations, but Roger himself was moving toward
a watershed period of his life. The draft was reaching out to un-
married men between the ages of thirty-five and forty.

Matters came to a head both for the Bureau and for Roger during
two short weeks. On August 31, 1918, the office of the National
Civil Liberties Bureau was raided by FBI agents assisted by a group
of self-styled patriots from the Union League Club. And on Sep-

* *Ibid.*, p. 94.

tember 12 Roger was called to register under the Selective Service Act.

The raid on the Bureau offices at 70 Fifth Avenue was led by FBI agent Rayme Finch whom Roger describes as a "seventy-five per cent good guy." The Union League Club contingent was led by Archie Stevenson whom Roger describes as a son of a bitch.

(7)

The Individual and the State

BY ALL ACCOUNTS THE RAID on the National Civil Liberties Bureau was a bungled job from start to finish. Roger was not on hand when the party of ten agents, all armed, from the Justice Department accompanied by the half-dozen or so volunteers from the ultra-conservative Union League Club took possession of the office in Room 710 at 70 Fifth Avenue. It was a Saturday morning at ten-thirty.

Walter Nelles was the first to arrive on the scene. As a lawyer he reacted instantly by demanding to see the squad's search warrant, which he at once pronounced invalid for "failure of supporting affidavits to show probable cause." Accordingly he ordered Rayme Finch and his men to quit the premises. Finch responded by pointing a revolver at Nelles's head and suggesting that he step aside. Wisely Nelles complied.

Roger was immediately summoned and hurried over to the office, but instead of confronting Finch and his men belligerently, he introduced himself politely and offered his full cooperation, while ignoring Stevenson's vigilantes, who were simply milling around making their presence felt.

Finch was understandably thrown off guard by this unexpected affability. According to Nelles, none of the Justice Department men knew what to make of Roger at all, especially when, as they started rummaging through the CLB papers, Roger stood beside them blandly telling them which items they wanted and which were of no importance to them.

On the other hand, Roger had nothing but scorn for Archibald Stevenson and his Union League volunteers, who went under the name of the Propaganda League and who were, Roger said sarcastically, "all doing their patriotic duty and escaping the draft."

"All were men of wealth," Roger wrote in his affidavit concerning the raid, "whose experience and views were obviously so narrow as to totally unfit them even to comprehend the issues with which they were dealing."

Furthermore, the affidavit continued, Stevenson had "stated in the presence of several persons that the purpose of the association he headed was to gather complete data on all radical leaders and radical movements, that they maintained a cross-reference index file of these leaders and movements which was becoming the most complete record of its kind in the United States . . ." (In other words, a 1918 version of Nixon's famous Enemies' List.)

Even apart from the raid, Roger had good reason to dislike Stevenson; he was counsel for the New York Lusk Committee — a precursor of the House Un-American Activities Committee — that had denounced the Civil Liberties Bureau for being "popular with droves of slackers, pro-Germans, Socialists (and others) who grasped at any chance to pose as conscientious objectors." *

And on a personal basis, Roger mistrusted Stevenson, "who called me Roger — and I called him Archie too. He was a Yale man as I remember it. He would get into private conversations with me around the luncheon table; two or three people would be there and he would use the talk we had as public testimony against me. So one day I said to him, 'Archie, you son of a bitch, I said that to you privately at a luncheon. You know I wasn't intending to be quoted.' But he would quote me just the same."

After the raid, Roger's collection is that Stevenson and his Propaganda League volunteers took all the papers from the CLB office and hauled them off to the Union League Club where they were tossed into such a disorganized heap that the Justice Department finally protested to Stevenson, "You fellows are no good. You're just a bunch of amateurs. You can't do anything with all those papers. Bring them back here."

So the papers were returned, not to 70 Fifth Avenue, but to the Justice Department office at 15 Park Row in New York where in due course Roger was to have a great deal to do with getting them back in order.†

* *Ibid.*, p. 176.
† Roger's affidavid, which incidentally was never notarized and therefore may never have been formally filed, states the matter somewhat differently. It says that a "pro-

Most of the CLB board of directors felt that the raid on the offices was only a curtain-raiser to a main event that would involve indictments and arrests, either of Roger alone as director, or of Roger and the staff, or even of the entire Board.

"Some of my committee were sure they would be arrested. I thought so too, and so our smart lawyers decided to get a most unlikely counsel to head off trouble. I never knew how they engineered it but they got the services of George Gordon Battle, who was prominent in Democratic politics [actually he was counsel to Tammany Hall], a southern gentleman and a strong war supporter. I had met Mr. Battle briefly and he knew of our activities and how innocent of wrongdoing such nice people as we were. So he persuaded the Justice Department that we were not worth their attention and all thought of prosecution was dropped."

"Meanwhile you had problems of your own, didn't you?"

"Meanwhile I certainly did."

On September 12, 1918, Roger Baldwin wrote the following letter to Local Draft Board Number 129:

Gentlemen: In registering today under the Selective Service Act, I desire to make the following statement as to my attitude toward conscription. I am opposed to the use of force to accomplish any ends, however good. I am, therefore, opposed to participation in this or any other war. My opposition is not only to direct military service, but to any service whatever designed to help the war. I am furthermore opposed to the principle of conscription in time of war or peace, for any purpose whatsoever. I will decline to perform any service under compulsion, regardless of its character. I am advising you of my views so that you may record my record with your board to show from the start where I stand. Very truly yours,

On October 9 Roger received a notice to report for a physical examination. He "respectfully declined to appear." In a letter to New York Attorney General Francis G. Caffrey * he gave substantially the

posal to take the papers for examination to the Union League Club instead of the Department of Justice was first seriously discussed in the affiant's presence and then it was dropped only when the impropriety of it was pointed out by an agent of the Department." Roger's comment on reading this affidavit, which he did not recall having written, was that he had been certain the papers *were* taken to the Union League Club but that "affidavits are usually better than memory. I accept it of course."

* Caffrey, it will be recalled, had been present at the luncheon with David Houston at the Century Club when Roger and John Graham Brooks had tried unsuccessfully to persuade him to tell President Wilson to lay off prosecuting the IWW boys.

same reasons for his refusal to comply as he had in his letter to Local Board 129, but added several further paragraphs:

I do not take this position against complying with a law without the most mature deliberation. I appreciate that there are several ways in which I might escape the serious consequences which I now face, but I reject them. First, I might get deferred classification on physical grounds; second, the war might be over before I would be called to service; third, by compliance with the law I would doubtless be recognized at camp as a conscientious objector and given the opportunity to perform agricultural service on furlough, as do most conscientious objectors.

But I prefer prison to gambling with the government, or to accepting an easy way of compromise. I cannot evade the clear moral issue which conscription presents to me. I can only resist it, regardless of consequences.

I do not seek martyrdom. I desire no public notoriety and I serve no cause but my own inner satisfaction.

All I ask of you is a speedy trial. I shall of course plead guilty. I shall handle my own case without counsel. I do not desire, and would not accept bail pending trial, because, refusing deliberately to comply with the law, I do not feel morally justified in purchasing a few weeks freedom.

Then, unable to resist the chance for a little gratuitous preachment, he added:

Furthermore I am opposed on principle to the institution of bail as one of the many devices by which the courts operate for the benefit of the well-to-do and against the poor. I would feel more comfortable not to accept before the law a privilege which is not equally shared by the poorest citizen.

Very respectfully yours,

A year earlier when Roger shifted his base of operation from Washington to New York, he had moved in with his Aunt Ruth Baldwin, who was living in an apartment at 1 West 83rd Street with her friend Elizabeth Walton. "It was a happy arrangement," Roger said. "I was devoted to my Aunt Ruth, the closest of all my relatives who shared my views of the war. Elizabeth Walton — the 'boss' I called her because she ran the house — was equally companionable on the war issues as a birth-right Quaker who stuck, as many did not, to the birth-right. It was a lively pacifist ménage."

And it was from this ménage that Roger Baldwin was arrested as a war resister the day after his letter reached Judge Caffrey.

"I knew it was going to happen, but somehow I was not quite prepared for the way it happened," he recalled. "I was getting dressed to go out to New Jersey to see my girlfriend for dinner when I was met at the door by a plainclothes man who said, 'The chairman of the draft board wants to see you.' So he took me to the basement of the American Museum of Natural History where the draft board had its office. The chairman was a distinguished lawyer whom I had known slightly in juvenile court work. His name was Julius Henry Cohen. He said, 'Mr. Baldwin, I have your letter. Why are you being so contumacious?' "

"His exact word?"

"His exact word. I hadn't heard it for a long time but I figured it fitted me so I said, 'Because I just am not going into the army in any service whatever, even under furlough to civilian work.' So then Mr. Cohen suggested that I had better think that over with a night in jail. He said he'd see me in the morning. I was taken to the police station after my guardian — the plainclothes man who had arrested me at my aunt's apartment — fed me, let me get a haircut and phone my girlfriend. I was put in a cold dark cell with nothing but a board bench and a toilet."

Since Roger had twice mentioned his girlfriend, I figured I had better pick up that cue — in fact, that he expected me to do so. "This girlfriend," I began —

"Was Madeleine Doty whom I eventually married."

I asked him to fill me in.

"Well, I first met Madeleine at the annual meeting of the National Conference of Social Work of which incidentally I am still a member — probably the oldest member — it's now called Social Welfare. But anyway I had met Madeleine at one of the meetings while I was still living in St. Louis. She was a well-known writer from New York, a prisoner reformer and a member of the New York State Commission who had volunteered to become a prisoner and had written about her experiences. She was also a lawyer — though she didn't practice — and a pacifist and a mild socialist and she was committed to feminism."

"She sounds formidable."

"She was intriguing," Roger said. "That is, she intrigued me, as

powerful, attractive women always have. And she was quite beautiful with the clearest blue eyes I have ever seen and a gay direct way
of speaking. She had a strong graceful figure and she dressed
charmingly — just unconventionally enough to stamp her individ-
uality."

"You say you first met her while you were still in St. Louis. Then
did you look her up when you moved to New York?"

"Well, I had seen her on several visits to New York before I actually moved there. And she introduced me to the most astonishing
group of people I had ever met. St. Louis had nothing like them.
They were the advance guard of social reformers known as the Liberal Club. We would dine at some bohemian restaurant in the Vil-
lage, some thirty or so socialists, feminists, free lovers and free
thinkers — I remember Max Eastman and his wife, Ida Rauh, Doris
Stephens, Art Young.* These were all exciting people to a midwestern youth who had only lately been exposed to those eastern here-
sies.†

"Then when I left St. Louis for good and came to New York,
there was Madeleine among the pacifists. She was living alone, writing for the big magazines, and we teamed up for meals and country
weekends. She had had her men friends but none was in atten-
dance at the time, fortunately. So our fast friendship grew and blossomed until it was more than a friendship. By the time of my arrest,
we had agreed to get married after I got out of prison."

I wanted to know what happened to him after he'd landed in his
cold dark cell. Was he taken in the morning to the chairman of the
draft board to see if overnight he had become less contumacious?

Rather to his surprise, he said, he was not. Instead, he was taken
out of his cell and was astonished to hear his name called out by
none other than Rayme Finch of the Justice Department, the man
who had led the raid on the Civil Liberties Bureau office a week
before. Finch said cheerily, "Come on out to breakfast — you're
going to have the fanciest little arrest you ever heard of." So after
breakfast, which was indeed very grand, Roger was driven down-
town in a black limousine to the Federal Building at 15 Park Row.

"There I hung around and learned that 'Washington' had ordered

* Edna St. Vincent Millay was also in this group.
† He was not, of course, a "midwestern youth," but in this context he chose to
regard himself as such.

them to go ahead with the case against me," Roger wrote in a contemporary account (November 15, 1918) entitled "How I Took the Veil." "In the afternoon I was taken to the assistant U.S. attorney. He read my letter stating my position, had an indictment ready in ten minutes and had me in court in fifteen minutes more. I was getting the speedy trial I asked for, all right."

In fact it was too speedy for Rayme Finch who wanted Roger available for a few weeks to try to make some order out of the NCLB papers that had been so badly messed up by the Union League Club patriots. So Roger was only arraigned that day and pled guilty. He was then assigned a special marshal deputized solely to look after him, and thus began a month's arrangement during which he was lodged each evening at the Tombs — New York's still-standing medieval-looking city prison — while each day he was taken to the Justice Department to work on the NCLB papers.

"If I had been an honored guest, I could not have been more considerately treated than by these government agents," Roger recalled. "I was a curiosity, of course, a man who wanted to go to prison, a Harvard man at that, and rich, they thought. My special marshal took me to a burlesque show one night before returning me to the Tombs. I remember we saw a tall comedienne named Charlotte Greenwood. He accompanied me to lunch with Norman Thomas and his family. And he took me to see my dying Aunt Sarah Briggs, who was well beyond eighty and hardly able to raise her head off the pillow. But she knew quite well why I was there. She said, 'I do not understand why you do it. You may be right. I don't know. But you have good blood in you and I do not think you can do wrong.' That was true Boston," Roger chuckled. "The family blood decides.

"One day," he continued, "my regular marshal couldn't make it and a strange one came for me, with handcuffs. I told him I didn't use those things, that I went freely, but he said he had to obey the rules, so he slipped them on. It was a five-block walk from the Tombs to 15 Park Row and I didn't want to meet anyone I knew while being dragged along by a cop, so I contrived to make *him* appear the prisoner and *I* the marshal by the simple device of keeping two paces ahead of him — he was short and fat — and dragging *him* along. Try that next time you get handcuffs on."

I said I would be sure to do so.

Diverting as Roger makes this sojourn seem, it must also have had its very unpleasant aspects, because the Tombs was old, decaying, dirty, bug-ridden and grim. Although Roger claims not to have minded it, his three weeks in the Tombs — even though he only spent nights and Sundays there — could hardly have made him very sanguine about what lay ahead for him when he finished with the Bureau papers at the Justice Department and faced trial and sentencing.

Finally, on October 30, 1918, he had his day in court, appearing before Federal Judge Julius M. Mayer. "I was taken over to the U.S. court from the Tombs by my own private marshal and greeted by the FBI and the district attorney's staff, out in force to see me on my way. The courtroom was well filled with my friends: Aunt Ruth was there, Elizabeth Walton, Judah Magnes, Scott Nearing, Rose Pastor Stokes, Norman Thomas — in fact, most of the board of the Civil Liberties Bureau, and of course my colleagues in the office."

The district attorney stated the case as a violation of the draft act — a willful violation; Roger responded with a prepared statement that he had written while sitting outside his cell in the Tombs and that he had shown to no one except Norman Thomas, who had made some minor editorial changes. His pronouncement (along with the extemporaneous response of Judge Mayer) was later published by his friends as a pamphlet entitled *The Individual and the State*. It is an extraordinary document: a sincere, straightforward, eloquent expression of Roger's most deeply felt convictions.

Reading it today, sixty-seven years later, against the background of all I have come to know and, I hope, to understand of Roger Baldwin, I have the feeling that those 1,500 words, spoken in a moment of high drama, are as truly idealistic as any he has ever uttered.

"I am before you as a deliberate violator of the draft act," he began, and after reviewing briefly the sequence of events since his initial arrest on October 9, he continued:

The compelling motive for refusing to comply with the draft act is my uncompromising opposition to the principle of conscription of life by the State for any purpose whatsoever, in time of war or peace. I not only refuse to obey the present conscription law, but I would in future refuse to obey any similar statute which attempts to direct my choice of service or ideals. I regard the principle of conscription of life as a flat

contradiction of all our cherished ideals of individual freedom, democratic liberty and Christian teaching.

He went on to describe his profound opposition "to this and all
other wars," suggesting that he was aware that his position was extreme, that "in the present temper it is regarded either as an unwar-
ranted egotism or as a species of feeble-mindedness." Thus, he said,
he could not "let this occasion pass without attempting to explain the
foundations on which so extreme a view rests."

The foundations, of course, were his forebears "of the stock of the
first settlers," his Boston birthplace and upbringing, his Harvard education, his early rebellion at "our whole autocratic industrial system," which led him to take up social work in St. Louis. He described his efforts through social organization and legislation
"gradually to free the mass of folks from industrial and political
bondage." At the same time, he said, he was attracted by the solutions to our social problems put forth by the radicals. He mentioned
his study of socialism, of the IWW, of European syndicalism and
anarchism, but said that however much he sympathized with those
programs he could see no way of translating them effectively into
practical daily service.

Then, in what seems a small discordant note and perhaps the only
disingenuous part of his discourse, he went on: "Six years ago, however, I was so discouraged with social work and reform, so challenged by the sacrifices and idealism of some of my IWW friends,
that I was on the point of getting out altogether, throwing respectability overboard and joining the IWW as a manual worker."

There is little or no evidence that Roger ever was really at the
point of throwing in the sponge and "getting out altogether." At
best this could have been no more than a fleeting romantic fantasy,
and, in all fairness, one that he himself partially acknowledged when
he added, "I thought better of it. My traditions were against it. It
was more an emotional reaction than a practical form of service."

However, it seemed altogether genuine when he went on to say
that ever since his period of discouragement he had felt himself
heart and soul with the worldwide radical movement for industrial
and political freedom. "Personally," he stated without equivocation,
"I share the extreme radical philosophy of the future society. I look
forward to a social order without any external restraints upon the in-

dividual save through public opinion and the opinions of friends and neighbors."

Then finally his closing statement:

I hope, your Honor will not think that I have taken this occasion to make a speech for the sake of making a speech . . . I know that it is pretty nigh hopeless in times of war and hysteria to get across to any substantial body of people, the view of an out and out heretic like myself. I know that as far as my principles are concerned, they seem to be utterly impractical — mere moon-shine. They are not the views that work in the world today. I fully realize that. But I fully believe that they are the views which are going to guide in the future.

Having arrived at the state of mind in which these views mean the dearest thing in life to me, I cannot consistently, with self-respect, do other than I have, namely, to deliberately violate an act which seems to me to be a denial of everything which ideally and in practice I hold sacred.

Judge Mayer made what Roger considered an eloquent off-the-cuff response. He praised Roger for his manly self-respect and for stating his position honestly, conscientiously and without a quibble. However, he said:

I am directing my mind solely to the indictment to which you plead guilty. You are entirely right. There can be no compromise. There can be neither compromise by you as the defendant, as you say, because you don't wish compromise. Nor can there be compromise by the Court, which, for the moment, represents organized society as we understand it in this Republic. He who disobeys the law, knowing that he does so, with the intelligence that you possess, must, as you are prepared to — take the consequences . . .

The maximum penalty, as I understand it, is one year in the penitentiary. You have already spent twenty days in imprisonment. You are sentenced to the penitentiary for eleven months and ten days.

"Two strong men looked each other between the eyes," ran the lead in the *New York Times* front-page story the next day, "and though one of the men sentenced the other to a term in prison, each of the men found no fault in the other. Roger Baldwin received with a friendly smile the sentence imposed by Federal Judge Julius Mayer . . ."

"I wish you could have heard him this morning," wrote Norman

Thomas to Roger's mother, "for it was one of the rare experiences of a lifetime and I think a sense of exultation of what he was doing would have overcome even your sorrow."

"Never shall I forget that scene in court, nor cease to be grateful that I was there and could see you and listen to your words," wrote Ruth S. Baldwin to her nephew. "I felt it was the most deeply moving experience of my life, and your bearing, simple and noble, your address beautiful, direct and convincing beyond what any words of mine can express."

"Baldwin has proved himself the most consistent of us all," wrote Emma Goldman to a mutual friend; "tell him I am prouder of him than I am of myself." (Which meant she was very proud indeed.)

Furthermore in *Living My Life* she wrote, "Roger Baldwin has proved a great surprise. In former years he had impressed me as rather confused in his social views, a person who tried to be all things to all men. His stand at his trial for evading the draft, his frank avowal of anarchism, his unreserved repudiation of the right of the State to coerce the individual had made me conscious of guilt toward him. I wrote him confessing my unkind judgement and assuring him that his example had given me a salutary lesson of the need of greater care in appraisement of people."

On July 24, 1974, I asked Roger, "How long since you've read *The Individual and the State?*"

"I read it not so long ago, and wondered — as I assume you were going to ask me — if I'd take the same stand today."

"And?"

"Well, of course my attitude toward the Second World War differed; the Second World War was primarily a defensive war because of the attack on Pearl Harbor. And almost everybody in the pacifist movement in the United States regarded it as a defensive — and inevitable war. And so there were not the tensions between opponents that there had been in the First World War and later in the Korean and Vietnam wars."

"But there were still conscientious objectors in World War Two?"

"Oh yes, of course, and the government by then was offering them civilian service. In my time there was only the army or jail."

"Although there were noncombatant opportunities within the army in World War One, weren't there — farm furloughs?"

"Oh yes, there were — but as you say *within* the army. It was still the draft. You see, Peggy, my objection was not only to the war but more to the whole principle of conscription. To be conscripted offends me, because the power that can force you to do good can force others to do evil — like killing enemies. I was against the power to draft for any service then, and I am against it now. I must admit though, that at times I have not been so positive and have thought I could be reasonable and accept the compromise of useful civilian service. But it is too dangerous a power to make exceptions. My whole pacifist philosophy denies coercion for any end, however good."

Twelve days after his sentencing, Roger's special marshal and another marshal corralled for the occasion set off to take him by subway from the Tombs to the Essex County jail in Newark, New Jersey.

There were no handcuffs. As the three men went on foot through lower Broadway en route to the subway their progress was much slowed by cheering crowds and showers of confetti. The date was November 11, 1918 — Armistice Day. The war was over, but not for Roger. Still, he said, he was cheerful about this "new adventure" and chatted amiably with his marshals all the way over to New Jersey. In Newark they stopped off at a bar for a farewell drink — Roger treating.

Then, Roger recalled, "They delivered me to a door in a high wall; behind was the old stone prison. I had been in many prisons as an officer of the juvenile and adult courts in St. Louis. I saw at once that this was the better sort of jail — small, informal, easygoing. I knew I would feel at home."

(8)

In the World and Out of It

Not only did Roger feel at home in cell 254 of the Essex County jail, he was almost lyrical about conditions there, which he found made for a "healthful, restful life of study and contemplation."

His practice of writing descriptive letters to be mimeographed and mailed wholesale "to my friends," which was to continue throughout his career whenever he was in strange places, began at this period. From these accounts, plus his frequent letters to his mother, and — surprisingly — his six or seven poems written from prison, one gets a very good idea of what his life behind bars was really like.

For the most part, it was a lark, largely, it seems, because Roger perceived it as such. "In contrast to the average county jail," he wrote to his friends, "we enjoy good light, sunshine, fresh air day and night, absence of smells (even of disinfectants), clean food and beds and freedom to spend our time as we like within the limits of our cells and corridors. As one of the half-dozen trusties I get outside the jail doors to work twice a day in the kitchen and wards. Our mail is unrestricted. We may all have visitors twice a week for two hours with, however, the embarrassment of straining conversations through double screens of heavy mesh, put up to prevent passing dope or sharp implements from outside.

"The trusties, however, are permitted to see visitors at other hours, outside the screens, and I am under practically no restrictions. Almost daily between four-thirty and six o'clock, when my work is done, some good friend drops over from New York to have a chat in the warden's office or outside the walls in the greenhouse."

Madeleine Doty, during his first weeks at Essex, came very regularly. "She has been a most faithful friend and brings me all the little things I need," Roger wrote to his mother, and added that he was sending her a copy of Madeleine's new book.* "I have read it with the liveliest interest and send it on to you because it's the kind of thing that will interest you. It's not hard reading."

It seems probable that Roger was carefully laying the groundwork for his mother to think well of his future wife. At least he hoped she would be his future wife, but the circumstances for nurturing a newly blossomed love were hardly ideal. "Dearest," Roger wrote to Madeleine, "It's hell to be away from you now when for the first time we understand and love together. I feel like a hunk of dynamite — ready to explode."

And in her autobiography (unpublished) Madeleine wrote, "It wasn't an easy time for our growing love. My telephone was continuously tapped. Our private conversations became public property."

She had even visited him when he was in the Tombs and she had acted as his attorney — or rather pretended to because it gave her the right to see him at any time. "I tried to look important and carried a briefcase," she wrote. "Frequently I found myself locked in the cell with him."

At Essex, they met always in the leafy serenity of the greenhouse. "But still we both felt frustrated," Madeleine recalled. "And even Roger's cheerfulness was put to the test." He wrote: "I don't know what is the matter. I never heard of a love so dumb. I am full of feeling I cannot voice . . . It isn't anything you have done or are, for you completely answer my underlying and essential needs."

Madeleine was six years older than Roger; she was convinced of their love, but she was not sure that marriage was right for them, and, as the strain of their relationship grew, she thought they ought to have time to think it over — especially as circumstances prevented them from doing very much else. So she proposed to Roger that she go to Europe to see the condition of the world as a result of the war, and also attend the congress of the Women's International League for Peace.

Roger readily agreed. Still a letter to her, written just after she landed in Liverpool on February 14, 1919, was a wistful one. "Dear heart — It was a long time ago you sailed away — and your two little notes from the harbor make it seem very long. I did not know until

* *Behind the Battle Lines: Around the World in 1918* (New York: Macmillan Co., 1918). The magazine *Good Housekeeping* had sent her abroad to gather material for this book.

you went how much I relied on your being close by — and how much my sub-conscious was engaged to you when my consciousness was on strike . . . But I'm really glad you've gone — glad for you, glad for me, glad for the thing we create together . . . Don't bother to tell me much, but say it often. My love — all of the real stuff I have."

He tried to fill the gap left by her absence with what Madeleine referred to as his "extraordinary love for all sorts and conditions of men." Soon he found himself falling again into his role of older brother-teacher-inspiration-guardian to three youthful prisoners (the youngest was eighteen), bright educable boys full of zeal. In a sense they were the Essex jail counterparts of Toto and Oral and he began to envisage a future life for himself and Madeleine that included them.

"I foresee you as the lady proprietress of a house for Roger's stray crooks," he wrote Madeleine only half-facetiously, "but they are fine boys and I love them — and you too — all the time." And again a few weeks later he wrote, "Being elder brother and exclusive solace is flattering to one's vanity (as the psychoanalysts would tell me). I have much of that protégé instinct in me, a form of ego, of course, all directed to developing youth. We will yet have our 'school' for big and little children — and we will do and teach them rustic and agricultural arts, trusting God to provide for them. Aunt Ruth says you will need an assistant, marrying a gang, and I have a hunch she is a candidate, but the boys need you — some of them fully as much as me and more. And you need them, my dear, for the same reason I need them. They are the eternal tests of our own integrity of mind and heart — the youthful examiners of our faith, the guarantors of our eternal childhood."

Roger's naturally ebullient spirits contributed to his enjoyment, not only of his three boys and his other fellow prisoners, but of his work as well. He was fortunate in being assigned to the warden's kitchen where the "pay" food — as opposed to the regular but coarser prison fare provided all inmates — and the special "diet" food was prepared. His "boss," the cook, was Bridget, "a character, an old Irishwoman, a grandmother worn by age and work but full of fire and oaths. 'God damn it, Roger,' she will bawl at me. 'And haven't I told you a dozen times that it's turnips for the paid dinners and cabbage for the diets. Jesus Christ how many times must I be telling you.' "

Bridget, Roger explained, was an habitué at the prison, committed regularly for drunkenness. After serving her time, she would keep on with her job as cook, going on salary and continuing to occupy her cell. Then she would go out, get drunk again, be arrested, recommitted, and go right on being cook, living in her cell, once more an inmate, minus the fifty-dollars-per-month wages.

"The head cook," wrote Roger, "is not a prisoner, and so is our superior — I must call her Mrs. Keane, and she calls me 'Roger' just as the warden and most of the prisoners do. There is a fine irony," he added, "in being the cook's servant which amuses me constantly."

After receiving his afternoon callers from New York, Roger usually spent an hour or so in the greenhouse watering and tending to the plants. On one occasion he lost track of time and was still outside when the gate closed at six. Only to Roger could it happen that he thus found himself in a position of being locked *out* of jail and of having to persuade a keeper to let him back in.

The political prisoners — there were fifteen in all — were looked upon with particular favor by the keepers, who were Irish and mostly Sinn Feiners at heart, and by the warden himself, who was an avowed and active Sinn Feiner (he had been suspected of running arms to the Irish rebels). All were vehemently against what they regarded as "England's war" and hence warmly disposed toward those men who refused to fight in it.

Roger was therefore welcomed to Warden McGinnis' quarters of an evening, sometimes to play the piano for "family sings," other times to lead a discussion with the warden, some of the evening keepers and a few invited prisoners on the foundations of social order, or some such cosmic subject.

Still, for all his privileges, and the variety of his pursuits, which made his days pass quickly, Roger was acutely aware that many of his less fortunate fellow prisoners were really suffering. Especially for those men accustomed to hard manual labor, the monotony and the physical stagnation were really a torture. "They felt the bars and the walls as a living tomb," Roger wrote.

Something, therefore, had to be done for those inmates who had no resources within themselves, and Roger, promptly accepting the challenge, set about purposefully to organize what soon became the Prisoners' Welfare League.

While Roger was mulling over in his mind just how to go about setting up his organization, he was visited one day by a Mrs. Sidney Colgate ("anyone who used soap knew her name").

Mrs. Colgate, who lived nearby, made rather a specialty of helping prisoners; she was rich, powerful, energetic and determined and she loved young men — particularly, it appears, those in stripes.

"Before I had anything to do with her," Roger told me, "she had already taken hold of a man on my tier, a fellow named Milton Mauman, a good friend of mine who was a burglar — a very capable burglar too until he got caught."

I smiled at the word "capable" applied to a burglar, then asked if Mrs. Colgate had also "taken up" with him, adding that I had heard stories to that effect — which indeed I had.

"Oh no," he answered agreeably, "nothing like that. After all I was thirty-four and she was fifty."

"But you said she loved young men."

"She did. She and her husband had a very poor relationship. He had a mistress of whom she disapproved, so she retaliated by more or less adopting young men. It was all very affectionate. No sex in it."

I asked if Mrs. Colgate had also adopted his particular three boys.

"Oh yes, she certainly did. They were her protégés as well as mine. One of them, the youngest, Harry Belair, even called us Mom and Pop jokingly. But I think we both had a particular favorite among them who was the liveliest and most devoted of the lot. His name was Fred Farnum. He had come from Massachusetts where he had been married in his teens and had a daughter — he was only twenty-one when I met him — whom he left to seek his fortune in New York. He was arrested and jailed for violating the draft act by not registering." ("Freddie may be the American Rupert Brooke with a dash of Thoreau in him," Roger had once written to Madeleine. "He has no complexes, no inhibitions. He is joy, laughter, wit and wisdom incarnate — and physical beauty too.")

Freddie Farnum was to be best man at Roger and Madeleine's wedding and to loom large for a time in their lives.

At Essex prison Freddie and Harry Belair, and Homer Wright, the third youth, all took an active part in helping Roger start the

Prisoners' Welfare League. Working from the outside, Mrs. Colgate (her first name was Caroline, but Roger always referred to her as Mrs. Colgate) was an efficient partner. It was she who persuaded the Newark public library to open a branch in the Essex County jail. "The librarian, the head of the whole works came out to see me," Roger said; "he was intrigued by the idea of a library branch in a jail.

"And then — maybe it was also through Mrs. Colgate — the head of the Community Service Society, or some such title — it was a social workers' family aid society — sent an agent out to see what he could do for the families of the prisoners. We also hired a lawyer, a very high-minded young man named Smith, who later became U.S. district attorney, to go into court and make pleas for various prisoners. And we paid him a couple of hundred dollars to do it."

"Who paid him," I asked, "and with what?"

"The gamblers — the professional gamblers in jail paid him. They could always put their hands on money and they were glad to help out."

At the same time Roger started a glee club, and, as the real core of the experiment in enlightened prisoner treatment, he organized a series of daily classes. Some were taught by him, some by the other prisoners. "There were some very smart fellows in that jail," Roger said. "I tell you we really had a great little piece of machinery going there in the Prisoners' Welfare League. And what was important about it was that that's the way I think all jails should be run."

"I gather, however, that that view was not entirely shared by the authorities."

"No, it wasn't. You know, I guess, that the sheriff of Essex County — Sheriff Flavel — closed us down."

I said that among his papers I had seen a number of clippings from New Jersey newspapers about the incident. It appears that Sheriff Flavel went out to the Essex County jail one day and was shocked to find a number of prisoners — members of the Prisoners' Welfare League — "playing the phonograph, singing and having a good time." He would have none of it. The League, Flavel decreed, was interfering with the management and discipline of the institution. A few days later, Roger was taken under guard — and by streetcar — to the sheriff's office in Newark where he was told by Flavel that the League would be disbanded at once.

"I was so mad," Roger recalled, "that I started to get up out of my chair and walk out of the office. But all of a sudden I realized that I couldn't. I was a prisoner — I didn't have the luxury of walking out — particularly out of the sheriff's office."

Flavel's action created an angry furor among the prisoners. When his ruling to suspend the organization was announced, 187 prisoners, a large majority of the inmates at Essex, signed a petition asking reconsideration. Flavel, thus put on the defense, countered by giving an interview in which he stated that "the reason for his order to disband was because Professor Baldwin was teaching members of the League socialism . . ." *

If Roger could not walk out of the sheriff's office in anger, he could, and promptly did, exercise his right of protest, by sending Flavel a sharp letter: "You state, according to the papers that I have been using the League to spread socialist views. I not only deny that charge in its entirety, but I state that on the contrary I have been scrupulously careful not to give voice to any sort of political propaganda. I challenge anyone to name any occasion on which I have voiced any views on socialism or any radical subject likely to be objectionable to the authorities."

Roger may have had the last word on the subject, but Sheriff Flavel had the last action, or rather he thought he did.

Before the smoke had cleared away and while the prisoners — aided by the redoubtable Mrs. Colgate — were still trying for a reconsideration of the disband order, Flavel had Roger transferred out of Essex County jail as a troublemaker and sent to the county penitentiary, which was a small country work farm in Caldwell, New Jersey.

Ironically, had the sheriff but known it, Roger had been angling for just such a change in his living arrangements. Spring after all was coming — it was May 14 when he arrived at Caldwell — and spring was no time to be stuck in a city prison. Spring was the time to move to the country.

"The penitentiary," wrote Roger "to my friends," "is located on high hills, open and wooded, with a marvelous sweep of horizon . . . It lies on the streetcar line about fifteen minutes from Montclair

---

* During this period the press took to referring to Roger as professor (justified in a rather far-fetched way by his brief teaching career at Washington University ten years earlier), presumably to point up the incongruity of his being behind bars.

. . . The grounds and entrance drive look like the gateway to an aristocratic country club — well-cropped lawns, beds of gay flowers, a great field of rye running up the hill to the grove of trees through which the long brown buildings of the institution show, capped by a tower."

Euphoric as Roger sounded and doubtless felt about his new utopia, he did note to his friends that Caldwell was a penitentiary rather than a mere jail (as Essex was), and hence considerably stricter.

Even though he was again a trusty, as indeed were sixty per cent of the 300-odd inmates — mostly short-termers, Roger was under much more rigid rules and discipline. All mail coming in and going out was read, and, although there was no censorship on the expression of political views, mail out was limited to two letters a week. Visitors were permitted on Saturdays and Sundays only.

In fact, Roger's description of a typical day included numerous features that easily distinguished Caldwell from the "aristocratic country club" he claimed it looked like. "Supper consisted of rhubarb, plain substantial white bread and tea. After it we were locked in cells until six o'clock, when we had an hour's walk in the corridor, talking or playing dominoes or checkers. At seven we were locked in again. At nine the lights were out."

His daytime activities were delightful, however. He was assigned to the garden work gang of ten men under the charge of a "deliciously eccentric German gardener named Gross whose frank comments and philosophy afford me endless hours of amusement."

Gross was a hard taskmaster, which Roger also enjoyed because the tasks included spading, digging, hoeing, watering, cutting grass and transplanting from the greenhouse and hotbeds to the gardens around the main building. It was very agreeable although often backbreaking work, which assured him that he would come out in August bursting with health.

Still in all, Roger concluded one of his letters, "it *is* a prison and as such is part of a wholly ineffective system of treating crime, doing society, in my judgment, more harm than good. A visitor said of it that it was 'a bad job excellently done' — an estimate which would be echoed by most of the men here."

Roger had been at Caldwell only a couple of weeks and was, for once, quietly minding his own business when for the second time in a month his name was again splashed in newspaper headlines.

The National Conference of Social Work of which he had been an active member since his earliest St. Louis days was having its annual meeting in Atlantic City. Jane Addams was president of the conference and Julia Lothrop (chief of the Children's Bureau) was presiding at the meeting. Committee appointments were under discussion when Miss Lothrop turned the floor over to Florence Kelley (of the Minimum Wage Commission) who was chairman of the Committee on Industrial and Economic Conditions. Miss Kelley put forward the name of Roger Baldwin for her committee.

"Instantly there was an uproar from all parts of the convention hall," reported the *New York World*. "When quiet had been partially restored," the dispatch continued, "George Thorne of New York leaped to his feet and demanded that Baldwin's name be stricken from the list. 'I make this motion because . . . I do not believe we can be party to an action that makes this conference in the eyes of the public endorse a man now in prison for having violated the laws of the United States in time of war.' "

Other delegates were even more vociferous. David I. Kelly of the New Jersey Department of Institutes and Agencies declared, according to another newspaper story, that "We have too much of this sliding back, we have too much of this excusing of persons who stab Americans in the back because of their convictions. I warn you that your entire organization will be cast aside and injured materially if you allow your sympathies and friendship to carry you in voting this matter."

Florence Kelley stuck doggedly to her position, favoring Roger as a man of convictions with the courage to stand by them. Her defense was greeted with "cheers and hisses mingled."

When finally the vote on the matter was taken it stood at 262 in favor of ousting Roger and 216 in favor of retaining him, one dispatch noting that "at least three-quarters of those voting to retain Baldwin were women." So Roger's name was dropped and the outcome was considered a defeat for the radicals.

Also meeting in Atlantic City at the same time was the National Probation Association, which was a branch of the National Conference of Social Work and which, as mentioned, Roger had helped to found. Great was the consternation at that meeting when it was discovered that Roger Baldwin's name appeared on the program. This circumstance was described in one newspaper account as especially repugnant to some of the New York City probation officers.

In addition, Judge Charles W. Hoffman of the domestic relations court in Cincinnati and president of the National Probation Association was quoted in the press as "indignant that a program with Baldwin's name upon it should have been 'put over,' on him by some of Baldwin's personal friends in New York. He called a meeting of the executive committee at once and Baldwin was vigorously repudiated."

One enterprising reporter managed to interview Roger himself at Caldwell Penitentiary to find out what he had to say about the fuss he was causing, but Roger's only comment was a laconic one. He was more concerned, he said, with his lumbago, brought on by all the shoveling and hoeing he was doing, than with the actions of the National Conference of Social Work.*

During his months in prison Roger received literally hundreds of letters. Several years after his release he put together a bound volume of this huge correspondence, dividing it into categories: immediate family, relatives, personal friends, friends in public work, civic work, social work, other political prisoners, acquaintances, strangers.

In an introductory note written in October of 1921, he explained that he had gone to the trouble of arranging the letters because he felt "they all bear testimony not so much to my position as to the writers' deep sentiments on public affairs and individual liberty, even when they appear most flattering to me . . . I am more than ever impressed with their value to me anyway as the most vital part of the experience . . . They were the bonds with the world outside prison which sustained my cheer and nourished love and as that they are the most precious souvenirs of those strange days when I was in the world and out of it."

Reading through the letters myself and recalling some of them to Roger opened up a great many new avenues. In some instances the letters introduced me to people who were of importance to Roger and about whom I would not have known to ask. In other cases they provided illuminating insights into his existing relationships.

* For the benefit of readers under thirty who perhaps have never heard the word, lumbago is what we used to call our aching backs before we learned about slipped disks.

Roger removed most of the family letters (and all those from Madeleine Doty) that he considered too personal to be included in a volume that he expected would be seen by many. However, rather to his surprise, three letters from his father — the only three that Roger thinks he wrote — are retained. They are quite long, written in a cramped but legible hand on blue stationery and signed only F.F.B.

The first, dated November 13, 1918, acknowledged "your good letter and your account of the trial. I think what you said to the court was well expressed and showed a finer feeling of spirit than could be expected from mere man. Yet I feel that Judge Mayer expressed his own feeling, viz. I regret that your theories led you to a defiance of the law. I admire your spirit and strength of character in holding to convictions and wholly respect you. In fact," he added in what must have been for this formidable Yankee a burst of sentiment, "I shall reluctantly admit to you that I am proud of you and feel a deep affection (this latter I presume because of your being in trouble)."

Roger smiled at this. "I didn't think the old boy had it in him," he said. "He loved his son, I guess."

"But did you maintain a warm relationship with him?" I asked.

"A warm relationship." Roger repeated the phrase doubtfully and left the question unanswered. "Once our period of not speaking after Father left my mother was over we never quarrelled about anything. Of course many of the things he stood for and would expound on so vigorously were things I completely disagreed with."

I showed him another letter from his father in which F.F.B. had "expounded vigorously" about the sorry state of the world and about the problems of labor and capital. "That which we formerly prized so highly — good common horse sense, seems to have utterly disappeared and we are overwhelmed by countless radical elements each of which tries to accomplish by revolution what should be worked out by evolution . . . I cannot for the life of me understand why capital and labor do not sincerely respect each other, each being so completely dependent on each other."

"He tried to be reasonable about these matters," Roger commented, "but he, after all, was a capitalist, and an apologist for business and he voted the Republican ticket."

I read on in his father's letter, "The only solution I can see for the difficulties which have arisen between the two is the profit sharing plan which I think has been successful where it has honestly been tried out."

"That," I said, "doesn't sound like the letter of a reactionary."

Roger conceded. "He was a very tolerant man in most intellectual ways. He was a freethinker in religion. He was a great fan of Robert Ingersoll, the atheist. And he went even beyond the Unitarians. He would have called himself an agnostic, I'm sure. But he was a man full of prejudices." He paused. "You know in the last years of his life he became quite demonstrative. He would always kiss me on the mouth, for instance, and I always felt it was just a little too much of a demonstration. As if he was really trying to make up for the past."

A letter from Anna Louise Strong (to whom it will be recalled Roger was once engaged) typified the many sides of her character. In keeping with her stern Protestant ethic she began, "The Press Dispatch says you've been given a year in the pen, so now you will settle down and plan what to do with yourself for a year. Something constructive, I'm sure; some educational improvement if they allow you to read in your off hours — some study into jail conditions and prison psychology . . . I cannot imagine a year of your life being really wasted. You will make it contribute one way or another."

Then, as the committed Communist, she went on to describe her first publication. "I took *Soviets at Work* by Lenin as published by the Rand School and I wrote a foreword and some catchy headings and even a complete digest of it so the speedy might read it. We are publishing it at ten cents a copy."

And finally reverting to the concerns of a mere woman, she ended with, "Good luck, dear. I hope the food isn't too bad. Do they let you get presents like knitted bed slippers for the cold floors?"

"I am delighted to know that you will soon be acquainted with the jug," began a letter from 5208 Market Street, St. Louis. "Am mailing jelly under separate cover in care of the Tombs, N.Y.C. and if anyone suspects me of disloyalty, they can look up the family Liberty Bond record."

The letter, which went on for several pages in this light, impudent, loving vein was signed Brownie. Somehow I had missed Brownie. Was he still another of Roger's adopted boys?

"No, he wasn't one of my adopted boys. He had perfectly good parents of his own, but he was one of my most intimate young friends. In fact, considering his intelligence, wit and power of expression, I would say my most intimate young friend. Brownie was an unusual boy I met at an IWW forum in St. Louis when he was eleven years old. His father was a socialist — Theodore Brown. Brownie was Harold K. His mother was a public stenographer at the St. Louis public library.

"Their story was that they had moved to St. Louis from southern Missouri where they had lived on a farm. The boy had never gone to school, nor had his sister, but because his father had weak eyes Brownie had read aloud to him everything from the Corn Law debates in the House of Commons to Marx. I at once took an interest in this remarkable kid and the family gladly accepted me and let me buy him a train and some of the toys he had never had and had set his heart on. I was so amused by Brownie's vocabulary that I took him to the City Club — eleven years old and in short pants — and introduced him to some of my highbrow friends. He astounded them by his talk: It was so adult, so beyond most of us and yet so unself-conscious. He was really two boys: the one his father brought up and the one I was bringing up. I often took him on country weekends with Oral and Toto. His father didn't resent it; he had other interests and soon he left the family for one of those interests and never came back. I hired the mother as my private secretary.

"When Brownie was fourteen I left St. Louis, but I didn't leave him nor he me. We wrote quite often — he in the spirit of an irreverent boy sassing his betters. He was amused when I went to jail as that letter shows. I'm sure he shared my views on the war; he had been trained by a socialist father and he felt most at home with people who had odd ideas of the world's affairs, people like me and my friends."

Another letter from Brownie berated Roger ("you poor boob") for being engaged to be married. "I sent you away from here a perfectly good bachelor, or at least if I didn't it wasn't my fault, for I always warned you that if you would insist on 'loving the ladies' that some day you would come to grief . . . But if the worst comes to worst, don't forget that I must have a look at the blushing bride, for I must know just how badly my idol has been stung."

Roger laughed. "Brownie affected to view marriage as bourgeois nonsense," he said, "but that didn't prevent him from getting married himself."

In fact Brownie's marriage would one day draw Roger into a bizarre and ultimately tragic sequence of events.

Both Roger's brothers were in military service and both wrote letters to the conscientious objector in Essex County jail. Herbert, who was an ensign in the navy, sounded a bit grudging, which would have been in character, for he never really approved of Roger — the less so as they grew older. "You may have spoken in jest," he began his letter of November 20, 1918, obviously in answer to one from Roger, "in referring to my 'prison on the sea,' but be assured by one who knows that it is a true prison. We live two in a tiny cell-like room and get mighty little exercise . . . It's too bad you had to 'enlist' for so long beyond the duration of the war, but then I am not going to lavish any sympathy or condolences on you for I know you don't want it. This is your lot as a result of the war and it is no harder physically than that of thousands of others."

Bob, the youngest brother, to whom Roger is devoted as is everyone else who knows him, wrote on January 18, 1919, a letter headed "On Active Service with the Expeditionary Forces."

"A little thing like a stay in jail is a wonderful booster for family closeness. Somehow I feel closer to you than ever, Rog. But still," he continued, "I can't see where your bolshevism or red flag policy would ever bring any kind of peace or happiness to the world. The more I run into individuals, no matter what their nationality, the more I can see the absolute necessity for having some sort of control over them in the form of centralized government. The *chacun pour soi* game will never work without more bloodshed, murder, rape, the world over, and there has been enough of that." This letter too was in character — a reasonable point of view, thoughtfully expressed by a reasonable man.

A significant exchange of letters between Roger in Essex County jail and Scott Nearing, the well-known Socialist who is still famous today for his books and lectures on "living the good life" on his maple sugar farm in Vermont, is important for what it reveals of Roger's thinking at this period of his life.

Roger and Nearing, who shared many mutual interests, had become good friends after Roger moved to New York, but clearly it bothered Scott Nearing that he could not persuade Roger to join the Socialist party, which is where he felt he belonged. Apparently the two men had therefore agreed that when Roger got to jail and found himself with plenty of time for marshaling his thoughts he would write Nearing a letter telling him why he continued to refuse to join the Socialist party.

On November 18, 1918, Roger did so in a well-reasoned dogmatic statement presented in a style Roger was wont to use, the paragraphs beginning *First, Second, Third* and subparagraphs 1st, 2nd, 3rd, 4th.

The gist of his case — if one can fairly cull a gist out of so closely woven an argument — was that the objective of the Socialist party was the possession of all socially necessary industries, which were to be operated for service instead of profit. This goal was to be achieved by careful control of the government and the *ballot* was to be the sole means for gaining such control. Roger disagreed with this basic purpose because he strongly favored economic over political solutions. He believed that the State, as we know it, based on the vote and on majority control, was a means of enslaving one group for the benefit of others. Therefore the State, as such, should be abolished and the control of industry and other organized processes needing control should be accomplished instead by *voluntary* associations in the economic field alone.

Unlike the Socialist party, the Socialist *Labor* party resorted to political means only to prevent the other side from using the power of the state against them. Therefore if he, Roger, joined any party in the United States today, it would be the Socialist Labor, but unfortunately as a party it was too weak to be of practical effect. He concluded by asking Scott Nearing — challenging would perhaps be more correct — to prove him wrong, which Nearing made a very creditable effort to do, using a few *First, Second, Third, Fourth* paragraphs of his own.

Faced with this correspondence, about which he had forgotten, Roger seemed pleased with how smart and how right he had been. "Remember this was just at the time of the Russian Revolution," he recalled, "and people were debating which way to go."

"Yes, but wasn't that why Scott Nearing wanted you to join the Socialists? To shore up the left wing of the party."

"Sure that's what he wanted but I didn't do it because I knew that what *did* happen was going to happen. I knew that the Socialist party was going to be split in two, which it was. And the radical wing became the Communist party. And Scott proved me right, because he himself left the Socialist party and went with the Communists."

Representatives of practically every liberal organization in the United States wrote to Roger commending his stand: the American Association for Organized Charities, the National Municipal League, the Society for Prevention of Cruelty to Animals, the Liberal Club of Harvard, the League for Amnesty for Political Prisoners, the National Populist Government League, the Society of St. Vincent de Paul, the League for Democratic Control, to mention only a few at random.

Other names, also chosen at random, appear in this volume of letters. Zona Gale, the well-known writer, wrote reminding him of their friendship ("a strong word, I know, but one I hope you will let me use"). Lillian Wald telegraphed on New Year's Day asking to come and see him "before the year is out." Judge Ben Lindsey wrote expressing his "respect for so brave a man." Ben Capes, friend of Emma Goldman, wrote a "Dear Comrade" letter; Manley Hudson of the American Committee to Negotiate Peace wrote an effusive one.

John Haynes Holmes, deputized by the board of the National Civil Liberties Bureau to be their scribe, wrote a flowery letter that was signed by eight of the directors. Meanwhile John Haynes Holmes sent frequent letters on his own, in one of which he said, "I think that your wonderful cheer and courage . . . exposes your friends to sore temptation. Many are inclined to take as easily the fact of your confinements as you do yourself. May I say, however, that there is one at least, and I believe many more, who are not forgetful of the fact that *prison is prison,* that you are suffering in a hundred ways that you never permit us to know anything about."

Crystal Eastman wrote urging him to send in stories about his experiences to *The Liberator, A Magazine of Revolutionary Progress,* of which she was managing editor, with her brother Max, who was editor along with Floyd Dell and John Reed.

Oswald Garrison Villard, with whom Roger had once corresponded about Booker T. Washington, wrote a "Dear Mr. Baldwin" letter, enclosing a laudatory piece he had written about Roger for the *Nation,* of which he was the editor.

Evan Thomas (brother of Norman) wrote concerning a problem that had arisen in Paterson, New Jersey, between the Amalgamated Clothing Workers, who were becoming less revolutionary and more opportunistic, and the IWW, who were fighting them. Roger was one day to have much to do with the Paterson situation.

A lady named Mrs. E. D. Church wrote that she was an old woman with no son, that she lived on a farm and that if Roger had no other home perhaps he would care to have her adopt him.

Other prisoners wrote. Agnes Smedley, who was in the Tombs because of harboring members of the India Freedom League and who first interested Roger in India's problem, wrote to commend his "noble action." H. Austin Simmons, a fellow absolutist whom Roger described as "the most articulate of the C.O.'s in the Chicago district," wrote saying, "We fellows at Leavenworth were sorry that you weren't sent to our part of the community housing establishment. We needed you." Oral James, of course, wrote often from the same "community housing establishment." Even the sailor who had been handcuffed to Roger when he returned to the Tombs the day after his trial wrote to say, "You're a real sport. I knew it the day I first saw you."

Louis Untermeyer wrote acknowledging receipt of Roger's six prison poems. "Damn you for an unscrupulous competitor," he joked. But it is difficult to tell from his letter whether Untermeyer, as a poet of distinction, praised Roger's verse because of its intrinsic value or because he had, as he said, a "prejudice in favor of convict poetry." Still, it seems only fair to permit others who may have a similar prejudice to meet Roger Baldwin, the poet. Here then is his "The Living Dead."

THE LIVING DEAD

I am the endless procession of men
Down the ages, around the world,
Marching in chains through the grim barred gates
Into the black and silent cells,
Into the pits of Fear and Hate
Where souls of men are eaten out.

I am the millions hanged and shot,
I am the countless legions lost,
Walled alive in the iron tombs.

I am the horde of the maimed turned out
Marked forever with brand of hate.

I am an old man bent and spent,
Hollow-eyed wreck of street and saloon,
I am a man who might have been . . .
I am a youth in the fire of life
Twisted in bonds the old men make,
I am a man who will never be . . .
I am a man with an infant mind,
Heir to the sins of the dead long gone,
I am a man who never lived . . .
I am the age-old slave of toil
Striving to lift the ancient yokes,
I am the man who yet will be . . .
I am a man who dared to speak
Against the wrongs that make men slaves,
I am chained, but my truth is free.

And I am the ghost at your cannibal feast.
I am your Hate and your Fear come to taunt you
With murder and theft and hideous want.
I am the terror that stares from your eyes.
I am the specter of all your wrong.

Not till the ancient march is done,
Not till I'm gone shall you be free,
Not till you've loved away Fear and Hate
And made of my millions a memory.
I, — the men who might have been,
I, — the men you never let be,
I, — your Living Dead make you free.

Essex County jail, 1919.

Roger was released from the penitentiary on July 19, 1919, which thanks to an error was one month earlier than he should have been free. He had been sentenced, it will be recalled, to *eleven* months and *ten* days (with his twenty days in the Tombs being credited to make up the twelve-month maximum sentence). But instead his commitment papers came through sentencing him to *ten* months and *eleven* days. Roger said he wrote to Judge Mayer pointing out the mistake, but the judge answered that it was too late to correct it. Roger had the feeling that Judge Mayer, who appeared kindly disposed toward him, would have managed to correct it if the clerical error had threatened to keep Roger behind bars for a month longer than he should have been.

As it was, with his two months off for good behavior, he was a free man after nine months of incarceration.

He left prison, he said, with only one thought in his mind — to marry Madeleine Doty as soon as possible.

(9)

Marriage on a Fifty-Fifty Basis

"ROGER! HOW CAN I DESCRIBE HIM?" asked Madeleine Doty in her autobiography. "He was gay and handsome. His charm was irresist-
ible. It was a great experience to be with him in the out of doors.
He knew all the birds and flowers by name . . . Once when we visited Smith College together [Madeleine was a graduate of the class
of 1900] President Neilson said that I had the most interesting man
in America to live with."

Certainly everything started out propitiously for them in the summer of 1919. Roger got out of Caldwell exactly one week after
Madeleine had sailed for home from Liverpool, so he was on the
dock, along with her parents, to meet her boat. Their reunion was a
joyous one.

They had twenty-four hours together before Roger left for Boston
to visit his family, whom he had not seen since his release. A few
days later Madeleine joined him there to meet his mother, his father,
his brother Herbert, his brother Bob and his wife Fran, his sister
Ruth and her husband Alan Snyder, his sister Deborah and her husband Roger Thomas. "I met the whole crowd and was warmly received, especially by Roger's mother."

"I feel very sure, very content, very peaceful," Roger wrote her,
"as you only can in a fixed, rounded, elemental relationship. I hope
to heaven you feel it similarly, and I have a hunch you do."

His hunch was apparently correct. They seemed in perfect harmony; both were fully attuned to their joint conception of marriage
as a relationship of "free comrades, each supporting himself and independent of each other" (Madeleine's words, but they could easily
have been Roger's).

The wedding took place on August 8 at the summer home of

Madeleine's parents in Sparta, New Jersey. The ceremony was out-of-doors, under a great tree beside a rushing brook. There was no dressing-up, no bridal veil, and not even a ring. Norman Thomas, who was still a pastor, officiated (or rather, according to Roger, "did whatever the law required"). Madeleine and Roger stood together and read, each to the other, their concepts of marriage.

Sixty-four years later, almost to the day, as Roger and I sat together in a small cabin on Martha's Vineyard, I showed him copies of those two solemn marriage vows. First I gave him Madeleine's: *"Today we enter into partnership, the union of man and woman,"* she began. *"Union, passionate love, all love is the creative force of the universe . . . The true test of love is does it make those who love bigger, finer and more creative?"*

"My goodness," said Roger.

"When this is so, the relationship is beautiful. It is a test greater and beyond all clergy. Believing this, my one desire is that our love may increase your power to live and to love . . ."

"Pretty pretentious stuff," said Roger. "She liked to think that way."

"I want to give and have a love that has perfect trust . . . The deep love that gives and does not seek, that respects and reverses, the love that springs from God and is for all mankind, that love I give you now and for always . . ."

"Highfalutin," said Roger. "Very highfalutin."

"All right then," I said. "Here's yours. See what you make of that."

"To us who passionately cherish the vision of a free human society," Roger's credo began, *"the present institution of marriage among us is a grim mockery of essential freedom. Here we have the most intimate, most sacred, the most creative relationship shackled in the deadening grip of private property and essentially holding the woman subservient to the man . . ."*

"My goodness," Roger said again.

"We deny without reservation the moral right of state or church to bind by the force of law a relationship that cannot be maintained by the power of love alone. We submit to the form of law only because it seems a matter of too little importance to resist or ignore . . ."

"I just can't believe it," said Roger.

"The highest relationship between a man and a woman is that which welcomes and understands each other's loves. Without a sense of possession there

can be no exclusions, no jealousies. The creative life demands many friend-ships, many loves shared together openly, honestly and joyously . . ."

"Grandiose," said Roger. "Much too grandiose."

"My primary interest and joy is the great revolutionary struggle for human freedom today, so intense, so full of promise. I regard our union only as con-tributing to that cause, making us both serve it the more passionately, the more devotedly."

"Too goddamned idealistic," Roger muttered. "Pretentious and idealistic." But by now he was beginning to grin as he read on.

"I come to this relationship with a passion for life growing with the years. I come without any ambition but to live fully the truths I cherish. Success, failure and practical achievement as they are commonly rated mean nothing to me. Not how far I go, but where I face, what values I see, what I can give and get of joy – that is the essence of living fully – with senses of abandon to a sure faith."

"Do you know what I think?" Roger was laughing as he handed the pages back to me. "I think — I don't know if you can use these words in a book — but I think this is full of bullshit. At least that's what I would say right now."

"But at the time?" I asked, feeling suddenly rather defensive for all those noble emotions and ideals, so earnestly felt and set forth.

"At the time I was quite elevated," Roger answered. "Marriage meant an awful lot to me. *She* meant an awful lot to me. I was very idealistic about our marriage and so was she."

Roger elected to take his bride (although that outmoded word was never used) to honeymoon (that word was permitted) at Caroline Colgate's estate in the Adirondacks. It was not an ideal choice since Mrs. Colgate herself was in residence, and despite Roger's entreaty to Madeleine to "please like my Caroline Colgate, she is a merry saint," Madeleine was less than entranced. Furthermore it had looked for a brief moment as if Freddie Farnum was planning to ac-company them on their honeymoon too, but here Madeleine re-belled. "Our marriage was a free union, but Freddie on a honey-moon, no . . . I won the day."

Mr. Baldwin and Miss Doty — as they were to remain — had two happy weeks together in the open air. They set up camp (Mrs. Colgate referred rather bitterly to it as "Forbidden Point") with two tents: one for sleeping, one for living. The weather was perfect. They cooked out-of-doors, went swimming, canoeing, mountain climbing. Bound together by their love of nature and of each other, the world and its problems were forgotten.

But before they could settle down to really test what they liked to call their "marriage on a fifty-fifty basis," Roger was off to test yet another hypothesis.

"I am still of a mind to go on the bum shortly after I get out of here with two or three of the radical labor boys," he had written Madeleine from prison. "About a two-to-three-month trip to get my feet solid on the ground of facts about the labor struggle. I cannot get it from books. My whole training must be overturned — and my fields of knowledge extended."

His romantic plan was to set off with just a few dollars in his pocket to see how he would fare as an unskilled laborer, living by his hands alone. He would head for the Midwest, where the labor movement was in ferment. Prospects of employment were good and with his prison experience he could both cook and handle a pick and shovel. First stop was to be the IWW headquarters in Chicago — Bill Haywood was there, still out on bail — where he would join the Wobblies and throw his lot in with them.

Madeleine, Roger said, cheered him on. Actually, according to her autobiography, she was rather depressed at the idea of having him leave her less than two months after their marriage, but apparently dared not protest after all her vows about a marriage of complete freedom.

Bill Haywood (Big Bill as he was always called since he weighed close to 300 pounds) took a frankly skeptical view of Roger's plan.* "While it is an experience that I'm sure you would enjoy for the limited time that you mention," he wrote Roger on September 17, 1919, "yet if my opinion were asked about the matter, I would suggest that your time could be spent to better advantage and more profitably than rustling a job and bustling around the country in boxcars. Excuse me please for expressing myself so bluntly, but this is really what I think."

Rustling and bustling was exactly what Roger did, of course, relishing all of it. He had a variety of experiences. He joined the IWW, sponsored good-naturedly by Bill Haywood who said, how-

* Roger recalled that the great wartime IWW trial that he had attended in Chicago had been designated in legalese *The U.S. vs. Wm. D. Haywood et al.* One of the IWW boys had commented that that was certainly correct. Haywood did eat it all.

ever, that he was not to try to get a job cooking in any of the IWW camps because "our boys like to eat good." Therefore, Roger decided he had better hedge his bets by joining the Chicago local of the A. F. of L. Cooks and Waiters Union, carefully hiding from the A. F. of L. the fact that he was also a member of the IWW.

Armed with both cards, he set off, stopping in St. Louis just long enough to show the cards and himself in his working clothes to his old friends, and of course to see Toto. He found two successive jobs in southeastern Missouri, shoveling lead ore for a week and then working in a brickyard heaving bricks from a wheelbarrow in a pit to the men standing above who placed them in the kilns. Roger had never been much in the athletic line; his aim was terrible and his throws were wild. After he had hit a couple of his fellow workers with badly tossed bricks he was promptly fired.

He did, however, have the pleasure of sending the first dollar he made in the brickyard (at thirty-seven cents per hour) to Haywood for the IWW defense fund. "I could not put the dollar to better use than to help the men persecuted solely for their loyalty to the revolutionary cause of industrial freedom," he wrote Haywood and received from him in response a letter beginning "Dear Fellow Worker," which Roger must indeed have loved.

Since neither of his jobs had been union ones, Roger figured that aside from his physical hardships (he had actually gone hungry for a day or so), he was not really learning what he'd come to learn. So with a ten-day stopover in Youngstown, Ohio, to work with a railroad construction crew, he moved on to Pittsburgh where the great steel strike in the Homestead mills was in progress. William Z. Foster, the A. F. of L. leader who was in charge of the strike, welcomed Roger although he had not previously met him. After Roger explained what he was doing and offered his services, Foster at once suggested that he could greatly help the cause by becoming a labor spy. He asked him to get a job in the Homestead mills and report on conditions from the inside.

Roger may have been an amateur, but he certainly was not unaware of the fate of labor spies if discovered. Still, he reasoned, this was the experience he had wanted to have "to get his feet solid on the ground about labor's struggle." Accordingly he went to Homestead (some eight miles east of Pittsburgh) and got a job in the plant cleaning the ovens. It was hot work but not so taxing that it did not allow him ample time to roam about the plant finding out the things he thought Foster wanted to know. Each night he made notes.

He stayed in a little hotel, ate in different restaurants every evening, was careful to know nobody and, he says, to talk to nobody. Nonetheless, at the end of a week he was told he was fired. No reason was given except that he was not needed. But Roger, of course, knew better. Clearly his role had somehow been discovered.

Back in his hotel he found that his room had been ransacked and his notes for Foster had all been stolen. He was thus placed on the horns of a nasty dilemma; he could not collect his pay until the next day but he was quite justifiably frightened by what he knew of the vengeance of company guards against labor spies. Should he take a chance and stay in Homestead until the next day or should he forfeit his pay and clear out while he still could.

It was hardly necessary to ask which course he followed, for two obvious reasons. Roger was not, then or ever, a man to pass up collecting money that was owed him, nor was he, then or ever, a man to run scared. He stayed in Homestead, waiting all night for an ominous call that fortunately did not come. The next day he got his pay-check (which he says he contributed to the strike relief fund, although he was getting down to the bottom of his pocket), went back to Pittsburgh and reported to Foster from memory, realizing that he never should have taken notes in the first place.

He stayed around Pittsburgh a bit longer to follow the course of the strike and to try to probe its inherent meaning (and, incidentally, to enjoy some of the dramatic excitement). Later he wrote that because he had been there it was easier for him to understand that labor's struggle, in substance, was not a "struggle for hours or wages, or for public ownership, but for control of the jobs exclusively by the workers themselves."

Brief and perhaps superficial as he admitted his experiences had been, he had the satisfaction of knowing that he had shared at first hand what he had previously only known academically. And in the end, as he said in his Oral History, "I recalled with insight a remark of Clarence Darrow's: 'I'd rather be the friend of the workingman than be the workingman: it's a lot easier.' "

A letter to Madeleine Doty from Roger's mother (usually a mild and self-effacing woman) demonstrated her strong disapproval of

Roger's perambulations and offered an insight that her son might well have heeded, and perhaps in part did. "I was intensely interested," Lucy Baldwin told Madeleine, "in all you had to say, especially in what concerned my runaway boy, Roger. I wish he could come home to his wife and *stay put* where he belongs . . . It seems to me Roger has reached a too visionary state of mind. He would better come home and be practical for a while."

Roger did come home in time to have Thanksgiving in New York with Madeleine and her parents, at which point their "marriage on a fifty-fifty basis" began in earnest. They settled down in Madeleine's studio on Waverly Place, just off Washington Square. The studio occupied one entire floor of a house and consisted of a large living room with open coal fire, a bedroom behind and two additional small hall bedrooms, one of which had been converted to a kitchen, the other to a bathroom.

Roger promptly put a tent on the roof to house what Madeleine referred to as his waifs and strays. Fond as she was of Freddie Farnum, who was their most frequent waif, she still was not enchanted to have him or the other boys "use my face powder, and the bathtub and fail to wash it out." But, she admitted, life was gay. Their two names on the entrance door to the studio created considerable interest and Roger especially enjoyed introducing her as "Miss Doty, my wife." Tongue-in-cheek he wrote on one occasion, "I am unalterably opposed to any woman taking my name. It's all I've got to identify me, and I am not going to give it away to a woman . . ."

Since Roger was determined to keep their expenses down to a working-class level, each contributed $60 a month to cover room and food. Even in 1919 this was difficult. The rent was $50 a month; they had many guests and a maid for three hours a day to clean and prepare the evening meal.

Madeleine found the carefully budgeted food shopping and the meal planning something of a chore so, with complete justification according to their fifty-fifty arrangement, she announced one day to Roger that she thought he should assume his share of the housekeeping burden.

Certainly, Roger said. They would each take a week at a time as housekeeper and he was ready to start at once. So he did. He got down the cookbook and methodically numbered all the recipes that he and Madeleine liked or that he himself had tried with good results.

The next morning before going off he left a note for the maid: "For tonight: Soup No. 5; Entrée 16; Salad 7; Dessert 21. Clean thoroughly and wipe behind all the pictures."

Suffice it to say when they returned home that evening no dinner had been prepared, the walls behind the pictures remained unwiped and the maid had vanished. Actually this was no great catastrophe, for as Madeleine ruefully conceded, Roger, in his carefree way, could produce a very nice Entrée 16 on his own.

Weekends were spent always at Roger's camp on the Hackensack River in New Jersey. It was a great retreat, which Madeleine enjoyed; she knew that Roger was in his element there. "We had many day parties and the oddest collection of people. I remember one Sunday vividly. Roger had invited a millionaire and his chorus girl, a Communist, a social worker, a businessman, Freddie and another ex-prisoner. Roger took the crowd walking until they were nearly starved. Then at three o'clock he produced a big dinner. Everyone declared he was the best cook in the world. After dinner he made the whole crowd do the washing up . . . It was all delightful and amusing," she concluded, "but I seemed to be getting nowhere with work of my own."

Roger on the other hand was moving steadily forward and getting somewhere very quickly indeed, which may not have been an ideal condition in this share-and-share-alike marriage. It was, however, an important augury for the many individuals who were prepared to join with him in waging a vigorous and unending battle against any denial of the civil rights of a democratic people.

(10)

The ACLU: Watchdog for the Underdog

DURING ROGER'S YEAR IN PRISON the Civil Liberties Bureau had continued to operate under the direction of Albert de Silver, assisted by Walter Nelles and, for a period of time, by the slightly mad Reverend William Simpson whom Roger said had "given up the ministry to become a Christian." By the time of Roger's release, Simpson had departed to try to live like St. Francis ("as carpenter, of course," said Roger) and de Silver was working only part-time. It seemed obvious to Roger that the Bureau was going to fold unless he rescued it.

All the Bureau faithful, and many others in the anti-war crowd, had been at a party given at Norman Thomas' house on East 17th Street the night of Roger's release, to celebrate his return to freedom. Although Albert de Silver decreed there was to be no shop-talk on this joyous occasion, it was clear to Roger and probably to everyone present that he was expected to take up the reins of the Civil Liberties Bureau once again.

A great deal remained to be done. Hundreds of war prisoners whom the Bureau had once aided were still in jail; so too were many, many conscientious objectors. The need for a shot in the arm for the Bureau was pressing. But still Roger hesitated. "I thought I would have a tough time mustering support as an ex-convict. So I agreed that if they would circularize all our supporters, I would accept if the agreement was general." This was done while Roger was on the road as a "common" laborer and when he returned he was told there had not been a single dissent among all the Bureau's pacifists and liberals about his reassuming the directorship.

But before he accepted, he made a further condition — also agreed to — that the Bureau be reorganized to serve (in addition to the remaining war protesters) "the cause of freedom of expression

in the industrial struggle." A memorandum written by Roger in
December 1919, and sent to the members of the old Bureau committee, stated unequivocally that "The cause we now serve is labor."

Three categories of people were to be sought, according to the
memorandum, to be active in carrying out the new work: "1) those
directly engaged in the labor struggle . . . 2) those who by their
writing and speaking are close to labor problems, and 3) [a great
catchall category] those who stand on general principles for freedom
of expression."

To point up the vastly wider scope of the new organization Roger
and others decided to change the name — the National Civil Liberties Bureau having been so exclusively connected in the public mind
with opponents of the war — to something more sweeping and impressive. Hence on January 20, 1920, the American Civil Liberties
Union officially came into being.

Its office was on the first floor of an old residence on West 13th
Street, shared, on the floor above, by the editorial staff of *The New
Masses* ("but otherwise unconnected," Roger carefully noted).

Before we went further, I wanted Roger to set the scene for me.
"January 1920," I prompted. "I need you to put that period in history a little into focus."

"Well, of course, it was a time of tremendous labor unrest, high-
lighted by the two great strikes in the steel mills and the coal mines.
And it was also, and I guess above all, a time of intense radical agita-
tion, brought on by the Russian Revolution that had happened
earlier — October 1917, I believe it was. And that changed everything. So by the time the World War was over we had a new war on
our hands — a different one. Then, instead of arresting and persecuting opponents of the war, we were arresting and persecuting
friends of Russia."

"For no reason except that they were friends?"

"Well, they were so-called subversives. The assumption was that
they were trying to do the same thing to our country that the Communists did to Russia; that they were dangerous because they'd
overthrown the czar and they'd overthrown the government in Russia so they might well try to do that here."

"In other words, it was the beginning of the Red Scare."

"That's right. The beginning and it's still going on today. People
are still scared of Reds right now, the same way."

I was about to ask, well how about you and your feelings toward Reds today, knowing how Roger in his nineties tended to seize any opportunity to disassociate himself from the extremist ideas of his thirties and forties. But instead, I put the question another way. "How radical do you think you were, Roger, about the time you came out of prison?"

"That's a relative term you know," he began, and I braced myself for the equivocation that invariably accompanies such a reply. But he surprised me.

"You can be intellectually radical and you can be practically radical. The question is, if you're intellectually radical, what do you do about it. And I never *did* much about it you know. My ideas were never really backed by my performance. I always *acted* like a liberal. I always stayed right with the liberal and social work profession. And what I did with the ACLU would be classified as liberal. But I never joined any radical organization, although maybe after I got out of prison I paid more attention to some of the more radical movements — the IWW particularly."

Since I knew that we would have more, much more, to say about his "extremist" views in future conversations, I contented myself now with saying only that I thought he would have qualified as a pretty radical man in the 1920's.

"You think I'm not now?" Roger asked.

"I think you've changed some," I answered. "For instance, I think you take a rather dark view of Communists these days."

"I always thought socialism and communism were good ideas," he said reflectively, "but as Mr. Nehru once said about them, 'They're great ideas, but when they're attached to the machinery of a police state, man must be against them.' So because I certainly am against police states, I don't want the Communists around here. But I wouldn't *do* anything to them. I wouldn't suppress them in any way. I'd just let them alone."

"You'd still defend them though, wouldn't you?"

"Of course, of course. I'd always defend them. I always have. Back in the twenties they deported over a thousand of them in one boat and naturally we defended their rights. That was in January 1920, in fact, just as we were forming the ACLU. The boat was called the *Buford*, I remember, and Emma Goldman was on it; Sasha [Alexander Berkman, one of Miss Goldman's most durable lovers] was with her. The Union began to get all those people who were deported — in fact aliens were a large number of our clients in 1920 and '21."

The wartime Civil Liberties Bureau had more or less fallen into Roger's hands as a result of the sudden need to protect conscientious objectors. But the new ACLU was far broader in its scope and more varied in objectives. Yet, the same principle continued to apply: Above all the new organization was pledged to defend the right of dissent. Its original Statement of Purpose defined the ACLU's position on "issues in the United States today":

> We stand on the general principle that all thought on matters of public concern should be freely expressed, without interference. Orderly social progress is promoted by unrestricted freedom of opinion. The punishment of mere opinion, without overt acts, is never in the interest of orderly progress . . .
>
> The principle of freedom of speech, press and assemblage, embodied in our constitutional law, must be reasserted in its application to American conditions today. That application must deal with various methods now used to repress new ideas and democratic movements . . .

The statement then went on to detail the most significant freedoms that were endangered by tactics of repression. They included Free Speech, Free Press, Freedom of Assemblage, The Right to Strike, Law Enforcement, The Right to a Fair Trial, Immigration, Deportation and Passports, Liberty in Education and Racial Equality.

To achieve these rights, which are guaranteed by the Constitution, the new American Civil Liberties Union pledged itself to "an aggressive policy of insistence." And to implement this policy, Roger set about putting together a national Board made up of prominent liberal activists — names that would command the respect of thoughtful people everywhere, or, as Roger also put it, "showcase personalities, good for letterheads." Sixty-four people were selected and agreed to serve. Of this number, twenty people, all living in or near New York, constituted the executive committee that made the day-to-day decisions. Diversity was the key word.

Together Roger and I went over the list of the sixty-four notable individuals who made up the first American Civil Liberties Union Board.* His memory of all of them and of their particular vir-

---

* *ACLU Annual Report,* Volume I, January 1920–May 1930 (New York, Arno Press, *New York Times*), p. 31.

tues — their strengths and their foibles, their dedication, their political attitudes and personal attributes — was extraordinary.

Many of the names have already appeared on these pages; more will appear later. All are important for having been founding members of an organization that is today taken for granted, universally referred to as the ACLU by many who perhaps are not even quite sure what the letters stand for. Some who doubtless know little of Roger Baldwin and his 1920 colleagues are nevertheless keenly aware that because the ACLU exists there is a bulwark, a last resort against prejudice and injustice.

The first chairman was Dr. Harry F. Ward, a professor of Applied Christian Ethics at the Union Theological Seminary in New York.

"I had not known Dr. Ward before he joined us," said Roger. "He was a supporter of the war, but also a strong champion of the rights of labor and of civil liberties on principle. For a while we thought very much the same way. I used to visit his house and I knew his wife and three children pretty well. He was a great gardener too and outdoor fellow, so we had that in common. I'd say we were friends although I'd also have to say that Dr. Ward was not conspicuous for any sense of humor."

Next, the two vice chairmen: Jeannette Rankin and Duncan Mac-Donald.

"Well, Jeannette was a great girl — she just died last year. She was an ardent pacifist, of course, and the only member of Congress to vote against both world wars. Duncan MacDonald was a very well known labor leader. He was president of the United Mine Workers in Chicago. He was the type of labor leader who liked to work with liberals. We had some others like that on the Board too. We had James Cannon, who was a very prominent labor leader — in fact I think he got hold of Duncan MacDonald for us — and then Rose Schneiderman, who was president of the Women's Trade Union League. And then we also had Julia O'Connor. Julia was president of the Telephone Operators' Union. They were the types of trade unionists who sought liberal support."

I asked who some of the other trade union people were and he said, reasonably enough, that he couldn't remember without looking at the list. But I said I thought I'd rather keep the list and read out names to him at random.

"All right. Anything you say." Roger was in one of his more docile moods.

"Helen Keller," I read.

"Well, Helen Keller was a kind of accident. She'd spoken out on some labor issue and I don't know who suggested that she would be a good member of the Board. But, of course, she didn't come to meetings."

"You mean you never met her?"

"Oh yes, I met her loads of times."

"What was she like?"

"Well, you were always aware with Helen Keller of the burden she was overcoming in being a blind deaf-mute. What she communicated was interesting enough, what she said about the war and civil liberties, but you could never forget that what she had to say, she had to say through Miss Sullivan — still, her heart was in the right place — always."

I consulted the list. "Jane Addams, of course we know, Scott Nearing, Norman Thomas, L. Hollingsworth Wood, Helen Phelps Stokes, Agnes Brown Leach, Crystal Eastman, Judah Magnes, John Lovejoy Elliott are all holdovers from the old Civil Liberties Bureau. Here's a good new name. How about B. F. Huebsch?"

"Huebsch," Roger corrected my pronunciation. "He was publisher of the Viking Press. He was a treasurer for a number of years and a very useful member of our Board."

"James Duncan," I read.

"James Duncan was president of the Seattle Labor Council. So that makes another one of the labor men."

"How about Furnass — Paul Furnass?"

"Paul was a Quaker; in fact he was at one time head of the Friends' Service Committee. But at the time of the first ACLU Board he was quite young, late twenties or early thirties. He and I had lived together with Miss Walton and my Aunt Ruth in New York. Miss Walton was also a Quaker. And we had several other Quakers on the Board. Let me see who — Well, we had Agnes Brown Leach, of course. She's still living. A lovely, lovely lady at ninety. And then we had Edward Evans, a very prominent Quaker down in Philadelphia. He's still living too, by the way. And then who else — Well, there was A. J. Muste — I guess he counts."

"What do you mean, counts."

"As a Quaker. He had been a clergyman, but he had no church and I guess by that time he had joined the Society of Friends. But he was on for two reasons: as a pacifist and also a labor organizer for the Textile Workers of America. And then later he became a Trotskyite. He was a very adventurous character. He went to North Vietnam on a peace mission and died shortly after he came back, sitting in his chair dictating a memo to his secretary about North Vietnam. I'd say he was one of the leading pacifists we had on the Board."

"Would you also say you had any pro-war people?"

"Of course, of course. I'd say the Board was about half labor-oriented and of the other half about half were pacifists and the other half were Wilsonian liberals who had supported the war."

I asked who some of the war supporters had been and Roger, after a moment's hesitation, came up with Norman Hapgood. "Who was he?"

"Norman Hapgood was editor of one of the big mass magazines. I think it was *Collier's*. And he was later ambassador to Denmark. He was one of Wilson's very close friends and he was definitely for the war." Then, after a moment. "John Codman — John was a very distinguished proper Bostonian. An untouchable, above reproach. He supported the war but he never hesitated to defend the AUAM [American Union against Militarism] before the authorities in Washington. I remember once during the war days he accompanied me on one of my most sensitive interviews. I was summoned by the advocate general of the army to explain my activities before the war." He chuckled. "I remember the occasion very well. The general said to me, 'When did you last see Villa?' 'Who?' I asked him. 'Pancho Villa.' I told him I'd never in my life seen Pancho Villa and wanted to know why he'd asked. Because, he said, army intelligence had reported that I was part of a band of Americans who helped Villa invade Arizona." Roger chuckled again. "So much for army intelligence."

And, I thought, so much for those war supporters on the ACLU Board. There may have been others, but they were not forthcoming. Talking to Roger I had the feeling, although he would deny occasioning it, that it was quite infra dig to have supported World War I. I went back to the list.

"William Fincke."

"He was a pacifist, a clergyman who lost his church — the Greenwich Presbyterian Church — because he was a pacifist. He went on to organize the progressive Munumit School, which was quite a success and is still going on."

"Felix Frankfurter, of course, was already a friend of yours by then, wasn't he?"

"So many of these people that I got on the Board were personal friends of mine. And I don't mind telling you, Peggy, that in all my days in public life I was always fraternizing with the so-called best people everywhere."

"By best people do you mean — "

"Reformers, they were all reformers."

"The best reformers."

"That's right. And that certainly included Felix Frankfurter, who was one of our staunchest founding members. He had been on the War Labor Board, and he had labor connections too. He stuck with us until he went on the Supreme Court. Then my differences with some of his decisions alienated us until his retirement, when we resumed relations again."

"Flynn," I read from the list, knowing that here was a name we would be hearing much more later on — Elizabeth Gurley Flynn.

"At the time Elizabeth was very active and well respected and liked in the labor movement. She was head of something called the Worker's Defense Union or Worker's Defense something. It was an organization she had started to help the IWW. She herself was a member of the IWW; in fact, she had been indicted with the others in the Chicago trial, but she somehow got a severance by order of the judge and was not tried with them. She was a great girl, Elizabeth, with a wonderful sense of humor. We were very good friends then."

"Was there a Mr. Flynn?"

"I don't think so. For years her consort [a favorite word of Roger's] was Carlo Tresca, the well-known Italian anarchist who was editor of *Il Martello* in New York. He was a wonderful guy too and also a good friend of mine."

I looked further down the Board list and put my finger on the name Granville S. MacFarland.

"Believe it or not," Roger grinned, "believe it or not, Mr. Granville MacFarland was the managing editor of a Hearst newspaper."

"I don't believe it," I said.

"Well, it's true. He was editor of the *Boston American,* and Hearst notwithstanding, he was a strong labor sympathizer."

I noted that while almost everyone who had been elected to the first Board had stayed on for a number of years, Granville S. Mac-Farland's name did not appear on the second, the 1922–23 roster.

"I don't remember why," Roger said. "I don't remember any incident. My guess would be that his boss just made him quit."

"Andrew Furseth?" I asked.

"Furseth. Now there was a man who didn't last a year either, but he got fired, I know. Andrew Furseth was president of the Seaman's Union. He was a labor man who didn't like the IWW and he took a position in favor of prosecuting the IWW. Since we were defending them, we couldn't have him on our Board, so we fired him."

"Mary MacDowell?"

"Mary MacDowell was the head of the Stockyard Settlement in Chicago. She was a friend of Jane Addams and Sophonisba Breckenridge and those other Chicago sages."

"Sophonisba was also on the Board, of course, but we haven't had her yet, have we?"

"No, I don't think so. She was a professor of sociology at the University of Chicago. She came from a very distinguished family in Kentucky."

"How about the men of God? You had quite a few of them on that first Board, didn't you?"

"I would say so, yes. Dr. Ward, of course, was our chairman and he was a reverend. John Nevin Sayre was a reverend. His brother Francis married Woodrow Wilson's daughter. John Sayre became head of the Fellowship of Reconciliation with which I was also associated. And of course, John Haynes Holmes, who was someday to succeed Ward, was a very prominent Unitarian; he was the minister of the Community Church in New York. In fact he was my Aunt Ruth's minister and I guess maybe I first got to know him through her. But he was well known, highly respected and very conspicuous because of his sermons and his writings in which he expressed his bold, challenging point of view with a deep conviction. I was very, very close to John."

"And of course you were very close to Norman Thomas who was also a reverend."

"Very close indeed. I suppose next to Scott Nearing, Norman was my closest friend on the Board. And I guess the only reason Scott was a little closer was that he was a country man, a farmer as well as a Socialist. Madeleine and I used to spend weekends with Scott and his wife and two little boys out in Ridgewood walking in the woods or swimming. It was a very relaxed, cozy outdoors atmosphere. Whereas I brought Norman Thomas to the country with me once and never tried it again."

"Why not?"

"Because he never left his business behind; he hardly knew where he was. The country meant nothing to him. He talked about public issues all the time. I got him up an apple tree to saw off dead wood and he talked about the socialist revolution. But he had the greatest longevity on the ACLU Board and in my life as well. After all, he married me to my first wife and he presided over the memorial service of my second wife."

"And did you ever vote for him for President?"

"No, I never did."

I remembered that Norman Thomas had stayed with the wing of the Socialist party that Roger had considered too weak to join, so felt there was nothing further to say on that score. Instead I went on to ask him about Judah Magnes, who had been involved with Roger and his anti-war activities from the beginning, having come from the AUAM Board. Roger seemed rather surprised, however, that his name appeared on the ACLU list because "I thought he had already gone to Israel by then. You see the Hebrew University in Jerusalem was started just about that time and he went over to be its first president and then lived there the rest of his life. His wife is still living there. But, my goodness, Judah was the most outspoken pacifist in the war. He lost his church, or rather, his temple — he was rabbi of the leading temple on Park Avenue — because of his views. He was a wonderful, wonderful man."

I said it seemed to me that there had not been very many Jews on that first ACLU Board.

"No, there weren't."

"Why not?"

"Because the Jews behaved badly, that's why not."

"By badly, do you mean — "

"I mean they were all for the war. Rabbi Stephen Wise and all those people went over to the war and Wilson. Wilson was going to save the Jews. Wise had some messianic illusions, of course. But anyway, they all went over to Wilson. And what's more they were not pro-labor either."

"They weren't?"

"No, they were not pro-labor," Roger repeated emphatically. "There were very few of them who were. Only the New York needle trades — people like Sidney Hillman and Morris Hillquit. Hillquit was on our Board by the way. Was on it for years."

"Yes, I see he was."

"He was a Russian Jew. He spoke with a very strong accent and was virtually head of the Socialist party in New York; he was the Socialists' candidate for mayor of New York, and he was also a very good lawyer with a big practice — largely in trade unions. And another one in that same category was Charney Vladeck, a delightful foreign-born — Polish, I think — Jew who spoke English badly and was a strong man in his personal convictions. He was a Socialist and the editor of the *Jewish Daily Forward*."

"A powerful man to have on your side," I said.

"Yes, the *Jewish Daily Forward* was important and powerful but more than that, Charney Vladeck was a good personal friend of mine. We used to lunch together and his son Steve Vladeck is a very good lawyer in New York today — one of our censorship experts."

"Speaking of lawyers, how many would you say were on this Board?" This time I handed him the list to consult. Quickly he ran his eyes over the page (no eyeglasses needed, incidentally).

"Frankfurter, Gilbert, Hays, Hillquit, Le Sueur, Moore, Stedman."

I held up my hand. "Slowly, Roger. Back up a little and give me a few words about those we haven't already mentioned."

"A. B. Gilbert and Arthur Le Sueur represented the Farmer's Non-Partisan League, which was based in Minneapolis. It was an organization of farmers who were against the war and who refused even to buy war bonds. Those two lawyers really stood out against the war in fine style. Seymour Stedman was a Chicago lawyer, a member of the directing committee of the Socialist party. He was a very smart Pickwickian sort of character with loads of good sense and a lot of clients. And — let me see — Hays, Arthur Garfield Hays. I don't think I can do justice to him in a few words."

I told him to take all the words he wanted.

"Of all my associates, Arthur Hays was the closest over the longest period of time," said Roger, notwithstanding the fact that he had said almost the same thing about Scott Nearing, Norman Thomas and John Holmes. Clearly he was a man with an admirable number of close associates. "Arthur was the ACLU's general counsel from

1924 until his death thirty years later. He was also my own lawyer and my friend — in fact, I lived almost a year with him and his family in his home at 20 East 10th Street. He was progressive in the traditional American sense of the La Follettes, Wilson and FDR, but the left never tempted him. He didn't get involved in the various United Fronts that I and some of the others in the ACLU got into, so he balanced some of the rest of us and gave the Union a more solid reputation as a defender of the Bill of Rights. I think he was the most extreme civil libertarian among us. He didn't believe in banning anything — not even Hitler, he said, if he could get anyone to hear him. He looked with intense suspicion on any restraint of thought or expression."

I said I guessed that took care of the lawyers.

"No," Roger answered briskly, "it does not. We didn't do John D. Moore. My goodness, he was a hot one," Roger grinned. "John was our professional Irishman. He was counsel for the Irish Republic. Wonderful sense of humor, he had. He hated the war, of course — England's war — but he was also a civil liberties man. He learned from the Irish experience to sympathize with other people who suffered too and he was all for the underdog."

I reminded Roger that he had once called the ACLU "the watchdog for the underdog," and then went on to ask him if they had had any other professional types besides their professional Irishman on the Board.

"Yes, as a matter of fact we did. We had a professional Southerner: James H. Dillard. Dr. Dillard was a famous Southerner. He was head of the Jean Slater Foundation in Charlottesville, Virginia. I think he taught at the university there too. Anyway, he spoke with a very strong accent, and I think he might originally have been a clergyman. So he was our big professional Southerner."

"And how about blacks?"

"Well, the fact is, the blacks were always so busy with their own organization that they weren't much interested in ours. Actually we almost never did succeed in finding a black whose attitude was not completely tempered by his racial concerns. Thurgood Marshall, I suppose, came the closest to taking the larger view, perhaps because he was a good lawyer. But on the first Board we had James Weldon Johnson, who was secretary for the National Association for the Advancement of Colored People. He was for the cause of organized labor, but as a Negro he couldn't see much beyond the use of civil liberties for the equality of blacks. Primarily, of course, he couldn't help thinking of civil liberties as a means by which his people would become full-fledged citizens. And the same was true for some of the trade union people. They thought primarily in terms of organized labor. You couldn't escape having a few special pleaders like that."

"Was Johnson the only black on the first Board?"

"No, we had William H. Pickens who was also in the NAACP as a field director. He was also president of Morehouse College in Atlanta and he was a very well known black speaker and a very good friend of mine. I went to Europe with him one summer."

"Just the two of you?"

"No, Toto, my adopted boy, went with us that summer — " his voice trailed off as his attention was diverted to the list he held in his hand. "Why," he burst out accusingly, "there are all kinds of people on this Board you haven't asked me about."

I started to say that I hadn't yet finished asking, but by then there was no stopping Roger. The excitement that had been building as we talked now burst forth in a torrent of enthusiastic recollection.

"Here's William S. Uren, the father of the great Initiative Referendum and Recall movement of the 1910's to 1920's. And Frederick C. Howe. He was a famous figure at the time; he was the commissioner of immigration at Ellis Island, in charge of all entries of foreigners into the United States. Yes, sir, a very good man to have on our side. He was also a single-taxer. And Henry R. Linville, who was president of the Teachers' Union of New York, and Vida Scudder, who was a professor of English at Wellesley College, a lovely lady of the Jane Addams type — I tell you I had forgotten how prominent these people all were. And Robert Morse Lovett, another professor. He was at the University of Chicago, a pacifist — a very outspoken one. He was a very controversial figure because he was big in the United Front and he was always mixed up in all the kind of things I did. He was a charming gentleman. He was finally government secretary of the Virgin Islands.

"And William Z. Foster, the A. F. of L. man who was very different then than he became later, and Farley Christensen from Salt Lake City who was once the Farmer Labor party candidate for President. And Herbert Bigelow — that's another of the reverends by the way — from Cincinnati. He was also a single-taxer. And, my goodness, we haven't even talked about Helen Phelps Stokes, who was our treasurer for many years. She was a dissident, very charming New York lady who joined the Socialist party with her friend with whom she lived — what was her name — oh yes, Miss Mary Stanford. And they both had money — they left some to me as a matter of fact — which of course I gave away. And they were lovely ladies — very determined. Helen's brother Anson Phelps Stokes became a bishop and another brother, Graham Phelps Stokes, married a little Jewish girl named Rose Pastor, who was prosecuted by the government during the war and went to jail.

"And here's Oswald Garrison Villard, who was the editor of the *New York Post.*"

I managed to tuck in that I thought it was the *Nation.*

"First the *Post,* then the *Nation,*" Roger answered. "In fact, I think he owned the *Nation.* His father was a very rich man. Mr. Henry Villard, who married the daughter of William Lloyd Garrison, the famous abolitionist." Finally he paused. "What a Board! What a distinguished bunch," he said with the air of a man surveying his own handiwork with satisfaction.

"And yet for all those great names," I said, "one kept hearing the phrase, 'the ACLU *is* Roger Baldwin.' "

"I know, everyone always said that. But it's ridiculous. Ridiculous," he repeated, sounding as if he meant it. "We had a very high-powered Board that met weekly, every Monday — that is, of course, the executive committee. I brought the cases to their attention but our decisions were always the collective decisions of a number of people."

"Were you often at odds with each other — I mean ideologically as to exactly why you were for civil liberties?"

"I expect if you took twenty or thirty members of our Board and polled them on why they were for civil liberties and the Union, you'd get almost as many answers as people. Some thought we were the greatest ally of the capitalists because we were helping to save the system by making it work. Others saw us as an extension of the revolution and the class struggle. Still others thought civil liberties had nothing to do with class but saw them only as a means of enforcing the Bill of Rights by legal means. Others — the pacifists — looked to civil liberties as the best way to avoid violence and bloodshed. Some on the Board saw civil liberties as a tactic to be sure that minorities would have an opportunity to be heard. Some believed — the socialists mostly — that civil liberties were a means of effecting the change that would bring about a noncompetitive society of harmony and brotherhood."

"And you?"

"I suppose I pretty much accepted the Christian underdog doctrine that in order to make democracy work you had to have due process and fair trials to protect the rights of the humblest citizens."

(11)

A Visionary State of Mind

THE YEAR 1920 WAS VERY BIG in Roger's life; all his prodigious energies, it seemed, burst out at once and in different directions. It was his year to give free rein to what his mother had referred to as his "visionary state of mind," and to implement his ideas by forming new and progressive organizations. In point of fact, the ACLU was only one of four that Roger started in 1920.

"It was necessary to start movements that year," said Roger, "necessary after the months of 'inactivity' [the quotes are mine] in jail, but more importantly, necessary because the war had stopped everything. There were dozens of movements that hadn't survived the war, so we had to meet the challenge by starting new organizations which were responsive to the problems of the day. For instance, I started the Mutual Aid Society in the spring of 1920, just a few months after the ACLU came into being, because there was a good deal of pressure on me personally to help radicals who were in trouble, who couldn't get jobs, or who needed bail, or defense money and lawyers. The ACLU itself couldn't provide help because these people weren't necessarily having civil rights problems. So we formed a society based on Kropotkin's principle of mutual aid: 'from each according to his means, to each according to his need.' Each person who was capable put in whatever money he could and the people who were in need took out what they had to have. We had a pretty big loan fund — I think it got up to thirty thousand dollars. To borrow money you had to have two endorsers who agreed to pay it back if you couldn't and enough well-heeled members to put up the money."

"When you say members, who exactly do you mean?"

"Leftist intellectuals, trade unionists, the radical fringe. The Mutual Aid Society was used exclusively for people on the left and people in the labor movement. We had a little office at 100 Fifth Avenue; one secretary handled mostly the whole job. I'm sure we never had more than two employees, but the Mutual Aid Society lasted fifty years. We had our fiftieth anniversary in 1970 and I came up from Puerto Rico, where I was teaching in the law school, to speak at it. But it has since dissolved; the need is over because those footloose radicals of the after-war years do not exist today."

"How about your other 1920 organizations?" I asked. "Do their 'clients' still exist today?"

"Not really, no. The International Committee for Political Prisoners stemmed from the deportation of those thousand radicals I told you about who were shipped off — Emma Goldman among them — on the *Buford*. Well, that was the beginning. The Justice Department deported thousands more, people who weren't citizens but many who had lived here for twenty-five years and who were considered dangerous subversives. Many times the husband would be deported, and not always to Russia either. They were sent to other countries, Scandinavia and France, and the wives would be put in the position of either following them to a place where they didn't know the language and had no roots, or doing without them in the United States. It was a terrible thing."

"But who was responsible? You say the Justice Department, but was there any one person or specific people?"

"Yes, first there was Palmer. A. Mitchell Palmer, who was Wilson's attorney general and responsible for the first raids on aliens. And he was followed by Daugherty. Harding's attorney general, Harry M. Daugherty [pronounced "Dockerty" by Roger].* They were responsible. And then what happened after the people were deported from this country was that they were arrested in their own countries. And then they appealed to me."

"Again to you personally?"

"Yes, in a good many cases. They wrote me at the ACLU because we had tried to keep them from being deported in the first place. So they wrote me saying, well, you tried and lost out before and we got deported, and now we're in trouble again so please try to help us out."

---

* Later implicated in the Teapot Dome scandal.

"So how did you?"

"By forming the International Committee for Political Prisoners — my first international enterprise, as a matter of fact. I organized it to raise money for the deported aliens and to get in touch with agencies in foreign countries that could help them. We set up a network of correspondents in the various countries, and we had contacts with the Communist movement and with the Socialist International in New York, plus a very strong committee."

"The usual ACLU people?"

"Yes, a lot of the same crowd. There were some new ones though: Freda Kirchwey of the *Nation* was one I think and Lewis Gannett of the *Herald Tribune* and Harry Kelly — "

"You mean Harry Kelly, the same male anarchist from St. Louis?"

"Exactly. The same one. He was the head of an experimental school in the East by then. I would say the Committee for International Political Prisoners was more leftist than the ACLU Board, though."

"Was it effective?"

"Well, I put considerable time into it, operating much as Amnesty International does today, but with far more limited means and results. We got some prisoners out — I don't remember how many, but we wrote a lot of letters to officials and put out a regular bulletin and irregular reports. Our most ambitious publication was *Letters from Russian Prisons,* which we published in 1924 and for which I wrote the introduction. The book consisted of scores of letters by political prisoners of the Bolsheviks that were brought out of Russia and translated by an American journalist named Henry Alsberg whose politics ranged somewhere between liberalism and anarchism. The letters — which were quite authentic, I checked on that — were written by social revolutionaries, many of whom were friends of Emma Goldman's and Alexander Berkman's. In fact, that was the reason Emma and Sasha were disaffected with the whole Russian experiment before some of the rest of us. They even went to Lenin and told him what they thought of the government locking up their best friends and Lenin said he regretted it but that they couldn't allow those Social Revolutionists and Social Democrats to stand in their way because they were obstructionists to the Soviet program." *

In the introduction that Roger wrote to *Letters from Russian Prisons*

* In her book *Living My Life,* Emma Goldman wrote at considerable length about her and Alexander Berkman's meeting with Lenin. The historic encounter turned on

his ambivalence was quite apparent. On the one hand, his idealism about communism and the revolution tended to make him color all things Russian with a rosy hue. Hence he wrote in the introduction that "many of the members of the Committee for Political Prisoners as individuals [and it is clear that he included himself] regard the Russian Revolution as the greatest and most daring experiment yet undertaken to recreate society in terms of human values . . . Many of them look upon Russia today as a great laboratory of social experiment of incalculable value to the development of the world."

On the other hand, the grim facts as set forth in the actual letters written from Soviet prisons forced him to state unequivocally that "the holding of prisoners by any government blocks progress by stifling ideas and forces necessary to growth," and that the committee was concerned that "this first working-class government should not perpetuate the evil practices of reactionary governments the world over."

"That introduction — the whole book really — was an ordeal to go through," Roger recalled. "Of course the introduction was somewhat naive in appealing as it did to the better sense of the Bolsheviks and deploring their conduct."

"How was the book received?"

"Oh, the Communists attacked it and me too," Roger said airily, "and nobody else paid much attention to it. But still I did not lose my faith in the Russian Revolution. It was popular among liberals then and I was sure it would correct its errors."

No such allegiance constrained Emma Goldman. Disillusioned by a "maze of revolutionary contradictions," sickened by the banishment of her beloved Peter Kropotkin, whom the régime had reduced to a state of near starvation, horrified by what she referred to as the "garrotte of the political machine," she had by 1922 abandoned Russia and left the country. In October of that year she wrote Roger from Berlin, presumably in response to a letter from him in which he, while reiterating his own continued belief in the great Soviet experiment, expressed understanding of her alienation. Her lengthy letter reveals something of Roger's thinking at the time, as well as of her own.

---

her insistence that she could not "cooperate with a regime that persecuted anarchists and others for the sake of mere opinion." Lenin brushed aside her scruples as bourgeois sentimentality. "The proletarian dictatorship was engaged in a life-and-death struggle," she quoted him as saying, "and small considerations could not be permitted to weigh in the scale."

I have no quarrel with my erstwhile American friends who have become obsessed by the Bolshevik superstition and have found it necessary to discard me or to impute ulterior motives to what I have written. I do not pretend to be superhuman. I am hurt deeply by a breach of friendship, but in the end I try to remember the light and let the shadow pass on.

However, I do not wish to deny that I am always deeply moved when friends prove themselves staunch and above all when they are understanding . . . I am glad that you have understood, dear Roger.

It is very kind of you to ascribe to me the great influence which has prompted you to "examine searchingly the foundations of life about me and to challenge them with courage." You forget that the principal requisite for any stimulus to become an urge is fertile soil . . . You must not, therefore, overestimate my influence. But I am glad to have been ever so little a spiritual force in your life . . .

Miss Goldman went on then to talk about Roger's attempt to "get close to the inside of the rank and file of the masses by becoming one of them," (quotes, Miss Goldman) referring, of course, to Roger's manual labor trip, and said that while she had not doubted the sincerity of his effort, she had never thought it would succeed (as actually it had not). "Perhaps," she wrote, "it is in the nature of things that we should understand better at a distance than we do through close proximity." She continued:

It is true that the great idealists who had consecrated themselves to the cause of the disinherited have idealized the masses far beyond the actual possibility and characteristics of the workers at large . . . I think that all of us have the tendency of putting a premium on the poverty of pocket as well as of spirit.

Because the masses have been exploited and robbed for centuries we are inclined to make peace with their deficiencies, with their readiness to kiss the hand of each new master. In so doing we have been guilty of a great deal of harm to the very people we wanted to help. After all, the masses are in the majority . . . They are capable of the most wonderful outbursts, but it is a fact that so far the masses have not shown the capacity for sustained effort . . . Please do not misunderstand; I do not blame the masses. I blame much more the teachers and prophets of the masses who have neglected entirely to throw the masses on their own responsibility and to point out the necessity of divesting themselves of their clinging attitude toward those from whom they won the new dispensation.

Her letter continued by praising Roger's work for the political prisoners and urging him to keep up that fight. She was encouraged, she wrote, that the wonderful IWW boys (those who had finally gone to prison after the Chicago trial) had "thrown their defiance into the teeth of smug society" and she was filled with disgust by the other IWW defendants at the Chicago trial who, led by Big Bill Haywood, had jumped bail and fled to Russia.

She concluded by saying that she was nearing the end of the book she was writing on Russia and predicted that it would arouse a storm — a prophecy that proved true. In America her book *My Disillusion with Russia* was received by liberals and radicals with contempt and outrage; only the conservatives favored her rapping of Soviet knuckles.

Roger once again was staunch in his support of her "uncompromising philosophy [which] stands out as a challenge and guide to many who have not your spirit," although there was certainly no indication that he shared her disillusion. Among his liberal colleagues who appeared to feel that she had betrayed the international proletariat, the reaction of B. F. Huebsch, publisher of the Viking Press and, it will be remembered, a prominent member of the Board of the ACLU (and ultimately its treasurer) was typical. "Emma Goldman, a positive force preaching revolution and the philosophy of anarchism was an interesting figure, but times have changed, and Emma Goldman, disappointed at finding that the Soviet government is not anarchistic and that the revolution is over, seems to me to be only a blurred carbon copy of herself . . ."

E.G. herself sent Huebsch's chilly assessment to Roger in a letter dated March 18, 1924, a letter in which she also urged her "dear boy" to read carefully an article she had written on Lenin in which she portrayed him as the modern inquisitor.

"Tell me whether you too do not think the silence of the American liberals in the face of such horror is the most damnable thing?" she asked Roger. "These people who shouted themselves hoarse for amnesty of political prisoners, how dare they keep silent now that their own 'pet government' is guilty of such heinous crimes. Any publicity you can give the matter will be appreciated by the unfortunate victims of Leninism."

Clearly Roger was not inclined to give those "unfortunate victims" any publicity in America, although in his "hasty acknowledgment" to

E.G.'s letter he did say that he was continuing his work to get the matter of Russian political prisoners effectively before the Soviet government.

Through the early to mid-twenties a certain armed neutrality prevailed between Roger and Emma Goldman with respect to each other's attitudes toward Russia. Then in the late twenties and early thirties it was to flare up into intermittent bursts of acrimony. And by the forties when Roger's viewpoint came to coincide with the one Emma Goldman had held through all those years, she was no longer alive to know of his ultimate disaffection.

"Of course we haven't talked about India," said Roger, "which was another one of my 1920 causes." (The speed with which one had to shift gears to keep up with Roger was sometimes quite dizzying.) "In fact, my preoccupation with foreign countries from 1920 on was primarily with Russia and India, and for the same reason; both were fighting for the freedom of oppressed people. There were many other struggles for the same end, but these were the key countries."

As always with Roger, I was curious to know exactly what had started him on this particular path. Did he seek out Indians and Americans devoted to the cause of India's freedom, or was he sought out by them? It seemed that circumstances (also as always) conspired to put him in the right place at the right time to be sought and in this instance the right place was the Tombs in New York City. While imprisoned there Roger came into contact with his first two Indian revolutionaries, Sailendea Nath Ghose and Agnes Smedley, an American woman. Both were fellow inmates, in jail on the charge of conspiring against the British and running guns to India.

"Ghose was an ingenious vigorous man; he and I had many talks about what could be done to arouse American support for India's freedom."

One might think that during his three weeks in the Tombs his mind would have been so full of his own problems as a conscientious objector facing a lengthy jail term that he would not have had much time or inclination to take on the cause of India's freedom. "What, in point of fact, did interest you about India just at that moment?"

"Well, I realized from the very beginning that India was the most vital country since it was the most populous in the whole system of imperialist power. Most of us had the feeling that if India went, all

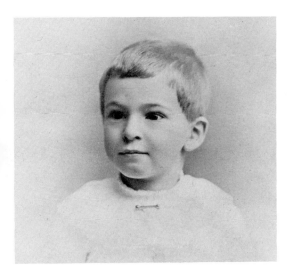

Roger Baldwin
at age two.

The Baldwin children: Roger, Margaret, Ruth, Deborah, Herbert and Robert.

Roger Baldwin in St. Louis, 1918.

Adopted sons, Toto and Oral.

Emma Goldman. *(Wide World Photos)*

Madeleine Doty. *(Sophia Smith Collection, Smith College)*

Roger at the time of
the founding of the ACLU.

Norman Thomas
and Roger Baldwin.

Roger at an ACLU meeting. *(Wide World Photos)*

Clarence Darrow and William Jennings Bryan at the "Monkey Trial," Dayton, Tennessee, 1925. *(Wide World Photos)*

Bartolomeo Vanzetti and Nicola Sacco arriving at courthouse, 1927. *(Wide World Photos)*

Morris Ernst and Arthur Garfield Hays, longtime counsels for the ACLU.

During the United Front days. Roger Baldwin with Herman Reissig and Evan Thomas, brother of Norman, at a test tribunal for conscientious objectors, 1940. *(Wide World Photos)*

Roger with Evelyn Preston, shortly after their marriage.

Daughter Helen, Roger and Evelyn at Windy Gates, Martha's Vineyard, 1941.

Elizabeth Gurley Flynn. *(Wide World Photos)*

General Douglas MacArthur in Tokyo, 1947.

Patrick Malin, new director of the ACLU, Dr. John Haynes Holmes, chairman of the ACLU Board of Directors, with Roger on the occasion of his retirement, 1950. *(Wide World Photos)*

Bill Mauldin's tribute to Roger at the time of his retirement. *(Princeton University Library)*

Roger in his beloved canoe.

Roger and René Cassin, original member and Nobel Prize Winner, at the United Nations Human Rights Commission, 1954. *(Leo Rosenthal)*

Roger and Nehru at the United Nations, 1957. *(Leo Rosenthal)*

Roger at 85.

of colonialism would go too. And the Irish made it very clear that they regarded India as the biggest obstacle to the freedom of colonial peoples and they made common cause with the Indians. I didn't know any of the Irish leaders, but I did know Ghose; I knew Agnes Smedley by sight only and she knew who I was, but she was in the women's section at the Tombs, and all we could do was wave to each other from one window to the other.

"Anyway when Ghose and Agnes Smedley got out of jail and when I got out, they came to me and asked me to help them with an organization. I don't know how Ghose got his support, but he managed to set up an American League for India's Freedom, or some such name, and we recruited liberals in the East, set up a little office and went to work with meetings and pamphlets."

"The same liberals again?" I asked. Sometimes it seemed to me they must have been the most overworked cadre of do-gooders in America.

"Well, some of the same, yes. John Haynes Holmes was one, and there was Bishop Fred Fisher and Dr. J. T. Sunderland and John Gunther and one or two senators and congressmen; mostly the pacifist–socialist–middle-class left, which was, of course, where I felt at home."

"Were there Indians in New York who were part of your organization?"

"Yes, there were some to assist us. Several were pretty violent revolutionaries, but I insisted on a commitment to nonviolence and got it. Our timing was good. By the early 1920's the cause of India was growing. We made contacts with an India League in London; the British allowed some of the leading champions of independence to travel abroad — those that were out of jail — and a stream of them came to the United States to lecture and in those early years we managed most of them through the League."

"Can you remember who some of them were?" I asked.

"Of course," Roger answered irritably (I should have known better than to ask). "I remember them most vividly. There was Villabai Patel, a bearded elderly gentleman who made us quite a lot of trouble by his unreasonable demands for VIP treatment. Then there was Shaukat Ali — he was Gandhi's only Moslem colleague who had any prominence in India — who appeared in native costume, very gaudy, all covered with stars and spangles, and he was a jolly color-

ful speaker. Then Mrs. Sarojini Naidu was a great success; she was
a remarkable orator with a commanding personality."

"Did Nehru or Gandhi ever come?"

"No, they didn't, although many urged them. I did not. In fact, I
discouraged Gandhi when I met him in 1931 because I knew the
United States press would never hear what he said when how he
looked was better copy. John Holmes gave him the same advice.
He toured Europe, but only Miraben came here. Miraben," Roger
answered my question before I could ask it, "was Margaret Slade, an
Englishwoman, the daughter of an admiral in the British navy. She
went to India and became completely like Indian women. She wore
saris always; she was very beautiful and she never married because
she was a servant of Gandhi. She lived with him in his ashram,
which is a sort of peace house — but Gandhi of course had taken a
vow of celibacy at forty, so Miraben was just his companion — his
slave really, and a good spiritual character. But both of them were
full of fun, joking all the time."

"Somehow," I said, "I never thought of Gandhi as much of a
comic."

"Oh, but he was. He was a big fellow for jokes. I remember
when I met him on a train when he was going through Paris — "

"Roger," I interrupted, "that's twice you've tossed out the when-I-
met-Gandhi line so casually. Please stop and tell me about meeting
him."

"Oh, I thought I had," said Roger ingenuously. "Well what happened was that Gandhi was on a train in France coming from Mar-
seilles to one of the channel ports, Calais I guess it was, and for some
reason the train was scheduled to stop for an hour in Paris, and I
was in Paris."

"What year was this?"

"Let me see, this was — the Indians would have been going to the
Round Table Conference in London, so that would make it 1931.
Anyway, I went down to the station because I'd never even seen
Gandhi and I was curious, and there he was with his bald head looking just like in the newspapers, leaning out the train window — I
remember he had a lei around his neck — and greeting people in
the crowd who were there looking up at him. And a little farther
down the train I spotted Mrs. Naidu — you remember I told you she
was one of our most successful speakers on India — leaning out of

the window too. And she saw me and called out, 'Oh Roger Baldwin, come and get on the train. We want to meet you.' So I got on the train and Mrs. Naidu introduced me to Gandhi. Miraben was there too and Gandhi said, 'Stay on the train! I'd like to talk to you,' so of course I said all right and I stayed with him in his compartment all the way to Calais. He hadn't had breakfast so he asked me to take breakfast with him. I was told, of course, that he was a very abstemious man — that he never ate very much — but I assure you that breakfast was as big as any I've ever had. It was made up entirely of fruits and nuts and goat's milk, but there was lots of it and Miraben kept serving us one fruit after another, over and over again."

"What did you talk about between bites?"

"Two things. One, the possibility of his going to the United States, which as I told you, I argued against, and the other, of course, was about India. He talked about what he hoped to accomplish at the Round Table Conference in London and how the British were misbehaving themselves."

"Who was to be at the Round Table Conference?"

"The British had called the meeting. The whole British cabinet was to be there along with the Indians to try to find an answer to the revolutionary movement in India. You see the British were willing to do almost anything except get out. And they didn't get out for seventeen years afterward. Not till 1948.

"Anyway, Mr. Gandhi talked about India and answered my questions about India and people I knew in India, and then do you know what happened? Believe it or not, I couldn't think of anything more to ask him. I ran out of conversation."

"That must have been a unique moment, Roger."

"It was. I couldn't believe it was happening, but it was."

"What did you do?"

"I got up and left his compartment and went to talk with Mrs. Naidu and some of the other Moslems on the train, and then just before we got to Calais, I went back to Gandhi's compartment."

"Fired up for one more conversational burst?"

"More or less. But the real problem was I was unprepared because I hadn't expected to meet him at all, so I hadn't thought up any topics ahead. But I hate to think how stupid I was in that meeting. Still, I wasn't stupid about India, because I knew right from the start that we were in a winning cause. I knew it right after Gandhi declared his policy and his leadership. It was evident the British could not resist such tactics except by killing him, and that would have meant a violent revolution."

"Did you stick to the League for India's Freedom right up until 1948?"

"Yes, I did. The organization changed its name and its leadership a few times. After 1940 it was the India League: I was treasurer and the spark plug was an Indian businessman named J. J. Singh, who was a resourceful propagandist with the knack of politics. We continued even after independence for a while to cement ties with the United States and the UN. But after the Indians got quota rights and resident Indians citizenship, the job was done well enough to disband. J. J. Singh, who by that time was a close friend of mine, returned to India."

"What had happened to Mr. Ghose?"

"After independence he was deported, protesting, to India to become the education officer of Calcutta. Agnes Smedley married an Indian Communist who served as a propagandist in Berlin; after his death she came back to the United States and published her autobiography. Of course I also knew Nehru very well, although I met him in another connection."

"Another connection?" I asked suspiciously. "Does that mean *another* league?"

Roger laughed. "Yes, another league. This time the League against Imperialism."

"Don't tell me that started in 1920 too?"

"No, it started in 1927 when I was asked to join the U.S. delegation to the first World Congress against Imperialism."

"Good," I said quickly. "Then we can take that up later. Now, what else did you found in 1920?"

After a moment Roger said, "It just so happened that in 1920 Charles Garland of Boston came into an inheritance at twenty-one years of age and because he had not earned it, refused to take it for his own use but chose to put it to public use. I had friends who knew Garland, so I went to see him with a proposal which shortly became the American Fund for Public Service, with two million dollars to be given away as speedily and as wisely as we could. We had a liberal leftist board of my usual colleagues; I was secretary and of course had been Garland's adviser in establishing the fund, so I had perhaps a greater responsibility."

A contemporary account entitled "Garland's Millions" was written by Roger at the time of the dissolution of the Fund twelve years after its inception, all the money having been disposed of.

According to Roger's report, Charles Garland had been greatly influenced by reading Tolstoi and the social reformers. At twenty-one he had a mature philosophy; he opposed the capitalist system of profit and exploitation and was committed to a "new social order." All the board members selected by Roger shared this overall view. Norman Thomas, Freda Kirchwey, Lewis Gannett, James Weldon Johnson, Scott Nearing, Elizabeth Gurley Flynn, to mention only a few of the familiar names, and others on the board worked together with comparative agreement, Roger reported, during the early critical years to shape the policy of the American Fund for Public Service.

"Later," he wrote, "we were moved by the intensity of the fratricidal strife in the labor and radical movements to judgments far less dispassionate." Further disagreements developed between board members because of the sharp difference between the "big spenders," who wanted to get rid of the money as fast as possible, and the "tight wads." Roger made no attempt to conceal which side he was on. "We tight wads were cautious," he wrote, "in letting the money go; we wanted to be sure we were not weakening the very agencies we served." The tight wads, it seemed, lost out. In the twelve years of its existence the Garland millions went to "almost a hundred enterprises of pioneer character directly or indirectly related to building up the power of the organized working class."

To cite only a few of the Fund's gifts: The great needle trades of New York City benefited lavishly; $50,000 went to the Furriers Joint Board and $100,000 to the International Ladies' Garment Workers' Union. Another $100,000 went to establish a bail fund for radicals; large sums went for workers' education; two resident workers' colleges were beneficiaries and periodicals, pamphleteering and book publishing took a large portion. In fact, the Fund directors themselves set up the Vanguard Press with a capital of $135,000 to publish radical classics in cheap editions and put out, in addition, a series of new books, chiefly studies of Soviet Russia.

"On the whole," Roger concluded his report on Garland's millions,

"I doubt if a wiser arrangement could have been made for doing the job we set out to do. Spending a million or two well is a tough job for anybody, and hardest of all for pioneering social causes which may or may not have survival value."

Today, his reaction to the Fund is slightly less charitable. "I do not feel so satisfied with our record of risks and compromises. We yielded too often to friendship and passing pressures. But wise investment in reforms is always chancy; that's their nature."

We had been speaking only of institutions that Roger founded in or around 1920 — not of the many dozens he joined in the early years of the decade. Far too many, according to his wife. Some of the people with whom he worked troubled her. "I could see they used Roger," Madeleine Doty wrote in her autobiography. "He was a member of at least twenty organizations. If the object of the organizations was worthwhile, he didn't question the personnel."

But at the same time she recognized that Roger was growing in stature. "His work prospered, he began to be a public figure. His fight for freedom of speech and press was bringing him renown. His name was now listed in *Who's Who*. It meant, of course, more and more entertaining, more and more people to see. My ideas on matrimony began to change. I came to see that running a home was a real job and a very fine one — to create a background where people could live and grow in harmony."

Roger was not sanguine. "No, I don't want to live à la Fannie Hurst," he wrote to Madeleine. "But perhaps you do. You are the chief sufferer from our domestic maladjustments."

It was true that life in the Doty-Baldwin ménage had been more than usually bumpy. Madeleine had had difficulty getting her articles published and so had taken a job editing a small news sheet for Roger's Friends of Freedom for India. But in the summer of the first year of their marriage she had given that up to go to Europe for three months with her mother and father, and more particularly to attend the Women's International League for Peace conference in Vienna.

She returned full of determination to make good on the fifty-fifty marriage and took a job with the Bray Moving Picture Corporation, producers of educational films. Her job was as a cutter, splicer and writer of titles, an occupation clearly inferior to her talents, but the salary of seventy-five dollars a week relieved her of further worries about her share of the financial arrangement in her marriage. She still found difficulty in managing the haphazard existence with Roger and the uncertainty of the dinner hour, uncertainty also as to who would be there, or even if engagements previously made would be kept. But, she wrote, "Roger's ideal of freedom applied to everything. To me freedom was intellectual and spiritual, a daily life was like the red and green lights of traffic. Without them there was confusion. But Roger, who had led a carefree irresponsible life for thirty-five years, found it hard."

He was, however, far from insensitive to Madeleine's malaise. "You are dead right about us," he wrote her from the Lafayette Hotel in Washington. "Much of my resistance is arguing against myself and against domination. I have an inordinate desire for a kind of personal freedom that perhaps isn't nearly as big as freedom shared."

And on another occasion he wrote her, "The thoughts I have of you and the state of matrimony which surrounds us are rather pleasant — amusingly reflective on the adventure of two trying to — oh, well let's say walk a tightrope over Niagara . . . When I am distressed or dubious it is because I don't like to see you *want* so much from life . . ."

Another letter was signed, "Much love Maddy — all I've got to spare from loving myself which is my first *duty!* (how's that for a husband?) Roger."

A sense of humor not having been one of Madeleine's more noticeable assets, it is probable that she did not greatly appreciate such touches of disarming candor.

In the summer of 1922 she again went to Europe with her parents, and although the following winter with Roger was less strained, her problems away from Waverly Place became ever more complicated. In the spring her mother died. Madeleine had always been exceptionally close to her father, who was completely lost without his wife, and so depended more and more on his daughter. Her life grew more and more hectic. Each day, while continuing her regular job, she would lunch with her father and then cope as best she could in the evening with Roger and "the folks he would bring home for dinner."

Such time and energy as she had left she tried to give to the

Women's International League for Peace. This organization founded by Jane Addams and Emily Balch (and in which Roger was also much interested) was the recognized leader in the women's movement for peace throughout the world. In the spring of 1924 the WILP held an important congress in Washington. Money had been raised to bring many of the most eminent European delegates, who were welcomed at a mass meeting and reception on the roof garden of the Hotel Pennsylvania in New York. Madeleine was very much in evidence; in fact, in her autobiography she quotes the following comment from an unnamed newspaper:

> Probably the most active woman in the whole convention is Madeleine Z. Doty, the best press representative of any large meeting coming here this season. She whisks here and there through the hall and the principal speeches come wet from the mimeograph under her direction only a few minutes after they have been delivered.

No sooner was the congress over when Madeleine once again went off to Europe with her father. On her return she gave up the uncongenial position at the Bray film corporation and took a job for half the money, but for infinitely greater satisfaction, with the New York branch of the Women's International League for Peace; she edited the League's bulletin.

But while her professional life may have improved, her private life was deteriorating. "My dad was a great anxiety. He had begun to take drugs to forget the loss of my mother. He needed constant attention . . . My studio needed care, dust and dirt accumulated. Neither my income nor Roger's were sufficient for a competent maid. Hours were uncertain; I never got enough sleep. I found myself breaking under the difficulties. And even more troubling than the physical aspect was the sense that my views had changed and were often not in accord with Roger's."

She objected to his basic philosophy of social and economic change, feeling that the appeal of workers striking for better wages and better conditions was always an appeal to self-interest. "Stand together that you may profit," she wrote, "instead of stand together regardless of the cost so your children may have better lives."

Such thinking led her to seek refuge in religion. She began attending Harry Emerson Fosdick's church with her father, a move with which Roger could hardly have been sympathetic.

Yet they both tried to hang on, knowing there was still much love between them. As a last resort Madeleine offered to give up her job entirely and to keep house for Roger and her father if they would support her. Neither her husband nor her parent considered this a good solution for her. Roger suggested separate apartments, which Madeleine considered no solution at all.

Finally Roger wrote her a letter in which he assessed with unvarnished honesty his own emotional condition.

> I cannot be content to let our present unhappy state rest without attempting to put in words what is so poorly said in the hit or miss of conversation. I only hope I can put it so you will understand . . . For your sake and mine I am unwilling to be party any longer to the kind of strain we have both suffered under, the last year particularly.
>
> You are unhappy with me most of the time, and I am unhappy with your unhappiness . . . [I am] conscious of my own shortcomings and alive to the probability that your unhappiness is justified by my failure to meet what you have a right to expect of a husband and comrade for life.
>
> There is, however, no question of my love nor yours. I have tested mine a hundred times. I am tied to you by profounder ties than to any other human being. Even at that they may not be, by fair standards, very profound. Next to my freedom in work you come — but you come only as the largest single *human* tie, *not* as the chief nourishment of my energies. That comes from many sides.*
>
> I am a crowd man. I need a variety of contacts to keep going in work and friendships. Without them I feel restless and unfulfilled. I know it is a shortcoming that I cannot also concentrate on a great personal love as do many other men who are also equally social. It is a beautiful expression of a fuller life but it is not mine. One of the reasons it is so hard to combat your challenge of my attitude is that I think you are right, that your way is the bigger way of life, but it is not mine.

By good fortune Madeleine learned that the main office in Geneva of the Women's International League for Peace was looking for a permanent secretary. It was, she wrote, "as though God had offered me a solution. He was again tapping me on the shoulder." She applied for the position and was at once accepted. Shortly thereafter she and her father left New York for Geneva.

Subsequently, Madeleine and Roger both made numerous trips

* Emphasis added.

across the Atlantic to be together, and they still had some happy times. But although the marriage was not officially terminated for ten more years it was to all intents and purposes ended when Madeleine sailed for Geneva on October 10, 1925.

Meanwhile Roger Baldwin, the "crowd man," gained not only the freedom that he held so dear, but continued to find the "variety of contacts" he had told Madeleine he needed to "keep going in work and friendships." Without them, he had said, he felt restless and unfulfilled. With them, there was no stopping him.

(12)

Strikes, Monkeys and Anarchists

"THE AVOIDANCE OF ANY ISSUE except the defense of the Bill of Rights has marked the Civil Liberties Union since its beginning," Roger pronounced.

"But surely there was some partisanship," I protested. "There must have been some issues, even within the Bill of Rights, that seemed more defendable to you than others."

"Well, it's true that I did not like the view of many of our clients or their activities, but I tried to be fair and impartial so far as emotion and prejudice would permit anyone to be. Still I was always more or less a victim of events. Our job, after all, was to protect citizens from the abuse of their rights by the government. So when labor's rights were under attack, the Union had to become their defender; the same was true when the Communists were the victims. We then became their defenders and apologists."

"And do you think people understood that you were defending the rights of Communists and the IWW, for instance, on principle alone?"

"No, I know that people certainly did not understand. Nobody would accept that. And so from the beginning the Union got the reputation of being left, and partisan and Communist. Our personnel didn't help correct that reputation either. As we discussed earlier, we had a very mixed bag on our Board, so our detractors could choose whatever label they wanted to put on us by picking their targets from the Board.

"I tried as director to keep an even-handed balance, to stick to principle, and to keep the spirit of resistance fresh and vigorous. I don't claim I succeeded, I just tried. Still we were lucky as an organization not to have been easily torn by inner dissension or to have been diverted from our aims by self-serving influences. Fortunately we also escaped bureaucracy by being too small and careerism by paying too little."

Small, dedicated, underpaid: Roger Baldwin hallmarks. Given those dimensions he was always in his element.

The ACLU office setup was particularly favorable since the team from the wartime Bureau that Roger had found so congenial continued. Albert de Silver was associate director giving full-time; Walter Nelles was counsel, giving part-time. Roger's salary as director was $125 per month; de Silver's was $75 (fortunately he had considerable personal means). The three men were joined by an excellent "field director" named Lucille Milner whom Roger had known from his St. Louis days.

A graduate of the New York School of Philanthropy, Lucille Milner (as Lucille Lowenstein) had worked for Roger at the St. Louis Civic League. She shared his interest in Oral James; she was also a pacifist. In fact, it was because she found her anti-war views so unpopular in St. Louis that she decided to go to New York in the summer of 1917 to renew her association with Roger and work as a volunteer for the AUAM. She kept up with Roger in the months he was in jail and one day received a letter from him saying he had great plans for her future and urging her to save herself for the "big cause" that lay ahead.

Writing of the early days of the ACLU in her book *Education of an American Liberal* Mrs. Milner says:

> From the start the Union was the target for attacks, and opposition to our work came from various quarters. Active support of the Union might mean social ostracism or economic ruin . . . It took a very brave lawyer to join with us in defense of civil liberties cases in the courts. Even so rock-ribbed an American institution as the *Atlantic Monthly* felt the pressure of the Iron Heel and declined to print our advertisements soliciting members; ". . . in the past few years," the editors wrote us, "there has been much civil liberty in the United States; what we need is not more but less civil liberty." *

At the ACLU office at West 13th Street, an old three-story brick structure that had once housed the fashionable and the rich, Mrs. Milner worked in what had been a "handsome drawing room with a beautiful old marble fireplace." Of her duties she wrote:

* Lucille Milner, *Education of an American Liberal* (New York, Horizon Press, 1954), p. 125.

From the moment I arrived at the office at nine o'clock until I left at the end of a strenuous day, I worked feverishly. One of my tasks was to record every civil liberties violation, as it occurred, for a weekly report to the Board of Directors and to our membership. Each day I scanned the metropolitan press and hundreds of liberal and labor publications sent to me by our representatives all over the country.

I clipped and had mounted and filed every case of mob violence, interference with freedom of speech and the press, every deportation for opinion, and every act of lawlessness by officials. Cases which required legal action went directly to our counsel. Those which called for unusual procedure or involved new policy went to the Board for discussion at the next weekly meeting.

Requests for our help became so frequent and so insistent that we had to keep reminding ourselves we were not a relief or defense organization or we would have been swamped. We could select only those cases to carry through the courts which involved new principles or established broad precedents.*

In many instances the ACLU acted to achieve what they referred to as a "manipulated test case." By confrontation and by direct intervention they tried to enforce civil liberties where suppression of them existed; they were able to dramatize their purpose and, they hoped, to awaken the conscience of an often smug middle-class society.

"We were always provoking cases one way or another," said Roger, "by sending our people into places where there had been a denial of the right to talk, and getting them arrested purposely in order to test whether these bans were legal. For instance we had a bishop of the Episcopal Church deliberately arrested in Newark where the police said the Communist party could not hold a meeting in the town. He was a very handy bishop by the name of Paul Jones — a saintly man, very Christian and quite left. He went over to Newark with the secretary of the Communist party and they both tried to speak in a public place and got themselves arrested and that was a big test case."

"Did you have any other such handy bishops?"

"Yes, we certainly did. We had about a half a dozen bishops available for duty in those days. Never had so many since. We had a bishop in Detroit and one in Buffalo and St. Louis and I forget where else."

* *Ibid.*, pp. 144–145.

"Did you just specialize in bishops or were there others?"

"There were others who spoke up. Monsignor Ryan — he was a Roman Catholic — I guess he was the only one we could ever get to speak up, but we had several rabbis. I remember one in particular in San Francisco."

"Why do you think you concentrated so much on men of God?"

"That's a very interesting question," said Roger. "I don't think we counted deliberately on them as men of God. It was more because most of them were men of conscience who were natural allies when they saw people suppressed. Their own doctrines required them to take a position, so many of them came to our attention because they had already expressed themselves publicly."

"Did you also have academics who spoke out for you?"

"We had a few. We had John Dewey, who was probably the leading progressive educator in the United States. He was on our Board for years; but he was more of a counselor than an activist. He would sign statements and speak at meetings but he didn't go on any missions."

"What about you and missions?"

"I rarely went. I sent others, but my job was primarily as manager of that office. If I went on missions it would probably take a week's time and there would be nobody back at the office."

"Didn't you have somebody to mind the store while you were away?"

"Yes, we had people who could take care of the store, but generally speaking it was a one-man show. In the years I was there nobody else made any decisions."

I recalled his firm denial of the "Roger Baldwin *is* the ACLU" line, but decided not to bring that up again. Instead I asked him if he had minded not getting out into the field.

"I preferred to lead the orchestra rather than play in it," he answered rather loftily.

"Well, you were certainly playing in it in the Paterson, New Jersey, case," I reminded him.

"That was an accident. I think there was nobody else I could send at that particular time."

It was an accident which came very close to landing Roger in jail for the second time and which was also one of the ACLU's early landmark victories.

In the fall of 1924, the Associated Silk Workers, an independent trade union, was conducting a strike of approximately 6,000 workers in Paterson, New Jersey. Suddenly, although the strike had thus far been peaceful and orderly, the strikers were informed by the chief of police that they could hold no more meetings in the private hall that they had hired. The reason given was that one striker had made disparaging remarks about the police and about a local judge.

As soon as the order was given, the Associated Silk Workers called on the ACLU to help them get the hall opened, and the Union responded by arranging that a test meeting be held in the hall under ACLU auspices. Thereupon the chief of police notified the hall owner that the meeting could not be held and backed up his edict by surrounding the hall with policemen.

Enter Roger Baldwin. Mr. Bill of Rights hurried to Paterson, met with the strike committee, and saw at once that since all halls were closed to them, only a public protest would get attention. Accordingly he advised a march to City Hall Plaza to hold a protest meeting on the steps of city hall.

Flags were secured, as was a copy of the Constitution; the strike committee, some thirty or forty men, and Roger set off from strike headquarters. As they progressed the few blocks toward city hall they were joined by hundreds of other strikers who had been milling around the streets awaiting the word from headquarters.

As the by then large crowd reached its destination, the strike chairman, John C. Butterworth, holding the American flag in one hand and the Constitution in the other, began reading from the Bill of Rights; this tactic had been advised by Roger to ensure that no charge of seditious utterance be lodged against them.

In his Oral History Roger describes what happened next:

> But far greater trouble than I anticipated broke. We had hardly got started before a whole squad of police descended on the throng, determined to break it up. In the trial later on the police testified that the captain had "read the riot act"; none of us heard it. Police clubs began to hit wildly right and left; heads were cracked; I saw blood stream from open wounds. The crowd scattered, running in every direction; only the flag bearers stood on the platform. The police promptly arrested them all — five of them. I looked on in some bewilderment; I had organized the affair and I was not arrested. I was determined I would be.

The culprit manqué spent the night in Paterson at the home of one of the strikers and the next morning went to police headquarters and asked to be booked, explaining his (and the ACLU's) part in the previous evening's happenings. The captain complied. A warrant was sworn out for Roger. Then he and the other five who had been arrested on the city hall steps were all bailed out and were thus free to make as much capital as they could of the wholly illegal police ban of a peaceful strike.

The ACLU publicity director (in a grossly underpaid post that, it will be recalled, was never occupied by any sufferer for very long) sent out nationwide releases announcing that another meeting would be held by the striking Associated Silk Workers at the same hall one week later: distinguished speakers from New York were to be on hand, the purpose being to force the issue into the courts. Wisely, the chief of police lifted the ban and permitted the meeting to proceed unhampered. Milking the situation for all it was worth, Roger had arranged for the strike chairman, John Butterworth, to walk down the center aisle and to begin reading the Bill of Rights exactly where he had left off one week earlier when he had been so brutally interrupted.

"His reception was tumultuous," said Roger, adding, "So was mine. A new spirit was infused into the strike and it was over and won within a few weeks."

The police, however, had been biding their time; they clearly had no intention of being bested by strikers and outside interferers, without extracting some sort of revenge. Accordingly, on the day the strike was settled, Roger, Butterworth and the others who had originally been arrested were all indicted for unlawful assembly based on an ancient 1796 statute. This curious document, couched in quaint language, charged that the defendants "then and there unlawfully, routously, [sic] riotously and tumultuously did make and utter great and loud noises and threatenings" with the intent to (among other evil purposes) "commit assault and battery upon the police officers and . . . to break, injure, damage and destroy and wreck the city hall . . ." *

The trial judge, Joseph A. Delaney, found the defendants guilty as charged, but singled Roger out for particular chastisement and retribution. He said:

* *The Victory in New Jersey* (pamphlet published by the American Civil Liberties Union, New York, June 1928).

As I recall the testimony in the case, Baldwin testified that he was the prime mover and was willing to assume the full responsibility. This is a rather serious crime — serious for the reason that we can see the possibility of serious consequences from meetings of this character. In this particular instance most of the men involved are not accustomed to our ways nor familiar with our government.

At the outset, Baldwin, you were primarily at fault. You felt that a test case should be made. The court feels that it should deal with you more severely than with the others. The sentence of the Court is that you be confined to the County Jail for a period of six months and that the other defendants pay a fine of $50 each. That will dispose of the matter.

The matter, of course, was far from disposed of, for although Roger claimed that jail held no particular terrors (or charms) for him, others in the ACLU felt that two jail terms in less than five years would hardly be desirable for their director. "One more strike," said Roger, "and I would be out — or in." So when the distinguished New York lawyer Samuel Untermyer volunteered to take the case on appeal to the New Jersey Supreme Court, Roger and his ACLU colleagues accepted with gratitude. But after a delay of nearly two years (due in part to Mr. Untermyer's absence from the country and to his illness), the decision upholding the lower court ruling was handed down. Again Judge Delaney sentenced the defendants to the same fines and Roger to the same six months in jail.

One more possible appeal remained, to the Court of Errors, the highest tribunal in the state. At this point Roger and all the ACLU lawyers came to the conclusion that Mr. Untermyer would have to be replaced. "They all said, including our Jewish lawyers, that a New Yorker, a rich Jew like Untermyer, would certainly get licked pleading before the Court of Errors in New Jersey. So we went out and got a local man who had high standing at the bar. Arthur Vanderbilt was the leading lawyer in Newark; he had been president of the American Bar Association and he knew all of the New Jersey judges on the Court of Errors. He pled the case for us with skill and wit and got the judgment against us reversed. After all," Roger added just a touch defensively, "you have to select lawyers to fit the case. It can be a very delicate matter."

I would have been more taken aback by Roger's rather cold-blooded pragmatism if I had not recalled a similar and perhaps even more blatant example of it. After a moment's hesitation, I decided to digress briefly. "The whole firing of Untermyer reminds me of Louis Redding," I said.

"What about Louis Redding?" Roger asked suspiciously.

I explained that I had been given an exchange of letters between Roger and a black lawyer named Louis Redding, that had been written early in 1942.* Redding, it seems, had represented the ACLU in the state capital at Wilmington, Delaware, until on February 6, he received a letter from Roger saying that the Union had recently decided to replace their state representatives — particularly those in state capitals — with lawyers "not identified in any way with minorities whose rights we commonly champion." Therefore, he was sure Mr. Redding would understand, "particularly in these difficult days," that the ACLU was replacing him in Wilmington with a lawyer "not identified with any special group interest."

Mr. Redding emphatically did not understand. "It seems almost supererogatory," he answered Roger, "to point out the incongruity between your letter of February 6, 1942, and the idealism implicit in the professed aims of the American Civil Liberties Union."

"It seems to me he makes a very good point," I said.

"I can appreciate his feelings, yes," Roger said. "But we took the action with regard to him deliberately. We all agreed on it."

"But why?"

"Because we had a general policy of not getting involved with race relations. We would not have had a Communist lawyer and we didn't have any Negro lawyers. I think he was the only one."

"I don't think you can really equate Communists and Negroes," I said.

"I mean minority interests," Roger said doggedly. "We had a policy not to have lawyers identified with the minorities we were defending."

"So your letter said. But in his answer Redding pointed out that in any event the ACLU had never championed the cause in Delaware of the minority to which he belonged. What he had been doing was representing persons *not* of that minority."

"In criminal cases," Roger pounced. "*Not* in civil liberties cases. He says that himself in his answer."

"True."

"The reason we had that policy was that you just cannot be effective

* From the papers of Corliss Lamont.

in court in civil liberties cases if you belong to one minority and you're representing another unpopular minority."

"Does that mean you can't conceive of a situation in which a black lawyer would defend, let's say, a Mormon who was prevented from holding a public meeting?"

"No, I can't conceive of such a situation."

"Then do you think Mr. Redding or any other black lawyer would be less effective in such a case *just because* he was black?"

"Yes, of course, that's what I think. He'd be less effective unless he was extraordinarily good. Because he'd have to be extraordinarily good to overcome a jury's prejudice."

"Whereas a white lawyer would just have to be average good, is that it?"

"Not necessarily," Roger said calmly. "It depends on the prejudice. For instance, we wouldn't use a New York lawyer in Alabama, and we wouldn't use a southern lawyer, particularly one with a strong accent, in a northern court. In New Jersey we all decided not to use a Jewish lawyer when we knew prejudice against him existed. And you have to remember that because of that tactic we won the Paterson, New Jersey, case, which was far more of a victory than just keeping me out of jail."

"I realize that, Roger, but still — "

"If the original judgment had stood in New Jersey," Roger broke in, now pressing his advantage, "it would have meant that men could go to jail for doing something which the Constitution clearly says they have a perfect right to do — peaceably to assemble and petition for redress of grievance. By pushing the case to the highest court, we raised, for the first time in the state's history, the issue of unlawful assembly; and by winning our case we knocked out as unconstitutional that ancient 1796 law."

I felt both unsatisfied and outmaneuvered; Roger had neatly managed to justify what I still considered his quite unforgivable dismissal of Louis Redding on the grounds of his totally unrelated victory in New Jersey.

By all odds the most important "manipulated test case" of the 1920's was, of course, the Scopes Monkey Trial, which the ACLU literally originated by creating a confrontation between an individual and the state in which he lived.

The Scopes case is by now a classic in American history, a classic dominated by three names: William Jennings Bryan, Clarence Darrow, and (almost incidentally) John Thomas Scopes. Often forgotten today is the role played by the ACLU, but the fact is that it was the Scopes case that largely won for the American Civil Liberties Union the national renown it has enjoyed ever since.

The Tennessee evolution case really began on March 21, 1925, when Governor Austin Peay signed into law the Butler Act, which "prohibited the teaching of the Evolution Theory in all the Universities, Normals, and all other public schools of Tennessee . . ." The act further provided a fine of not less than one hundred dollars for any teacher found guilty of teaching "any theory that denies the story of the Divine Creation of man as taught in the Bible, and [of teaching] instead that man has descended from a lower order of animals."

In New York Lucille Milner, combing newspapers as was her daily practice, saw a small news item noting the passage of the anti-evolution act in Tennessee. In some excitement, she clipped the piece and hurried in to Roger, who glanced at it and according to Mrs. Milner "saw its import in a flash." He told her "laconically" to bring it up at the Board meeting the following Monday.

Members of the Board agreed at once and without a dissent that the suppression of academic freedom, of free speech, and of religious liberty as embodied in the Tennessee act was of the utmost importance — important enough to be carried to the Supreme Court of the United States. A special fund was voted to finance a test case and to implement such a case a story was sent to the Tennessee press announcing the ACLU's willingness to test the constitutionality of the anti-evolution law by defending any teacher willing to challenge it in the classroom.

A few days later came a telegram from the small town of Dayton, Tennessee, announcing, "J. T. Scopes, teacher of science, Rhea Central High School, Dayton, will be arrested, charged with teaching evolution . . . for test case to be defended by you. Wire me collect if you wish to cooperate and arrest will follow." The message was signed G. W. Rappelyea, who, it turned out, was a young Dayton businessman whose motives were slightly mixed. He sincerely objected to the anti-evolution act, but at the same time he saw an opportunity to put his town on the map. The ACLU reaffirmed their offer and instructed Scopes to go ahead and present himself to the prosecutor and await indictment.

John Thomas Scopes was a willing victim. Although a modest, unsophisticated young man, he nonetheless had no qualms about assuming his historic role because he simply did not think it was possible for anyone to teach biology without considering Darwin's theory.

At first the ACLU Board in New York did not seem quite aware of the magnitude of the issue they had raised in that little town a thousand miles to the south. But they all knew from the outset that their objective was to get the case to the United States Supreme Court. The question was how.

In his chapter in the 1965 anthology *D-Days at Dayton: Reflections on the Scopes Trial,* Roger has written of the Board's early dilemma.* "Should we enlist a conservative constitutional lawyer and make it a top issue of separation of church and state, freedom of teaching the truth as laid down by the very textbook which Scopes taught, approved by the state? Or should we make it a contest between religion and the unreasonable restraint on science imposed by law? Should we attempt to get into the federal courts with an injunction against enforcing a state law violative of the First Amendment guarantees?"

The ACLU Board did not have long to debate these basic questions; the decision was, in effect, made for them when William Jennings Bryan offered to appear as counsel for the prosecution, "assisting" the attorney general of Tennessee.

As Scopes himself has written, "Mr Bryan's entry into the case . . . had thrown a monkey wrench in the gears of all their [the ACLU's] plans." †

And, as Roger wrote, "it was immediately apparent what kind of a trial it would be: the Good Book against Darwin, bigotry against science, or, as popularly put, God against the monkeys." ‡ Furthermore, with Bryan for the prosecution, it was almost inevitable that Clarence Darrow, the agnostic, would volunteer for the defense, as indeed he promptly did, thereby deepening the conflict at the ACLU. For if it was inevitable that Darrow would enter the case as soon as Bryan had volunteered, it was equally inevitable that with these two classic antagonists facing each other, the real issue might well be obscured. The trial, argued some of the Board, would be-

* Jerry R. Tompkins, ed. (Baton Rouge: Louisiana State University Press, 1965), p. 57.
† *Ibid.,* p. 18.
‡ *Ibid.,* p. 57.

come a carnival and any fight for civil liberties surely would be lost.

Some few others, most notably Arthur Garfield Hays, who was the Union's chief counsel and very influential in its policies, strongly favored Darrow. Roger himself claims to have expressed no preference but to have left the matter up to "the man whose party it was, after all." John Scopes was brought to New York from Tennessee to meet with the Board and with other interested participants in this increasingly dramatic case. The meeting, Roger recalls, was held at the Town Hall Club at 45th and 7th Avenue. The Union first offered young Scopes the services of Bainbridge Colby, who, like William Jennings Bryan, had been secretary of state under Wilson and whom most of the lawyers (and doubtless Roger) felt would argue the case as it should be argued on strong constitutional grounds.

Then Dudley Field Malone, an eminent lawyer in his own right, arose officially to offer the services of Clarence Darrow, as well as his own services, for the defense. (Hays was already committed to work with these two lawyers.) Scopes was then given an opportunity to voice his preference. "Now it was my turn to speak," he wrote in his chapter ("Recollections Forty Years After") in *D-Days at Dayton:*

> I pointed out to the group that if they thought that Darrow would have too much influence on the course of events, then they had forgotten apparently that . . . the major headlines and news stories had already begun to drop the issues and to play up Mr. Bryan. As to creating a carnival atmosphere, my hearers should have been in Dayton the day Neal and I had left to come to New York. There was not enough room in that part of Tennessee to accommodate any more medicine men, traveling evangelists, and screwballs than were already there. If the carnival atmosphere and the shift of the tenor of the news stories from Dayton meant the loss of all our efforts up to now, then they were lost already. We could thank Mr. William Jennings Bryan for the loss . . .
> I concluded by stating that I would like to have Darrow and Malone join the battle in our behalf.*

Scopes then recalls considerable tension between the hard-core opponents and proponents of Darrow. Finally the showdown came; the vote was taken and Darrow's offer was accepted, "but just barely." He makes the whole episode sound very exciting. Roger, on the other hand, says it wasn't exciting at all; it was just plain dull be-

* *Ibid.,* p. 20.

cause, Scopes's description notwithstanding, Darrow was a foregone conclusion.

So too, from the ACLU's point of view, was the outcome of the case. Bryan and Darrow did indeed put on an unforgettable show, in which the fundamentalist doctrine of revealed religion and the Book of Genesis clashed with the scientific doctrine of evolution. Bigotry against enlightenment, dogma against freedom — yet nothing was settled in Dayton, Tennessee, in the hot summer of 1925.

When John Scopes was found guilty (it took the jury just nine minutes to decide) and fined a nominal $100, the way finally seemed open to take the case to the United States Supreme Court, for it was considered probable that the highest court of Tennessee would uphold the lower court's finding. In effect the Tennessee Supreme Court did so, as indicated by the opinions rendered by the judges on its bench. But then, deliberately, they *reversed* the conviction of Scopes on a blatantly specious detail. The fine on Scopes, they said, had been imposed by the presiding judge instead of, as the law of the state provided (inexplicably), by the jury. The strategy was obvious; Scopes's conviction was thus overturned. There was no possible justification for him to take his case up through the federal courts on appeal. By thus reversing the lower court on a technicality, the Tennessee Supreme Court neatly forestalled a test of their state's anti-evolution law in the federal Supreme Court. For forty years it remained untested until, in 1968, a similar Arkansas statute finally did reach the highest court, which ruled anti-evolution acts unconstitutional.

Given this inconclusive result, it is perhaps not surprising that today Roger's attitude toward the Scopes case is, to say the least, haughty. For the most part, he simply rises above it. For example, Scopes receives only the briefest passing mention — a mere few words — in his Oral History. And, in my frequent attempts to draw him out on the case, he usually responded sparsely and often rather grumpily. He did not even refer me to his own chapter in *D-Days at Dayton* (without which I would not have had a plausible explanation of his obvious, although always unspoken, disappointment in the outcome of a case that he himself had initiated).

But given all these justifications, I told him I still found it puzzling that throughout the entire Scopes case, neither before, nor during, nor after the trial, had he ever once traveled to Dayton, Tennessee, to witness the spectacle or be part of the action.

"I didn't want to go because I was in New York raising money and paying bills," he said.

"But I understood this was one case where you had little or no difficulty in raising money."

"Yes, that's true. There was no problem financing this case; in fact the money poured in."

"So," I persisted, "you could have got away. Weren't you even tempted to go to Dayton?"

"No," Roger answered sulkily, "I never had the habit of attending trials. They're a waste of time, most of them. And besides I was managing things from New York."

But it appears in this instance that he wasn't really managing very much from New York, since everything was happening in Dayton and was being reported in minute detail by hordes of newspapermen, most notably by H. L. Mencken. The ACLU had rented and furnished an unoccupied house — known locally as The Mansion — to accommodate their legal staff and the numerous eminent scientists they had brought to Tennessee to appear as expert witnesses on the facts of evolution. (None of them was allowed by the court to testify, but they all gave informal press conferences almost daily, so their planned testimony was widely publicized.)

Still Roger stayed miles away from this heady atmosphere; it seems probable that there were two reasons why. First, he was bitterly disappointed that the great constitutional issue that had moved him to institute the case in the first place had become totally obscured. And second, because, through no fault of his own, the reins had slipped out of his hands. What was happening at Dayton would have happened whether or not he had been there, and he either could not or would not visualize himself in the wholly unfamiliar role of fifth wheel.

In the three other famous cases of the era — the Sacco-Vanzetti, the Mooney-Billings and the Scottsboro boys — the ACLU never held any reins at all. In all three instances their connection was peripheral although, of course, supportive of the defendants. However, in the Sacco-Vanzetti case Roger had a relatively close personal connection.

It will be recalled that Nicola Sacco and Bartolomeo Vanzetti — both Italian-born — were accused of having robbed and murdered a paymaster and his guard in a shoe factory in South Braintree, Massachusetts. Although both men carried firearms and were believed to have had access to the car identified with the crime, both had witnesses to prove that they had been elsewhere at the time of the murders that took place in broad daylight. But the exculpatory assertions of their witnesses were later allegedly discredited. Still much of the evidence against the men was refuted and as the case became a cause célèbre, it was widely held, particularly among liberals, that they were being victimized because they were labor agitators, draft dodgers and anarchists. Seven years after the crime was committed Sacco and Vanzetti were executed.

"From the beginning the case was handled exclusively by the Italians," Roger recalled. "They formed a defense committee and hired the lawyers. All the rest of us were just assistants; we never had any inside authority of any kind. The Union appeared on the letterhead of the defense committee as one of the sponsoring organizations, of course."

"But you were friendly with Sacco and Vanzetti."

"Yes, I knew them well, especially Vanzetti. I used to visit them both in jail every time I went to Boston during those years. Vanzetti took rather a shine to me. His English was very poor, but he liked to chat about anarchism and events and literature. He once gave me a very bad translation into English of Proudhon, the French philosophical anarchist. Poor Vanzetti, he tried to be a literary man, but he really wasn't. He was such an innocent really."

"You were closer to him than to Sacco?"

"Well Sacco was a difficult character compared to Vanzetti. Vanzetti was an open, naive fellow, but Sacco was passionate, suspicious and militant. His English was good — much better than Vanzetti's — but he didn't welcome visitors unless you really had some business with him."

"Tell me how you got to know them both in the first place."

"Through Mrs. Evans, Mrs. Glendower Evans, who was one of my closest friends — in public matters, that is — and someone that I admired very much. Her husband was Welsh obviously, and she was what they call 'well connected.' She was also rich and she was a widow and she devoted herself completely to the Sacco-Vanzetti case. She financed a lot of moves in it. In fact she was the principal character — by another name, of course — in Upton Sinclair's novel *Boston,* which is about the Sacco-Vanzetti case."

"Well, how did you get to know her then?"

"She was on our local Civil Liberties Committee in Boston. It was a very active committee there; Mrs. John Codman, Mrs. Horace Davis, who was a Hallowell from Medford, all the so-called best people in Boston. They were untouchables and they could do a job for civil liberties just because they were untouchables."

I pointed out that the Boston committee does not call itself the ACLU, but rather the CLUM — Civil Liberties Union of Massachusetts.

"Something like that. A lot of our local committees kept their own identities, especially in those early days. But anyway, Mrs. Glendower Evans brought many hesitant liberals into the case and raised a great deal of money. She was also the one on the committee who had all the contacts with Sacco and Vanzetti. She was allowed to visit them right in their cells and when she went she took me along. She acted almost like a mother to Vanzetti; she used to discipline him. I remember hearing her scold him for having flighty ideas."

"Such as?"

"Such as trying to get the miners from Pennsylvania to come up and blow up the jail to let him out. With Sacco her relations were not so warm, but with his family they were fine — with Rose Sacco, and their boy, Dante, and their little girl."

"Vanzetti was not married?"

"No, he had just a sister. But Mrs. Evans and Mrs. Gertrude Winslow, who was also on our Boston committee — two lovely ladies — they constituted themselves as guardians of the Sacco family. And after the execution I was trustee of a fund of about fifteen thousand dollars which was raised by French workers for the assistance of the Sacco family."

"Did you also know Mrs. Sacco?"

"Yes, I knew Rose, and Dante — he was an engineer. I think he's dead now, but he came to see me a few years ago when I was speaking at the Boston Community Church, which has over the years kept alive the memory of those two men and their tragic end."

"And what do you think after all these years? Are you still convinced they were absolutely innocent?"

"Well, I don't say they were *absolutely* innocent. I just say they were never guilty beyond a reasonable doubt. Never! They may have known the so-called Morelli gang that probably did the job. Whether they actually benefited from the robbery I don't know. The money was never recovered. But I don't think they shot anybody. I don't think it's possible that they shot the payroll master in South Braintree in broad daylight. Years later Fred Moore, their trial counsel, told Upton Sinclair that he thought Sacco was 'probably guilty' and Vanzetti 'possibly.' But Fred Moore has to be discounted for his irresponsible behavior. He was an unstable man — he took drugs I think — and he was finally discharged by the defense committee. In the last analysis I think the outstanding issue really was that they were condemned because they were Italians and anarchists."

Roger was in Russia in August of 1927 when Sacco and Vanzetti were executed. I asked him if he was aware that there was a letter from Vanzetti written just two months before he died to Roger who was then in Rome.

He said that he had had numerous letters from Vanzetti but he thought he had loaned the last ones he received to Tolstoi's son and literary executor to put up on the bulletin board of a state bank in Russia where he worked (the Russians were much interested in the case), and he had never seen them again. He seemed pleased, as I handed him the letter, to know that at least one of them was still extant. It was dated July 25, 1927:

Dear Roger,
Your good letter from Rome was received in due time and very much pleasure. As for my translation, I am satisfied of your assurings, but I would like you will put only my first name in it, followed by the second name of he who corrected it. That would be a square deal.

To heard from you in my land, it is a thrill — and your report is more optimistic than I could have expected. I presume to know what my people want, what they need and which their task should be. Too bad that the great Idea has so many too little men. But there are also the great ones — to bad that they are misunderstood by their own followers and that the large masses prefer cheaters and demagogues to real men.

Your trip is certainly important . . . And if Fuller will not doom me before your return, I am writing and will lend the whole of my to ears to your rapport on Europe affairs.

Be well, dear Roger, salute for us all the friends and Comrade you
will meet, and have from Nick and I our best. Ah! Since you are in
Europe I cannot refrain a note on the case . . .

The commission appointed by the Gov. to investigate the case has just
began its study and, safe a reprive, it will have only three weeks of time
to study a case that lasted seven years, with two trials lasting, globally 10
weeks, and five appeals and two motions for a new trial, one more volu-
minous than the others. The defence asked for a reprive before July 1,
in order to give the commission sufficient time to study the case and to
avoid our deportation to the death house on July 1 — as the laws
request, except a reprive . . . Now listen Roger, if you will know that
we will have been carried to the death house, on July 1, that would
mean that the Gov. is decided to have us executed or burried alive for
ever in the malebolgie [sic] of the State Prison. To delay a reprive intill
after we will have been confined in the death house is the only way to
have us there before giving the decision — which can save the ap-
parance, conceal the intention and keep the people suspended by hope
and anguish.

It would also happen that no reprive will be ordered and a contrary
decision given before the actual date fixed for our execution. I like
to believe and hope that Gov. Fuller is a better man than I thought
and will act decently and manly. But if we are taken to Charlestown on
July 1 — beware, beware, beware.

With a strong and most cordial shake hands,

alway your friend BARTOLO

Roger shook his head as he gave me back the letter. "It was a tor-
menting case," he said.

(13)

Liberty under the Soviets

A STRANGE AND QUITE UNCHARACTERISTIC LASSITUDE overcame Roger in the year 1926. Suddenly, he says, he could not stand going to the office and answering all those phone calls and seeing all those callers. Suddenly he was not even sure he wanted to continue in civil liberties work. He felt restless and purposeless. He wanted a respite and he took it, staying first at the country home of Morris Ernst (the ACLU's eminent, and with Arthur Garfield Hays, most durable lawyer), then going on to spend three months in Carmel, California, visiting Miss Mary Bulkley, one of his "older women" friends from his St. Louis days. After that he traveled around a bit, visiting other friends, accomplishing nothing, taking each day as it came, sometimes enjoying the impromptu casualness of his schedule (or lack of it), sometimes — more often — feeling restive and aimless.

"I found it difficult, and I still do today, to account for this confusing period in my life. I never had anything like it before, nor have I since."

Certainly, I said, it seemed quite foreign to his nature.

"It was. I always felt that a day without some purpose was a day lost."

"Had your malaise anything to do with the breakup of your marriage, do you think?"

"Oh yes, I think so. I still had a wife and yet I didn't have a wife. I had no real home. But more than that, it may have been that these were just uninspiring years; there was no great challenge to civil liberties. These were the Coolidge years of prosperity and peace. We had had the monkey trial in Tennessee a couple of years before; I was still out on bail in the Paterson, New Jersey, free-speech case. I had started both those cases and participated actively in the second one; that had been the real excitement for me. But in 1926 my motivation was low. The fun seemed over. Nothing in sight aroused me. But Madeleine was in Geneva and the thought of Europe was the only thing that did stir me. I hadn't been there since the year after I graduated from college. I had a mission — working for political prisoners — and a wife. I asked for a year's leave of absence."

"What about the office?"

"I left that in good enough hands to meet the demands, which were not great because we weren't doing any pioneer work."

"Are you saying there really was none to do at that time?"

"No, I'm saying it was a mistake not to have found some to do. The ACLU should have been playing a more thoughtful role in those years. Instead we seemed to consider ourselves a sort of firehouse to respond to fire alarms."

"And you left enough firemen behind to go to Europe!"

"Exactly. I left enough firemen. Forest Bailey, a teacher who had had administration posts, became associate director.* And besides our chairman, Dr. Ward, John Haynes Holmes, our vice chairman and a stalwart, was always at hand to be counted on for integrity and sticking to principle. Norman Thomas, my closest colleague, never missed a single weekly meeting — in fact, for years they were held at his house — except when he was campaigning in the presidential years. And there was the faithful Lucille Milner and our team of lawyers, Hays and Ernst."

With the store thus minded — or the firehouse thus manned — Roger sailed for Europe on the day before Christmas of 1926. Being Roger he had by the time he left lined himself up another "mission" in Europe besides his planned work for the International Committee for Political Prisoners — in fact, as it turned out, he had several other projects in hand.

Through his connection with the India League he had been asked to be a member of the United States delegation to the first World Congress against Imperialism in Brussels. And the Vanguard Press, on learning he was taking a year's leave of absence, had commissioned him to write a monograph in their Russia series on liberty in the Soviet Union.

* Albert de Silver had by then been killed in a strange accident, falling off a train between cars while on his way to New Haven, Connecticut.

He set off, he says, armed with a card from the Quakers to help in his work with political prisoners and with a press card from the Federated Press, a left-wing news service highly appropriate for the very radical Congress against Imperialism and also, as Roger was gratified to discover, easily confused with an Associated Press card.

As soon as he landed in Europe, Roger went directly to Paris to check in at the office of the International Committee for Political Prisoners at 11 Rue Scribe, which was to be his official headquarters throughout the year. For no matter how many fascinating, gripping other activities he engaged in, his primary mission abroad was not only to carry on the fight against the persecution of political prisoners, but to combat the very fact of their existence, that is, of persons being incarcerated for the opinions that they held.

Reporting in one of his well-known "to my friends" letters (this one dated February 13, 1927), Roger wrote:

> The countries where political persecution flourishes are of course the dictatorships and the colonies. In the order of their present degree of oppression, I should list the dictatorships and near-dictatorships about as follows: Italy (in a class by itself), Hungary, Poland (much alike), Russia, Turkey, Spain, the Balkans and the Baltic States. That is about half of Europe — excluding Russia . . . Among the colonies, the oppression most complained of is in Syria, under the French mandate, in Georgia under Bolshevik rule, in "independent" Egypt, in the French colonies in North Africa and in the Far East, in India and Korea.

Paris, he reported, was the historical haven of political refugees. They were there in greater numbers than ever before, with committees meeting constantly and issuing little weekly papers, circulars and pamphlets. Paris was also the headquarters for the anti-Fascists.

Paris for Roger was one more thing — the place where he and Madeleine were reunited. She came from Geneva to meet him there and, as he wrote his mother, "We played around for a week, even descending to the Moulin Rouge leg show. It is really an 'all-over' show, excusable to us high-minded folks on the ground of magnificent color and scenic effects. A sort of glorified peasant art. I could hardly tear Madeleine away. One evening," he added, "we put in dancing at a fashionable café — just to pretend we weren't highbrows." They spent a few days at Fontainebleau walking in the forest, in the woods and over the old palace grounds and found the

French country people "friendly and gay and always ready with a humorous reply." In fact, Roger wrote, "I have fallen quite in love with the French and could easily settle down for a long stay most anywhere in France if I weren't an agitator looking for trouble."

As it happened, he had little trouble finding trouble, but first came a peaceful interlude in Geneva. Madeleine had fixed up very comfortable quarters for him at the Maison Internationale where she lived with her father and various young boarders. Writing his mother the details he presumed mothers liked to hear, he described his "quiet homey spacious room, bright and warm (steam heat), gay hangings and electric lamps [hardly notable one would think in 1927] and a private washroom. I look out on a little garden still green [this was January] and a holly tree and vines and little shoots waiting for a warm spell." Although Madeleine was busy all the time, each evening they had someone in for dinner, and often for tea as well. Once a week they went to a friend's house for an "old-fashioned American party with charades, guessing games and general high-jinks, attended by some ten to fifteen people of all nationalities." Certainly very harmless-sounding "high-jinks" for an "agitator."

As an afterthought in his letter to his mother, Roger wrote, "Oh yes, the League of Nations seems to be here too, but nobody takes it very seriously. I went to a session of the Opium Committee and it is enough."

In retrospect, Roger is slightly less supercilious about the meetings then being held at the old Palais Wilson, although he says, "I listened to the speeches as I have in the years since at the United Nations, always with the feeling that they were more for the record than for any practical application." Still he did manage to become involved, although there were no NGOs (Nongovernmental Organizations) in the League but many volunteers, in two practical commissions set up to deal with two specific problems: the administration of the mandates taken from Germany and the rights of the minorities in the Balkan countries. The latter was of particular importance, he thought at the time, because of the political prisoners involved. However, it was all very frustrating; despite his efforts, no action of any sort was taken in behalf of the prisoners by the League of Nations.

On February 10, 1927, Roger left Geneva and went to Brussels for the first meeting of the League against Imperialism; this marked his first involvement with the United Front organizations that were to dominate his life for the next decade.

"The auspices of the congress were supposed to be very nonpartisan," said Roger, "but the actual operation was in the hands of the Communists. It took me a while to find that out after I got to Brussels, but I suspected it by the makeup of the American delegation. I almost had to be introduced to my fellow countrymen; we had people I hardly knew except by reputation, a couple of colored people and others who were fellow travelers at least."

"Did you know any of the delegates from the other countries?"

"I knew Luis Muñoz Marin because I had been on a committee with him in New York when I had expressed sympathy with the struggle to get the marines out of Haiti. But I knew many of the others by reputation and there were some towering reputations there too. Nehru of India — I told you that was when I first met him; James Maxton and George Lansbury and Ellen Wilkinson of England, a couple of Chinese generals representing Chiang Kai-shek."

"How would the Chinese be regarded as colonial people?"

"Because they were trying to throw off the yoke of the war-lords and Chiang Kai-shek was trying to unify China. The Egyptians and the Sudanese, of course, were under strong British control and they were represented by their so-called freedom fighters."

"How about Africa?"

"Oh, there was a delegation of black Africans. And there was Georg Ledebour, the head of the German Left Socialist party, and the French soldier-author of *Under Fire,* Henri Barbusse, and Edo Fimmen, the Dutch secretary of the International Seamen's Union, who had a very forceful personality and played a large role, and other assorted Socialists, Communists, liberals, labor leaders and colonial subjects. It was surely the greatest collection of subversives I had ever seen. They were gathered together and held together by a secretarial team headed by Willi Muenzenberg, who was not only a German Communist, but a member of the Third International Executive Committee. His sidekick was an ingratiating Hungarian of many languages named Louis Gibarti, who was one of those faithful party agents who didn't admit it.

"Anyway, the purpose of the whole congress was to unite liberal political parties in the controlling countries with leaders in the colonies who were struggling for independence. The program was quite passionate. This was the first time that the Communists had appeared openly under Russian influence to make colonialism a major issue. And they still do today; right now on the Cyprus issue you see the Russians are backing the Turks whom they regard as the oppressed people." *

"What exactly was your role in all this, Roger? After all you didn't represent an oppressed people."

"That's right, and all through those first meetings in Brussels, I said not a word. But even so I was elected to the executive board of some fifteen or twenty persons, evidentally because they figured I had some influence and contacts in the United States that would be helpful to the cause of anti-imperialism. So the rest of that year in Europe I attended all the meetings of the executive committee that were held in Brussels and Holland and Paris and got to know the other members very well, especially Nehru and his family because his wife had TB and they were staying in Geneva where I was also staying with Madeleine. Jawaharlal's father stopped in, too, on his way to London and Moscow. His name was Motilal and he was an exceedingly elegant gentleman who, it is said, had his shirts laundered only in London. And Indira was there — a charming girl in her late teens — the subject of great admiration among my European colleagues." †

After the Brussels congress, Roger had planned to meet Madeleine and her father in England and to look into the situation regarding political prisoners there; then he wanted to go on to Ireland for the same purpose. In England they were to be the guests of Madeleine's good friends the Pethwick-Lawrences. Emmeline Pethwick-Lawrence — Melani — who was a well-known suffragette, had visited Roger and Madeleine in New York in their Waverly Place days and had found Roger a delightful kindred soul. ("They were

* The date of this interview was July 25, 1974.
† When I asked Roger in December 1975 how he had reacted to Indira Gandhi's surprising — to say the least — disregard for the civil liberties of her citizens during the past chaotic months in India, he said that he had, of course, been deeply shocked, that he had sent the prime minister a cable saying, in effect, "How could you?" Indira Gandhi had replied promptly, sending along three of her speeches that justified her actions, and explained them as merely temporary measures. Said Roger, quoting an unknown savant, "There is nothing more permanent than the temporary."

exactly suited," Madeleine wrote.) This prior affinity was fortunate since Melani, and more especially her husband, F. W. Pethwick-Lawrence, M.P., were both to have their hands full coping with a Roger Baldwin suddenly turned "dangerous subversive." In point of fact, the Brussels meetings had so badly "damaged" his reputation that when he applied at the British Passport Control office in Paris for a visa to enter Great Britain (necessary in those days), he was refused one "at any time and for any purpose."

He thereupon called upon the good offices of Pethwick-Lawrence, as a member of Parliament, who wrote at the end of February a "dear Baldwin" letter saying that in taking the preliminary steps necessary to clarify Roger's ambiguous position, he had stated to the Home Office that "1) though you are a Communist [which of course Roger was not], you are rather what one would describe as a philosophic Communist; 2) that you are wholly opposed to violence and that it was really on this account that you had come into conflict with your Government; 3) that I think you are only coming to England for a short visit and are not coming to take any political part whatever while you are here."

Roger was to write agreeing that he would limit his visit to two weeks, that he would leave at any time during that period if the Home Office requested it, and that he would refrain from all political activities. Since Pethwick-Lawrence was to be entirely responsible for his good conduct, Roger wished to be sure before agreeing that he fully understood what was meant by political activities. The reply from Lawrence made clear that he was to eschew meetings of a public or a quasi-public character, that he was not to confer with executives of the Communist party ("if such an idea should enter your head"), nor was he to give interviews to the press or write any articles himself. He was also required to enter the country at the port of Dover.

The prohibitions, Roger thought, were ridiculous, but he decided to "play the game" and go to London, partly because he hoped that once in England he could persuade the Home Office to let him go to Ireland and partly because he clearly enjoyed acting out his assigned role of "dangerous agent of the revolution" who scared the daylights out of the British.

In London he and Madeleine stayed with the Pethwick-Lawrences in Lincoln's Inn, and Roger saw his Labour party friends, Quaker friends and pacifist friends while uttering not a single subversive word. Ellen Wilkinson, the fiery left-wing member of Parliament, wanted to bring the case of his visa refusal and subsequent restrictions up as a question before the House of Commons. Pethwick-Lawrence was "agitated" by the thought of it, feeling that such an action would be violating the spirit of the agreement with the Home Office; that, "having elected to negotiate, we should not fight too."

Roger was unmoved by this argument, he wrote Ellen Wilkinson from Amsterdam just after his departure from London. "When similar situations have arisen in the United States," he said, "we have thought it wisest to fight such restrictions on principle and our wisdom has been vindicated by the results." However, he added that he was not sure whether a question before the House raised after his departure from England would be effective, and the matter was finally dropped there, but not before the ACLU in New York had managed to get out a press release on the whole story.

For Russia Roger's credentials were more acceptable. Although his critical position on the Soviet treatment of political prisoners, as expressed in his introduction to *Letters from Russian Prisons,* caused him some difficulties obtaining a visa, this strike against him was counterbalanced by his recent participation in the League against Imperialism.

Further militating in his favor was his involvement four years earlier with a Russian-American project called the Kousbas Autonomous Industrial Colony, which was a United States–financed enterprise backed by liberals and more particularly by many members of the IWW. The Wobblies and the American Communists had obtained options on a vast tract of land in the Siberian Urals where they hoped to develop a mechanized "autonomous" farm.

Roger was corralled to join the board — an organizing committee of nine progessive-minded people eager to help build up the promised land. He liked the fervor and the adventure of the project; he liked the Wobblies; and he was encouraged by reports from Russia that indicated that Kousbas participants would have a free hand, with no government control or supervision, but with the Russians willing and eager to make any concessions to ensure the success of the industrial colony.

Shares were sold — the board with Roger's strong leadership was said to have raised approximately half a million dollars — and eager potential colonists sold their homes and took their savings to make a new life in the new land. Some 460 American men, women and children were reported to have been sent to the Siberian colony on two-year contracts.

Trouble started almost as soon as they arrived; complaints began to filter back to New York indicating that the situation in Kousbas was not at all what their prospectus promised. There was, Roger concedes, a certain amount of mismanagement, and the situation was aggravated by the extreme hardship of life in Siberia. Colonists began to return home full of bitterness, complaining that they had been exploited. Some took their complaints to the district attorney who presented their charges to a grand jury, which ultimately brought an indictment against the nine members of the American Organization Committee, Roger's name being perhaps the most prominent among them. They were charged with grand larceny on the grounds that colonists had paid money based on misrepresentations in the prospectus.

Roger and several of the others were accused of having converted money or property to their own use — a patently ridiculous charge; the books of the Kousbas enterprise satisfactorily accounted for every dollar. Arthur Garfield Hays, chief counsel for the ACLU and Roger's great friend, took the case, which was generally conceded to have had strong political overtones (inspired by what Roger termed "anti-Russian hysteria"). The judge dismissed the indictment before it ever came to trial. Roger, however, had gained some kudos from the left for his participation and because of the unjust accusations against him — kudos that stood him in good stead in gaining entry into Soviet Russia in June of 1927.

He had spent the spring traveling around in Amsterdam, Berlin, Prague and finally in Italy with his brother Herbert and his friend Crane Garth, a rich young bachelor from Pasadena whose mother was on the Board of the ACLU. In June he and Garth journeyed through Bulgaria to Istanbul — then still called Constantinople — where they were joined for their trip to Russia by a young Austrian Quaker named Fritz Schubert whom Roger had met at the League of Nations in Geneva.

In Istanbul the three young men "full of illusion and ignorance" boarded a passenger freighter and sailed to Georgia in the Black Sea, which was to be their first stop in the "promised land."

There is no question that Roger entered the Soviet Union with a strong predisposition to look favorably on what he saw. In those days there was no Intourist to screen visitors; foreign critics of the regime were not discouraged. Roger was astounded, for instance, to learn that Abraham Cahan, editor of the *Jewish Daily Forward* and a bitter foe of the Soviets, was holding forth in Moscow; he felt it augured well for the free expression of thought that he hoped would prevail. What he did not at the time acknowledge was that *foreign* critics did not count. He encountered few, if any, citizens who openly challenged the revolution or the system.

Roger had an introduction to a local journalist in Georgia who spoke excellent English and who offered to act as his guide. ("Craney" Garth and Fritz Schubert went off on their own to see the more obvious sights, including what passed for the night spots.) "He took me everywhere," Roger recalled, "even to the local Soviet where I found the committee in session. I was impressed by such elegant gentlemen in silk shirts, well fed, middle-aged and very, very busy. They were big shots — revolutionary big shots — the kind of party men whose drive brought them to the top. My guide said it was useless to inquire from them about political prisoners and it was pretty obvious, when they found out I was just a curious tourist, that they would ignore me and any requests I made."

Through his journalist guide, however, Roger did manage to visit the local jail and thereafter during his three months in Russia to go to half a dozen other jails from Georgia to Leningrad. In each instance he was impressed with the conditions he found. Even inside the prisons that we would term maximum security he was surprised at the freedom: the open dormitories, social rooms complete with samovars and tables for games, the enlightened trusty systems, the provisions for rehabilitation, particularly of short-term offenders.

Yet he was not so naive as to be unaware that in all the prisons he visited he saw only criminal offenders and never the political prisoners whose cause he hoped to espouse. Still, he says that while he did not accept the patently false excuses that kept him from seeing the political prisoners, he sympathized to a degree with the reasons given. He had, after all, found the same strictures in Italy and the Balkans and he understood the reluctance of officials to let dissident prisoners talk with foreigners who might thereby gain a distorted impression of the regime.

The same willingness to see or hear no evil — or perhaps more accurately to see and hear but to discount evil — obtained when on his last night in Georgia his journalist guide broke down and confessed how bitterly he hated the whole system.

"He confided to me at our final dinner that he had concealed the facts and his own views," Roger said. "He told me that I would not be told the truth by any official, nor would I read the truth anywhere. He said nothing I had seen really mattered because the real control was the OGPU [Secret Police]. He said, 'You saw their building, I pointed it out, but I would not even let you walk in front of it. It is a terrible place of torture and of people never heard of again.' "

"Didn't even that shake you?" I asked Roger.

"No," he said ruefully, "I'm afraid not. I was too prejudiced in the beginning to let signs — even clear signs like that one — count heavily in my total picture. Great upheavals like the Russian Revolution have their price, I told myself. Violent storms had to run their course. Oh, there was a certain ambivalence, but somehow throughout my three months in Russia I seemed to give more weight to the great and unprecedented upheaval of all bourgeois values than to any real moral judgments. I went on making allowances for what I should, in my own mind at least, have condemned and rejected."

Next stop for Roger and his companions was the Caucasus where they spent a week among the peasants on the Russian Reconstruction Farms, another Kousbas, only more successful, with which Roger had been only marginally involved. Talking about his "carefree, happy week," Roger said, "I was struck by the spirit of the peasants and the workers, their vigor, their cheerful talk and banter — I couldn't understand it, of course, but I judged there were a good many wisecracks by the laughter — and the merriment at night with singing and accordions."

Such is his recollection today. But writing to his mother at the time (on July 4, 1927), he tells rather a different story: "My net impression is that the peasant is apathetic and wholly uninterested in what the Communists want to do for him, but that the Communist program of collective agriculture will make headway in spite of it. Alcohol," he went on to say, "is a universal evil among the peasant men. I have seen more drunkenness and more beggars in Russia than in all of Europe. But," he added loyally, "they tell me it was worse in the Czar's days."

Somehow Roger's "net impressions" always managed to remain

positive and hopeful even in the face of countervailing evidence. And by the time he reached Moscow, he was able to bolster his own rose-colored views with the comforting realization that Trotsky was, after all, still functioning as an open adversary of Stalin and that furthermore an anarchist book store, so proclaimed by a large sign, was open for business just opposite the gate of Moscow University.

Roger had a letter of introduction to Madame Sophie Kropotkin, widow of his ideological hero, Prince Peter Kropotkin. After he had been in Moscow a week, staying at the Hotel Metropole and for once behaving like a plain ordinary tourist, Madame Kropotkin invited him to live in her large and imposing house for the rest of his stay. She herself planned to be absent most of the summer at her dacha outside the city, so Roger had the house more or less to himself, except for two Kropotkin nephews who turned up occasionally.

"I had a room, kitchen, bath and, of all luxuries, an icebox that miraculously got filled with ice every day," Roger recalled. "I would go to the market, basket in one hand, dictionary in the other, to buy the food I cooked for myself and for any friends I invited in. It was fun and homey. Madame Kropotkin had engaged a neighbor boy who spoke English to come in and translate the daily papers for me, but after a week he quit; he was afraid of trouble, working for a foreigner, he said, because he came from an old bourgeois family. I suppose it was a real fear. Anyway I accepted it as such."

"What was Madame Kropotkin like?"

"A very dignified lady in her sixties. She welcomed me for my interest in her husband, but she did not confide her views to me; in fact, I would say she only tolerated me in her royal way. I assumed she was opposed to the regime but like most Russians I met, she endured it without complaint."

After the neighbor boy quit, Roger hired a guide-interpreter who spoke only French (Roger's French was up to this) but who was helpful and had good entrée everywhere and probably was — at least so Roger now suspects — an agent of the OGPU.* With the help of this knowledgeable, resourceful man, Roger embarked on a schedule of research on the topics he planned to cover in his projected book

---

* In his book *Liberty under the Soviets,* however, Roger says quite explicitly that at no time was he conscious of being under any surveillance.

on liberty under the Soviets: such broad headings as Economic Liberty, Religious Freedom and Control, Freedom in Education, Control of the Press and Printing.

To deal with this wide field of research, he had allowed himself a mere month's time, and to make matters worse he was frequently thwarted and frustrated by red tape.

"Work is very hard and slow here," he wrote his mother from Moscow on July 23, "both because of the summer vacation and the bureaucracy whose sole slogan appears to be 'Come back Monday.' " It was the old czarist system, he wrote, that the Bolsheviks were fighting but at the same time were themselves caught in. Still, he marveled at the optimism of the people and at their fighting qualities in the face of so many obstacles.

There was fear and repression, he conceded in his letter, but not among the city working class that is "free, in the saddle and bossing the whole show." "Recently," he wrote, "just after the break with England and the murder of the Soviet ambassador at Warsaw, there had been a scare of possible war with England which was followed by 'executions and arrests galore.' " However, he assured his mother, he himself was not in the slightest danger. In fact, he added, "my trouble is getting anyone to pay any attention to me at all."

"What about civil liberties," I asked Roger. "Did you ever question any Russian about things like equality before the law or due process?"

"No, I knew better than to bring such matters up because there was no claim that they even existed in the Soviet regime. The dictatorship was acknowledged — a temporary necessity, they all explained, until things got straightened out."

"But you didn't really accept that rationalization, did you?"

"I tolerated it," said Roger. "Despite all my contrary conditioning, I tolerated it because I believed that somehow the education of masses and the elimination of exploiting owners and employers would dissolve the dictatorship. You must remember, Peggy, that the withering away of the state as a process had long appealed to me as a goal."

"And as a possibility?"

"Well, Lenin had said it would come when the classes were fused into one. And in 1927 I still had a strong hope that he might be right. Sometimes I look back on that feeling I had in 1927 with a lingering hope that it might still be right, but there is no evidence, after nearly fifty years, that it is so."

As it turned out, Roger acquired a large part of the material for *Liberty under the Soviets* only after he left Russia. "I did not do a good job of research," he admitted. "When I got to Paris in October of that year to write up the material, so much was missing I had to go to all kinds of sources including the Soviet Embassy to supply my lacks."

Yet he was determined, he wrote his mother, to write the book while he was still in Europe. "I shall not leave Paris until it is done. Once back in New York I would never finish it. It will take me a month to write it," he added, in what must surely qualify as either the most wildly optimistic estimate or as the most telling comment on the superficial level of his proposed project.

Actually, it took him much longer. He did not complete the book in Paris, although he worked very hard at it — and for more than a month. He was fortunate to have two old friends turn up (as Roger's many old friends had a habit of doing) to help him with his task. One was Brownie, who it will be recalled was the youth whom Roger had befriended (although not adopted) in his St. Louis days — a brilliant, uneducated but exceedingly well read iconoclast who adored and mocked Roger at the same time and who was also an experienced stenographer.

The other was Alexander Berkman (Emma Goldman's Sasha) whom Roger hired ("I paid him but not much") to translate some of the supporting tracts and documents he had brought out of Russia. Berkman was a committed anarchist who looked upon Roger's general acceptance of Soviet attitudes and practices with a disdain that he tried to conceal because of his friendship for Roger and because of his need for the small fee he received for his services. Roger was not fooled. "He was gentleman enough to hide his view of me as naive," he said.

When he returned to New York in December (1927), he was still working on the book and indeed as late as March 1928 he was still asking searching questions — at that point from a Boris Skvirsky of the Soviet Information Bureau in Washington. Brownie had come back to the States by then and was dividing his time between working with Roger on the book and doing public relations for the ACLU.

Liberty under the Soviets was published late in the fall of 1928 as a part of the Vanguard Press series on Soviet Russia. On the title page was a quotation from Lenin:

> While the State exists there can be no freedom.
> When there is freedom there will be no State.

"Personal reactions color most of what is written about Soviet Russia," Roger wrote in his first chapter, entitled "The Problem and Its Background."

> Where one puts one's emphasis is a matter of feeling and opinion [he continued]. Anyone who writes of Russia owes it at the start to confess his personal bias; and on Russia everybody has a bias, conscious or not . . . My own prejudices are amply conveyed by the title of this book. Though over half of it is devoted to a description of the controls by the Soviet state, I have chosen to call it *Liberty under the Soviets* because I see as far more significant the basic economic freedom of workers and peasants and the abolition of privileged classes based on wealth; and only less important the . . . new freedom of women, the revolution in education — and, if one counts it as significant — liberty for religion and anti-religion.
>
> Against these liberties stand the facts of universal censorship of all means of communications and the complete suppression of any organized opposition to the dictatorship or its program. No civil liberty as we understand it in the West exists in Russia for opponents of the regime — no organized freedom of speech or assemblage, nor of the press. No political liberty is permitted. The Communist Party enjoys an exclusive monopoly . . .
>
> Such an attitude as I express toward the relation of economic to civil liberty may easily be construed as condoning in Russia repressions which I condemn in capitalist countries. It is true that I feel differently about them, because I regard them as unlike. Repressions in western democracies are violations of professed constitutional liberties, and I condemn them as such. Repressions in Soviet Russia are weapons of struggle in a transition period to socialism. The society the Communists seek to create will be freed of class struggle — if achieved — and therefore of repression.

Liberty under the Soviets is filled with this type of rhetoric; sometimes balanced, sometimes slanted, sometimes insightful, sometimes deluded. Throughout the book runs one strong theme — to Communists all liberties are class liberties. Individual rights cannot exist until classes based on economic exploitation are destroyed.

As Roger himself pointed out, "Anyone who tries to see both good and bad in Russia is constantly divided between depression and hope, friendliness and criticism." Logically enough, reviews of his book were likewise divided between reproach of him for having been gulled to respect for his fair-minded presentation of his material. Overall, however, there seems to have been a slight tilt in his favor as a man of probity, even-handedly trying to give reasons for the lack of democracy in Soviet Russia.

Not unexpectedly, the person whose opinion he probably valued the most was hardest on him. Emma Goldman (who did not actually review the book) was savage in her condemnation of what she looked on as Roger's benign attitude toward the Soviets.

While I have no hopes of helping you to see things as they really are, and not as you have been made to see them through the solicitous help of Soviet representatives, [she wrote him] I feel that some of the things you say cannot go unchallenged . . .

You write, "I deplore the same evils in the Soviet regime that you do, but I see so much to be said for the destruction of privilege based on wealth that I will stand for Russia against the rest of the world." Let us see whether what you say is really correct. First, do you really deplore the evils in Soviet Russia as I do? Do you deplore them as much and do you protest against them as much as you do against the evils in Italy and other countries under the iron whip of dictatorship? If so I have never heard about it or seen it in cold print. Oh I know that you have spoken up on occasions and have written against the abuses in Russia, but you have always done so in a very faint voice, Roger dear, and with so many apologies for the so-called good of the Soviet regime that your protest was fairly swamped, and made no impression whatever. Unless you have become an apologist for dictatorship I cannot understand how you can cry out indignantly against the horrors going on under the capitalistic regime and only whisper your protest against the crimes committed in the name of Revolution and Socialism . . .

You are not the only one, of course. Everyone who goes to Russia for a short time, without the language, and chaperoned, is as shortsighted as you. Dear old Dreiser, for instance, although I must say that he had a much more penetrating eye than you — he at least saw some evils — you saw nothing . . .

I do hope someday we will get together again and talk, but I frankly admit that people as naive as you are hopeless. They see the world and the struggle through romantic rosy eyes as the young innocent girl sees the first man she loves. However, I like you well enough to continue my affection for you, largely because I have faith in your sincerity. Always glad to hear from you. Affectionately,

Roger answered this blast promptly and without rancor. Only at the very end of his letter did he get in one little jab. "You are good to say you have faith in my honesty," he wrote, "although none in my judgment. I feel just the same toward you. I don't think you are naive, but I think you are hopelessly prejudiced."

In the end, however, Roger was to change his views radically and, in fact, to do an almost complete about-face. Today he is almost as harsh with himself about *Liberty under the Soviets* as Emma Goldman was in 1928.

(14)

The United Front

ALTHOUGH ROGER INSISTED THAT HE KNEW within a year after the publication of *Liberty under the Soviets* that he had made a serious miscalculation and that his conclusions were wrong, his actions and utterances during the next decade did not indicate any real disaffection with the Soviet Union.* On the contrary, in the years 1934 and 1935 he made two of his most unqualifiedly pro-Communist statements.

The first was an article published in a magazine, *Soviet Russia Today* (September 1934), which was less measured and more revolutionary than anything he had written before.† (Dwight Macdonald in his *New Yorker* profile refers to it as the article that marks Roger's swing "Farthest North — that, in fact, went all the way to the Pole.")

In the one-page piece entitled "Freedom in the USA and the USSR," Roger rhetorically stated the question most frequently (and justifiably) asked of civil libertarians: How can you consistently fight to support free speech and free dissent in capitalist countries and at the same time defend a dictatorship that permits no dissent at all against its rule? He then proceeded to answer the question.

> Our critics are in error in denying us a class position . . . All my associates in the struggle for civil liberties take a class position, though many don't know it . . .
>
> I too take a class position. It is anti-capitalist and pro-revolutionary

---

* Roger said he wrote an addendum of about eight pages stating his revised position which was printed and added to later copies of the book. He himself does not have a copy of his emendations, nor did one come to light among his Princeton papers.

† Nor does he have a copy of this article, which was kindly supplied to me by the magazine *New World Review,* successor of *Soviet Russia Today.*

. . . I champion civil liberty as the best of the nonviolent means of building the power on which worker's rule must be based. If I aid the reactionaries to get free speech now and then, if I go outside the class struggle to fight against censorship, it is only because those liberties help to create a more hospitable atmosphere for working-class liberties. *The class struggle* is the central conflict of the world; all others are incidental.

When that power of the working class is once achieved, as it has been only in the Soviet Union, I am for maintaining it by any means whatever.

The article went on in this vein (emphasis and all), regretting that the means had to be dictatorship with its concomitant "personal distress" for many victims, but justifying even brutality: "I couldn't bring myself to get excited over the suppression of opposition when I stacked it up against what I saw of fresh, vigorous expressions of free living by workers and peasants all over the land . . . No champion of a socialist society could fail to see that some suppression was necessary to achieve it."

Roger hates to be reminded of this particular piece of prose, which he wrote for what he calls "that stupid publication." But he says, "What troubled me at that time was not the character of the Communist state but of the Fascist states. We already had Mussolini and, by the time I wrote that article, Hitler had risen to power and I was very scared of him. I felt that if I had to choose between the Communists and the Fascists there was no doubt about which side I was on."

Somehow I failed to point out, as I should have, that nowhere in his piece in *Soviet Russia Today* was there so much as a mention of the Fascist states, let alone of the threat they posed. Instead I asked him if he did not think, in 1934, that it was still possible to be on the side of the democracies.

"No, I didn't think so. I didn't think democracy was much of a choice at that point, because as you looked at it from the outside, the Communist powers and the Fascist powers were on a collision course and the democracies were nowhere. The British and the French and the rest of the countries — including us — who represented the democracies were appeasers, most of them. They appeased the Nazis and the Fascists. Hitler had them all buffaloed. And that's what caused me for a brief period to be so fearful of the triumph of Fascist powers that I thought the Communists looked pretty good. I shouldn't have said it the way I did. But I did. After all, people's ideas do change around. Still," he added, "it wasn't so much that I changed. It was that events did."

"Which brings us," I said, "to your other radical statement of that period."

He looked at me quizzically, but I knew he knew that I was referring to his celebrated statement in his 30th reunion classbook at Harvard. If his *Soviet Russia Today* article caused him some discomfort, his report to his classmates, which was an out-and-out leftist statement, defiant and unequivocal, culminating in the line "Communism is the goal," seemed to give him a certain sardonic satisfaction. Still, in answering me he backed and filled to a certain extent, claiming that he had been sent a questionnaire by the class secretary and that the editor of the Class of 1905 volume had simply run his answers together in one statement, without reference to the particular questions that evoked his responses. Nevertheless he broke into an impish grin as he read the copy that I handed him of his entry in *Thirty Years Later*.

"Gracious," he said.

"What prompts that 'gracious'?"

"Well, I wouldn't take exception to that statement even today if it had been expressed less violently. For instance, the questionnaire they sent must have asked, 'What is your chief aversion?' and I wrote, of course, that my chief aversion was "the system of greed, private profit and privilege which makes up the control of the world today. At bottom I am for conserving the full powers of every person on earth by expanding them to their individual limits."

"Well, surely there's nothing very violent about that."

"No. In fact that still represents my basic philosophy." He read on, " 'I am for socialism, disarmament and ultimately for abolishing the state itself as an instrument of violence and compulsion. I seek social ownership of property, the abolition of the propertied class and sole control by those who produce wealth. Communism is the goal. It all sums up into one single purpose — the abolition of the system of dog-eat-dog under which we live.' " He handed me back the page. "Now that really is a very revolutionary statement."

"Indeed it is. Especially since the people for whom you were writing it — your Harvard classmates — were, many of them, prominent members of that propertied class that you were all for abolishing."

"That's right," he grinned again. "And I was mad at those boys; I was trying to defy them. They were so smug."

"And so upper class?"

"Yes, I was mad at those upper-class boys who said to me whenever I got together with them at a class reunion, 'We don't want to change things; we like it the way it is.' I remember one of my classmates said to me once, 'You're a great fellow, but I don't agree with you.' So I asked him, 'What exactly don't you agree with?' and he said, 'I don't know exactly what you stand for, but whatever it is I don't agree with it.' "

"Roger, I notice that in this 'infamous' statement of yours there is one line that should have pleased your privileged classmates. You said you were opposed to the New Deal."

"Yes, probably that did please a lot of them, but of course for the wrong reasons. And I was wrong — very wrong — to have said so myself."

"Why did you?"

"Well, I voted for Frank Roosevelt," he said defensively. "As a matter of fact, I've only voted for one Republican in my life and that was for Dwight Eisenhower because he was standing by the United Nations. And in 1920 I think I voted for some minor party — not for Norman Thomas — but I guess the Socialist Labor candidate, because it was useless to vote for either Harding or Cox that year. Then in 1924 I voted for La Follette. But, to get back to your question; even though I voted for Roosevelt [pronounced "Ruesevelt" and always referred to by Roger, who knew him slightly at Harvard, as Frank not Franklin], he scared me. He had a general * who was head of an institution called the — " Uncharacteristically Roger stopped and groped for a name.

"The NRA?" I supplied.

"That's right. The NRA. National Recovery Act I guess it stood for and I thought, here is the state again, trying to control everything and everybody and, as I said in the class report there, I thought it was leading to the protection of the propertied classes as against other classes. All of us at the ACLU were leery of the government getting into the relations between capital and labor, because we were pretty sure the government's influence would be on the side of capital."

"What changed your mind then?"

"As soon as Frank Roosevelt began to talk in terms of distributing

* General Hugh Johnson.

power and money to the forgotten man and we began to have a social security system, why I changed my views, of course. We had a National Labor Relations Act, which we were also afraid of at first because we were sure it would put the government in the business of discouraging trade unions. But that too turned out the other way; the board started with a very strong pro-labor bias and remains so to this day. So those events really constituted a revolution, because they gave the federal government many more powers to help people and not to oppress them. First we thought the power of the federal government was dangerous because it could be used in favor of the status quo versus change. It could also be abused. But it was not."

I pointed out that today we were seeing the abuse of that very power that Roosevelt assumed, for this conversation was taking place on July 24, 1974, the day the Supreme Court ordered President Nixon to give up the tapes to the special prosecutor's office.

"That's right," Roger said. "But what's more important, we are seeing *what happens* when the powers of government are abused. And that's good."

For a moment or two we took great satisfaction in the Supreme Court's unanimous decision that curbed Nixon's villainy. Then Roger shifted back into reverse.

"You know," he said reflectively, "as it turned out, I think those few paragraphs for the class report were the last favorable words I ever wrote about the Soviets."

Roger may have made no more public pro-Soviet utterances (although I have some reservations about that), but he certainly continued his Communist-oriented activities through his participation in United Front organizations. He belonged, he said, to scores of such committees, but concentrated his major efforts on three, in all of which he was a prime moving factor.

A United Front, as Roger described it, "is a device of people who are too weak to exert the influence they desire, so they seek strength in unity with others sharing the same purpose — others who do not share common ground on anything else." The Communists in the 1930's were weak in the United States, but extremely energetic and determined. So they both inspired and ultimately dominated all the United Fronts. Furthermore, Roger pointed out, because they were so effective, the temptation to place them in key positions within the organizations was too great to resist. "So that non-Communists were deceived, as I was, into accepting the assurance that the officials we put in top spots were not party members. They simply lied about it, as some of them who quit the party told me later."

"Specifically, what was the problem about having actual party members instead of just plain Communist sympathizers in the United Fronts?"

"The problem was that the party member was using the United Front organization as a recruiting center for the Communist party. Lists could be taken, sympathizers spotted and enrolled and if the treasurer happened to be a party member, the funds could be siphoned off for party purposes. All this was true of the three big Fronts in which I played a role as officer, but I didn't know it until afterward."

"Or was it that you didn't want to know? After all, wasn't involvement in the United Front an almost obligatory action for a man like you who was so identified with liberal causes?"

"Of course. The only choice was to join or stay out. I joined. I don't regret being a part of the Communist tactic which increased the effectiveness of a good cause. I knew what I was doing; I was not the innocent liberal and I was not a fellow traveler either. I wanted what the Communists wanted and I traveled the United Front road — not the party road — to try to get it."

The first of Roger's three principal United Fronts was the League against Imperialism which, it will be recalled, he had originally joined at the Brussels Congress of 1927. Subsequently, on his return to New York, he became chairman of the American section. For some reason, none of the regular standby names from Roger's pool of liberals joined him in this enterprise, which was perhaps understandable since imperialism was really no issue as far as America was concerned. Roger's initial interest in the League against Imperialism had been his concern for India.

At any rate the League lasted only four years. The American section was small and not well run, Roger says, by a man named Charlie Phillips, who called himself "Manuel something — " Roger remembered vaguely. "He took a Latin last name to pretend he was not an American. But he was a Jewish boy from New York City who had gone to Columbia and was a party member. I thought he was a pretty good guy, even after he got me thrown out."

"What do you mean 'thrown out'?"

"Just that. They fired me, as chairman."

"But why?"

"Because the line changed. The Communist line changed. Most of the disruption was caused because the Communists had decided about that time to throw off Chiang Kai-shek. Mao was just beginning to emerge, so of course Chiang Kai-shek became a bourgeois liberal. I never thought much of him myself, but anyway they decided to throw off all the other bourgeois liberals like me and to depend entirely on the revolutionists."

"So what happened? I mean, how did your ouster come about?"

"Very simply. Charlie Phillips, or whatever his party name was, called a meeting, which he had a perfect right as secretary to do. I remember it was at a hall on 88th Street and since I was chairman of the American section of the League against Imperialism, I presided over the meeting as I had always done in the past. Only this time, there must have been forty people there whom I'd never seen before. They had a right to be there I guess, but at least they were there. And as soon as I called the meeting to order, one of these people stood up and introduced a resolution stating that I was a friend of Mr. Gandhi, that Mr. Gandhi was a compromiser with the British, that I was supporting bourgeois liberals in India, that I was not faithful to the struggle for independence and calling for my ouster as chairman and as a member." He chuckled. "It was all so ridiculous. Phillips, of course, had packed the meeting and gotten his pals to introduce the resolution and they passed it. After it was over I asked the ones whom I'd known all along to come downstairs and have coffee with me, and they did — they sat around downstairs and had coffee with their deposed chairman and that was the end of that. The organization disappeared very shortly afterward in America and everywhere else. Nehru was kicked out of the League at the same time, by the way."

"Meanwhile had you already got involved with the League against War and Fascism?"

"No, I'd say that wasn't until afterward, although the League against War and Fascism started in the same place — Brussels — and at about the same time as the League against Imperialism. Some of the same people — Willi Muenzenberger, the German Communist, and his man Friday, Louis Gibarti — were also the moving spirits. But I didn't join the League against War and Fascism until the American section was formed and I was asked to serve on the board; I accepted, despite my recent ouster from the other organization."

Ever the optimist and eternally against war and fascism, Roger threw himself with vigor and dedication into the new League. This time things would be different, he told himself; the board was made up of many of his regulars. The chairman, J. B. Matthews, was a pacifist-leftist-socialist whom Roger knew well through his association with the Fellowship of Reconciliation, a Christian pacifist organization of which Roger was also a member. But Matthews was unstable and, as it turned out, something of a rascal.

"He was a careerist of the left; when he came to us at the League against War and Fascism he was what you might call a revolutionary socialist. Then later he wrote a book called *The Odyssey of a Fellow Traveller* in which he confessed his connection with the Communists, which we had not suspected. And then, still later, he made a professional career of anti-Communism and became research director for the House Un-American committee and also briefly for Senator McCarthy."

However, in the 1934 period of the League against War and Fascism, Matthews' posture was only as a left-wing socialist, and this led to considerable disharmony on the board since the Socialists and the Communists were always squabbling. The Communists were much more aggressive, according to Roger; they would attack anyone who did not agree with them. For example, early in August 1933, the *Daily Worker* lashed out at the Socialist position on war — so unjustifiably that the Socialists, led by Matthews, threatened to resign from the League board. It fell to Roger personally to get matters back on track; to prevent the Socialists from resigning and to try to smooth rough waters in the interest of the greater cause that they all served.

"I was always doing that," said Roger. "That was the role I was supposed to play — it was expected of me as a sort of civil libertarian neutral."

It became more and more difficult for him to play this role, however. A few months later in February 1934, the Socialist party staged a huge meeting in Madison Square Garden to protest the actions in Austria of dictator Engelbert Dollfuss, who had dissolved the

Socialist party (and all other political parties), permitting only his reactionary Fatherland Front to continue.

The Communist party — or at least some unruly factions of its
membership — chose to put on a wild and noisy demonstration that
broke up the Socialist party meeting in Madison Square Garden.
Their rationale is difficult to pinpoint; Roger himself is somewhat
confused as to their motives, for certainly the Communists could not
possibly have *favored* Dollfuss. He assumes, however, that they had
chosen to adopt a hands-off position about events in Austria. But
since the Socialists were reacting so strongly, the Communists seized
the opportunity to goad and discredit them, primarily because both
parties were at the time engaged in a bitter rivalry to win the support of the laboring class in America.

The Madison Square Garden incident came very close to destroy-
ing the League against War and Fascism altogether. This time there
was obviously no mollifying the Socialists; Matthews resigned as
chairman; the others withdrew. Roger himself thought of resigning
for, as he wired Matthews, he felt that the incident had made cooperation with the Communists too difficult and had destroyed any
possibility of extending the United Fronts to the labor movement.

But then Earl Browder, secretary of the Communist party, came
to see Roger, along with some of the other party officials, to express
regret — privately, although never publicly — at what had happened. As Roger puts it, "They came to me and said our United
Front has been split, 'we're very sorry, it was a mistake, it shouldn't
have happened, we weren't in town to control things and our people
got too enthusiastic and broke up the meeting. We would like to
repair the damage. Will you help us?' So I asked them what I could
do, and they said, 'Will you ask Dr. Harry Ward to be chairman? We
would like to have him.' "

Since Dr. Ward was chairman of the Board of the ACLU, one
might think that this request would have posed something of a problem for Roger. Could both the chairman and the director of the
Union be so heavily involved in a United Front organization without
making the League against War and Fascism seem like a branch office of the ACLU?

Apparently they could. Harry Ward accepted the new post en-
thusiastically, and it is perhaps a tribute to both men's determination
to keep the main objective — the fight against war and fascism — so

firmly in the forefront that they allowed no secondary considerations
to divert them.

As far as the Communists in the United Front went, Roger and
Ward appear to have taken pretty much the same position. Both
agreed that there were too many of them, that the Communists did
try to take over, but that they also did a great deal of the work that
needed to be done. Furthermore, after Madison Square Garden,
the Communists seemed, to Roger at least, to be "enough chastened
by events to be very conciliatory." Hence, accept them for what they
were worth and attempt to minimize their dominance by continually
trying to bring other elements into the organization and by working
to get the Socialist party back.

With this in view, Roger wrote to Earl Browder in July 1934 concerning the forthcoming second congress of the League against War
and Fascism to be held in Chicago in September. "We ought, we all
agree, to have less Communist party representation in proportion
to the whole. Special efforts should be made in Chicago to get out a
large non-Communist representation, particularly of foreign language groups, trade unionists and the middle-class church and anti-
war crowd. I am willing to write letters of invitation to speakers
selected whom I may be able to influence to accept. By all means invite Norman Thomas. I will do so if the committee agrees."

The committee did agree and Roger did invite Norman Thomas
to appear. "Speak as an individual or for the Socialist party," he
wrote him. "Be as critical as you like of the United Front inspired
by the Communists."

Norman Thomas could not be tempted. He was, he answered,
convinced that a United Front with Communists — and especially almost controlled by Communists — was impossible until there was an
understanding within the Communist party itself "of a democratic
and fair basis of action." And he had little hope that there would be
such an understanding.

Looking back Roger was surprised that he would even have
thought of asking Norman Thomas to speak at the congress after the
Madison Square Garden affair. And, in any case, even without Madison Square Garden, the Socialists, he said, were never comfortable
with the League against War and Fascism.

"Were they comfortable with any United Front organizations?"

"More so later in '38 when the Spanish Civil War broke loose, but in general they didn't want to be part of organizations where the Communists would be so much more vigorous than they were. The Socialists were weak-willed. They didn't feel strongly enough about what they were committed to to make sacrifices. Whereas the Communists were sacrificial people, most of them. They would work twenty-four hours a day, weekends, anytime. They didn't care. They were fanatics. The Socialists were not fanatics. The Communists are salvationists. They will go to the stakes. Some movements attract salvationists like that. The American fight for independence was led by the give-me-liberty-or-give-me-death kind of people. And then there were the other kind who said, oh what the hell, there's no use fighting for it; the British aren't so bad."

"So would you say — or are you saying — that the major difference between the Communists and the Socialists is their willingness to sacrifice?"

"I think it is practically that, yes."

"But what about the ideological differences?"

"The common distinction made is that the Communists are for revolution and violence and the Socialists are for evolution and peace. And there is something to be said for that distinction because the Socialists *do* generally want to use parliamentary methods of getting ahead. And the Communists, while they don't practice violence, don't oppose it. What they say virtually is, well if we have to have dictatorship to maintain our ends we will have dictatorship. The Socialists say no, we don't believe in corrupting our ends by means of this sort; we are going to stick with democracy; we are going to do what the majority says and we are going to have peaceful evolutionary process. The Communists say, we don't care what the majority says, *this minority is right,* and if we can impose our will on the majority, we will do so. The Socialists say no, that is wrong, we are not going to impose our will on anybody, we are going to *convert* a majority to our side. So," he gave a satisfied nod, "that is the ideological difference."

I thanked him for a straightforward answer, then asked him: "When and why did the League against War and Fascism change its name to the League for Peace and Democracy?"

"That was my idea," he answered. "In the first place I always prefer a positive line; I'd always rather be for than against something. But also in this case, some critic — I forget who it was — brought up a very good point. He said, 'Why aren't you against war, fascism *and* communism.' Well, of course we could hardly say in the name of our organization that we were against communism when we had so many Communists working so effectively for us. So I suggested to Dr. Ward that we change the name to the League for Peace and Democracy." *

Under the new name and Dr. Ward's chairmanship, a certain degree of peace did in fact prevail in the organization for a few years. Then on August 20, 1939, came a political bombshell that to Roger was cataclysmic; on that date the Nazis and the Soviets signed their Non-Aggression Pact.

"I remember," said Roger, "that I was walking along the beach in Chilmark [Martha's Vineyard] when someone came up and told me about the deal between the Soviet Union and the Nazis. I think it was the biggest shock of my life. I never was so shaken up by anything as I was by that pact — by the fact that those two powers had got together at the expense of the democracies."

Rather reluctantly playing the devil's advocate here, I pointed out that he had been accused by one or two of his friends of having overreacted to the pact.

"You couldn't overreact to it," said Roger fiercely. "It was too shocking. I had thought that the Communists could at least be relied upon to be anti-Fascist. But no, they couldn't be. The Nazi-Soviet pact made you feel that suddenly the Communists were different people. They had abandoned us and got into bed with Hitler. It changed everything, of course. I resigned from the League for Peace and Democracy the next day — " he broke off and looked crossly at me as I shuffled through my papers, often a sign that some document from his Princeton files might be produced to contradict his present memory of events. "Didn't I?" he demanded.

I said, no, it wasn't the next day, and I showed him two copies of his letter of resignation, one, a draft dated September 17, and the other, presumably the final version, dated October 21.

"I didn't think I waited that long," Roger said.

I said I thought the date quite unimportant. What was much more significant was his excellent, well-reasoned and temperate letter of resignation. He read it and snorted.

"Much too reasonable," he said.

* By which name the organization may still be remembered today by many middle-aged or older liberals who supported it and who often were blacklisted by the House Un-American Committee for having done so.

"But why?"

"Because I *argued* the case. I should have given it in one sentence. I should have said simply, 'As long as the Communists follow the Soviet foreign policy, any United Front with them is quite impossible. Very truly yours.'"

I said I thought it was to his credit that he had not been so summary at the time, and then pointed to the final sentence of his letter of resignation, which read: "I shall of course continue to work with the Communists, as with all others, on specific issues of civil rights in the United States in which they are engaged. The notion that Communists are outside the pale of cooperation because of their adherence to Soviet policy is so irrational as to be almost hysterical."

Roger looked very sour indeed. "I was just being considerate of my colleagues," he said.

I suggested that this was perhaps not the only reason, that he had, in truth, stiffened his attitude against the Soviet Union in retrospect. In fact, even after the Nazi-Soviet pact, he had his most involved and tenacious association with a United Front in the Spanish Refugee Relief Campaign, which was equally dominated by Communists.

"I am by nature a conciliator in contentious circumstances," said Roger, referring to the extreme complexity of his activity in the United Front established by the left to try to save the Spanish Republic from Fascist attack. The organization duplicated all the elements backing the Spanish Loyalist government — anarchists, Communists, Socialists and plain liberals. As chairman of the executive committee of what after several incarnations came to be called the Spanish Refugee Relief Campaign, Roger found himself virtually in the eye of a continuous storm.*

Although the problem of Communist domination and control was just as it had been in the other United Fronts, in this Front there was stronger opposition. For one thing the Socialists were deeply committed to the Spanish Loyalists, and certainly could not be taunted into walking out. Furthermore, there were anarchists, there were

* The first organizations were the North American Committee to Aid Spanish Democracy set up in early 1937 with Bishop Francis McConnell as chairman, Roger as chairman of the executive committee and Herman Reissig as executive secretary, and, started at about the same time, the Medical Bureau to Aid Spanish Democracy with Dr. Walter B. Cannon of the Harvard Medical School as founder and chairman. In 1938 these two organizations merged to become the Spanish Refugee Relief Campaign with Bishop McConnell and Dr. Cannon as co-chairmen and Roger and Herman Reissig continuing in their respective positions.

trade unionists, there were Quakers, and there were many famous names on the board of fifty.*

"While the non-Communists objected to the dominance of the Communist party," said Roger, "I as executive committee chairman would insist that as long as we held to our program we could not complain. And the non-Communists accepted my good faith. We were fortunate in this United Front in having an executive secretary who was no Communist or fellow traveler. Herman Reissig was a Protestant clergyman whose courage and oratory at public meetings had endeared him to the left. But he was well aware of the politics of his new 'congregation' in the Spanish Relief Campaign, and I always backed him up with the necessary diplomacy to keep the peace.

"As I look back over those few tragic years for the Spanish people, I'm impressed with the memory of one of the greatest national campaigns I've ever had a part in. In city after city, from coast to coast, we held great mass meetings with speakers who had come directly from the war front. We showed war films; we capitalized on every atrocity. So did the Catholics, who conducted a holy war in support of Franco and against the godless anarchists and Communists who had burned churches and killed priests.

"Today one forgets the passions of that war and how deeply it struck at the hearts of youth — the hundreds of young American men who volunteered and died, many of them fighting in the Lincoln Brigade for the Loyalists."

"Did your committee actually recruit the young men?"

"No, but I remember I made a speech approving their participation. Even as a pacifist I justified it on the ground that it was a police action in aid of a legal government. I took the same position later in the Korean war in support of UN intervention as a police force, but I am aware, and was aware then, that the lines are pretty fine on what kind of force is morally admissible. I know how easy it is to find good reasons for what you want to do.

"Of course we were all deluding ourselves anyway in the Spanish war. The Loyalists were doomed the moment the democracies declared their neutrality and the Fascists entered the war. We knew it,

* Mary McLeod Bethune, Louis Brandeis, Malcolm Cowley, Helen Hayes, Lillian Hellman, Ernest Hemingway, Fannie Hurst, Rockwell Kent, Edna St. Vincent Millay, to mention a few of the personages who appeared on the letterhead of the Spanish Refugee Relief Campaign who had not previously been on Roger's lists of "liberal middle-class do-gooders."

but we hated to believe it. It took me a long time — almost to the
end — to despair. And as the war went on, badly for our side, our
meetings in the Spanish Relief Campaign became more and more
tense. We non-Communists had a majority of the board, but the
Communists often controlled a quorum. So we were often forced to
absent ourselves from meetings in order to prevent a quorum until
we could count on a majority of our non-Communists to be there.
This went on for weeks of trying everyone's patience, mine most of
all as chairman."

"Until what happened?"

"Until the Communists went too far in attempting to use the organization for specifically Communist purposes. The money and medical supplies sent over were directed by the Communists to their own
detachments. There was a bitter struggle over which refugees
streaming out of Spain were to get relief. In the end the Communists were outnumbered and defeated and decided to withdraw."

"But surely not without a fight."

Roger snorted. "Certainly not without a terrible fight. In fact the
steps leading up to their withdrawal are so complicated I don't think
I can still recollect them accurately. But really all that matters is that
when they pulled out, they tried to take our name, our mailing list,
our letterhead and our files with them. That took some straighten-
ing out; a government inquiry into their good faith, with a court
order against them and a few citations for contempt of Congress.
We purer folk continued for a while longer, but the Front was over.
And then the war came to a tragic end for the Spanish people."

Roger had spoken so eloquently and feelingly about his participation in the Spanish Relief Campaign that I felt churlish about
mentioning that during those weeks and months (when he was trying so hard to keep peace between the Communist and non-Communist factions), the Nazi-Soviet pact, which he had so vehemently
insisted made any further attempts at a United Front with the Communists quite impossible, had long since been signed. I temporized,
"Exactly when did all this happen?"

"In the forties," he said, and then, answering my unasked question, "I can't believe I was involved in a United Front that late, but I
suppose I must have been."

"And for excellent reasons, it would appear."

He sighed. "I guess I was romantic enough to hope for miracles."

(15)

The Home Front

ROGER WAS GLAD, HE SAID, TO WITHDRAW after the end of the Spanish Relief Campaign to the civil liberties fight on the home front. Not, he hastened to point out, that he had not been right there on the job at the ACLU all during the United Front days. In fact, he said, the period between the Depression and World War II was probably one of the busiest and most important in the life of the Union.

It was also quite an important decade in the life of the Union's director, most particularly in his private life. Although Roger had known Evelyn Preston casually in New York liberal circles as a "rich girl who had gone into the labor movement," his friendship with her did not blossom until the summer of 1928 when both were guests for a week at the Barnhouse on Martha's Vineyard.

The Barnhouse, a unique cooperative, was founded in 1919 by a judicious mix of lawyers, artists, businessmen, academics and reformers. These twenty or so persons — personages would perhaps be more accurate — sought a summer retreat by the seaside, a communal utopia for themselves and their families that would offer simple living, modest expenditure, high-minded contemplation, stimulating dialogue and lively and often whimsical activities. In this sympathetic and slightly fey atmosphere, surrounded by a spacious and varied natural setting that they both relished, Roger and Evelyn Preston were inseparable during this memorable week.*

Evelyn Preston came of a very well-to-do family. "I remember Helen Meiklejohn, who was on the Vineyard that summer, telling

---

* Still in existence today, the Barnhouse, while perhaps less utopian than originally envisaged, nonetheless qualifies as a durable tradition. Both Roger and I are "members" of the cooperative, and about half our interviews took place there.

me about the swank in which Evelyn lived, the big estate, the enormous house, the servants, the racing stables, the endless acres," Roger recalled. But from the beginning he simply rose above the privileged background of the young woman who had so strongly attracted him. Her wealth was neither a plus nor a minus as far as he was concerned.

There were, however, two serious drawbacks to a continuation of their promisingly begun relationship. Both had ties elsewhere. Roger was still married — although not in a very active sense — to Madeleine Doty, and, far more of an obstruction, Evelyn was engaged to be married to a man named Steve Raushenbush, also an active liberal, who was at the time on the staff of Governor Amos Pinchot of Pennsylvania.

Evelyn, in fact, soon married Raushenbush and moved to the capital city of Pennsylvania. Still she and Roger never lost touch; Evelyn, who was far from stimulated by life in Harrisburg, returned often to New York to keep up her contacts in the labor movement. (She was particularly interested in the Brookwood Labor College at Katonah, New York, which was, it happened, one of the institutions Roger had helped support during his Garland Fund days.) At the time her first child — Roger — was born, she took an apartment in New York to be near her doctor. Shortly thereafter she bought a house on West 11th Street and with other friends created Bleeker Gardens, another cooperative.

Soon after the birth of her second son, Carl, it became clear that Evelyn was going to leave both Harrisburg and Steve Raushenbush for good.

Meanwhile Roger had suffered two very unhappy personal losses. In February 1930, his adopted son Toto (Otto Stoltz) committed suicide. Although he and Toto had never had a great deal in common intellectually, they were nonetheless bound by close ties, and Toto's death was a great blow to Roger. They had spent a part of the previous summer together in England and France — a trip that was not an unqualified success as Roger remembered it. On his return Toto, who had been living and working in St. Louis since the war, gave up his job and decided to move to Los Angeles, thinking he would prefer the climate there. He found employment promptly in Los Angeles, but soon gave it up for a job at a larger salary in an oil camp in Santa Fe. Here he found conditions so distasteful that he returned to Los Angeles, but was unable by that time to find another position. After some months without work, he received a telegram from St. Louis offering him back his former job. According to Roger's mimeographed account of Toto's death, the thought of having to return to St. Louis after failing in the West was too defeating for Toto to accept. He drove his Ford roadster to a public park late one evening and shot himself with his service revolver.

"He had plenty of money," Roger wrote in his 1930 account, "for he had saved carefully for years. He had no love affairs or personal relationships which troubled him. His habits and health were always excellent. I can charge his collapse only to failure to find in Los Angeles the relief he sought and to being out of work for the first time in his life. Toto was always a lonely figure but very self-reliant and apparently satisfied with his simple routine . . ."

Others who knew Toto thought differently. Roger's Aunt Belle, who had moved from St. Louis to Los Angeles and had known Toto in both places (in reality she was almost his only friend in Los Angeles), wrote Roger saying, "He came to my house every five days and always started talking about you, for time and again he said he could not understand your line of thought. He would have liked to live nearer you, but after his visit last summer he said 'that was all over.' "

Roger did not go west for Toto's funeral, but left the details to the public administrator whom, he said, could handle matters better and more cheaply. The funeral expenses totaled $65. "He was buried with taps," wrote Aunt Belle. "He looked so nice in his coffin."

Toto left all his money — between seven thousand and eight thousand dollars — to Roger, who put most of this inheritance aside and used it to help boys in need. (The balance he spent, twenty-nine years later, for a round-the-world trip with his daughter, Helen, and a friend.)

Speaking of Toto today, Roger ascribes a somewhat less simplistic, if not wholly realistic, motive to his suicide. "At the time of his death," he says, "I was satisfied that his suicide was not deeply rooted. But looking back I have an uneasy feeling that some of his childhood wounds did not heal and that I could have done more to overcome his mother's rejection of him. I could not have been more companionable; he was the closest of anyone to me for a decade, but it was not the closeness of love. I was not a competent enough psychologist to see so earlier or I might have treated him differently."

One can perhaps probe a bit more deeply, as did the sister of

Roger's protégé Brownie, who knew Toto well (and who was soon to face tragedy of her own). "Toto was the most tremendously lonely person I know," Frances Brown wrote Roger. "That he wanted to dig deeply into life I do not doubt. That his pick always struck on rock I am almost sure. I know that Toto felt this inadequacy of himself as an individual . . . He fell socially between two groups and was acceptable to neither. Through association with you he had learned to find distasteful a vapid glamour of tinsel and roadhouse parties . . . He wanted social intercourse with people who were finding life a vital experience . . . He longed for love and tenderness . . . He saw something of great passion and beauty in other people's lives. He knew nothing of it in his own."

Less than two months after Toto's death, Roger received a second blow when Brownie, who along with Oral James was perhaps the closest of all his young wards, also committed suicide. The circumstances could not have been more different; in contrast to Toto's solitary ending, Brownie's came about because of his involvement in a *ménage à trois*.

He had come back from Paris where he had been helping Roger with *Liberty under the Soviets,* rejoined his wife, Ruthie, and gone back to work briefly for the ACLU.* Shortly afterward he and his wife were joined by another young woman, a friend of Ruthie's whom Brownie loved so much that they all agreed to live together. Roger, who at the time was seeing Brownie daily at the office, expressed doubts to him that such an arrangement "which defied convention and natural law" could possibly last. But Brownie laughed at Roger's misgivings and assured him that they were all very happy. "He was proud of his harem, proud of being the male supreme," Roger said, "although he wasn't really all that male nor very sexy either."

Some time later (long after Brownie had left his job at the ACLU) the girl walked out of the ménage saying that she could not continue a life that had no future for her. Brownie pursued her but to no avail. "Brownie was very depressed," said Roger; "he was usually so

* Brownie was another in the long line of short-lived publicity men whom Roger brought into the ACLU and soon let go. A letter from Roger to Brownie concerning their relationship illustrates what Roger expected of his underpaid staff and how at least one of them who was otherwise devoted to him reacted. "You do not act as a member of the staff who takes and shares a common responsibility," Roger wrote Brownie. "You insist that I so dominate the job that you and all others in it are my hired men. Your attitude in matters of wages and conditions is characterized by resentment and opposition, not by a spirit of understanding and cooperation."

gay and self-assured that his new mood troubled me. I tried to make him see how unfair it would be to his wife and the other girl to try to get the girl back. But that he thought of suicide for such a reason never crossed my mind."

Unhappily though Brownie did think of this solution to his problem. On March 25, 1930, he took his motorcycle and a borrowed pistol to New Jersey to the apartment of his girl. After one final entreaty to her to come back to him (and his wife), which she refused, he went upstairs and shot himself. He left identical notes to the girl and to Ruthie, each saying, "Dear, I cannot go on without you both. Forgive me."

"When I heard about it that afternoon," Roger said, "my reaction astonished me. I felt anger — anger at Brownie for doing such a thing, doing it to his wife, to his girl, to me, to his family."

From Geneva Madeleine Doty sent Roger a tender understanding letter. "I can well believe how you are hurt in your innermost being," she wrote, "to have two such friendships — children almost — swept away in such a fashion so devastating and I know it isn't only the loss of the gay companionship, but the sense of failure you feel after having put so much into the lives of both Toto and Brownie. But, old dear, what more could you have given them than you did? Doesn't the difficulty lie rather with the boys you have chosen to help? You chose them, or they chose you, because they needed your strength. You fed and sustained them. They lived off you and with you. I know you wanted to give them everything, but that inner thing — that inner vision is something we all have to find for ourselves. It can't be given. So you mustn't let a sense of failure torment you in your memory of Toto and Brownie.* Sometimes I think we are like Ford cars. Someone can show us how to drive and the best road to take — as you did for those boys — but we ourselves have to know where to get the essence or gasoline that will keep us going . . . They were dear boys," she ended; "much of what they were is due to you."

In 1934 Madeleine came back to New York to spend a year with Roger in an effort to rekindle their marriage. She took an apartment next to the one he shared with Eduard Lindeman, his oldest

* Freddie Farnum, Roger's "protégé" from Essex County jail who was best man at his wedding, also had died some years earlier, a probable suicide, from an overdose of drugs.

close friend from the St. Louis days, at 132 West 12th Street. "She was back and forth in my apartment all the time," said Roger. "She had a key."

"Well, after all, she was your wife."

"Yes, she was my wife and she acted like it too. Until she realized what was going on with Evelyn."

"By then was something going on with Evelyn?"

"Oh yes. She was living by herself in her New York house with her two little boys, of course, but without Steve Raushenbush. She had decided it was no go with him, so she'd come back to the house she'd bought in Bleeker Gardens on West 11th Street. Of course Madeleine didn't know that I was already interested in Evie when she came back to spend that year with me. But she soon found out. It does not take women long to draw conclusions from very little evidence."

"Did she talk to you about it?"

"No, she hardly mentioned it to me except to let me know that she saw it."

"And did you then ask her for a divorce?"

"No, I didn't. Of course we had talked about divorce before, but that year it wasn't discussed at all."

I said I found that hard to believe.

"Until after Evelyn went to Mexico and got her divorce," Roger continued, as if I had not spoken. "By that time Madeleine was back in Geneva and we started correspondence about it. Then I spent a large part of the summer of 1935 in Geneva — living mostly with my father, who by chance had a villa there that summer on the lake — and it was during that period that Madeleine and I got a friendly divorce."

"And when you came back you moved into Evelyn's house in Bleeker Gardens, is that right?"

"Before I went to Geneva I had moved into the house *next* to Evelyn's," Roger enunciated carefully. "She owned them both but she lived in number 282 West 11th and this was number 284."

"Oh come on, Roger, they were connected, weren't they?"

He chortled. "Yes, they certainly were connected."

"And how soon after your divorce did you get married?"

"We waited a respectable time to make it official and even then, it was so obvious a step — we were clearly in love, and no other course had ever occurred to us except to get married — that we made no fuss about it. We had a Quaker-like ceremony on the lawn at Dellbrook one Sunday morning. We were married by Judge Dorothy Kenyon, Evie's great friend who was also her lawyer and who had invited her to the Barnhouse where she and I first met."

"And this was in what year?"

"March 6, 1936."

I asked Roger if he could possibly describe and somehow evoke Evelyn Preston for me, since I had never met her; she died in 1962 at the age of sixty-four.

"Well, Evie was at heart a retiring personality; I think her lack of social success was due to shyness and her awareness that she was no beauty. She was too tall, for one thing — over six feet — and, as ratings of pretty girls go, she was plain. Some might even have found her without sex appeal, though after our marriage I doubt they would have. She may have been reticent, but she was a strong character just the same who knew exactly what she expected of life and what she rejected. She could turn her face on a person she found dull or unresponsive and forget his or her existence. She just refused to be around people who bored her or to make efforts to be nice when she didn't feel it."

"But didn't that make it rather difficult for a gregarious type like you?"

"It could have, but I didn't let it. It was simply a matter of compromise. Evie submitted to small private occasions and welcomed a few guests at a time — more than four or five was too many though — and left the larger parties and public affairs to me."

"You make her sound a bit forbidding," I said.

"I know. I suppose she might have seemed to be to some people but only because she was bashful and uneasy. It was entirely different with those she liked and loved. She had a wonderful hearty sense of humor. Her deep rollicking laugh could be heard a room away. She enjoyed wit and jokes, even on herself. She loved the theater too, and she was an omnivorous but choosy reader. I'd say that all the great emotions found a response in her, but she didn't speak much of what she read or saw. She was not particularly articulate but she could say what she meant and pointedly.

"In all our thirty years together we never had a single argument," Roger went on, and then seeing me looking as doubtful as I felt, insisted. "It's true. I know that's a remarkable comment for a husband to make but the reason was simple. We both hated conflict and disagreement. If we felt them, we kept them to ourselves. Each would state his case and then we would leave it at that, never trying to convince the other. And I think it was this mutual tolerance that made our marriage so happy."

"Would you say you each went your own way a good deal of the time?"

"Often we did, yes. We rarely traveled together, for instance. Evie didn't like traveling — too much confusion, she said, and I was always too preoccupied; the beds were not as comfortable as hers and she hated to live out of suitcases. And I, of course, had to travel a great deal and liked it. So yes, we did go our separate ways with separate friends and interests, but the important thing is that we had the right basis for that kind of independence. We loved each other always without a break and with no other emotional excursions.

"I was fifty-two years old when I married Evie, and I had inherited a whole new family — a wife and two little boys. We continued to live as before, I in number 284 and she in 282, because the house was full of children and servants. But we took our meals together and spent evenings and often our nights together. Weekends we went to Dellbrook. We both wanted a child, a girl, if possible. Two years later, after Evie had had two miscarriages that were devastating for us both, Helen was born, just as ordered — a very joyful moment."

I asked Roger to back up for just a moment and tell me about Dellbrook, the New Jersey estate where he and Evie were married and which, it seems, looms larger in his life than even Bleeker Gardens (where he still lives with Helen and her family) or than Windy Gates (the choice 280-acre property in Chilmark on Martha's Vineyard that Evelyn had bought in 1923), partly because it was he who had discovered it.

"Well," he explained, "I had had a camp in New Jersey on the Hackensack River from 1923 on — a portable shack, it was, on leased land. Then in 1932 I was notified that I had to give up the land, so I went hiking around with a friend to see what I might acquire on the Ramapo River. By good luck we chanced on Dellbrook Farms, a beautiful large piece of land with a good many buildings that had just come on the market for lease or sale. Naturally there was no question of my buying it, so I got together a group of my outdoors friends and we leased the property for one thousand dollars a year. Evie joined the group in 1933 — she loved the country and she always felt the most alive then; she occupied one of the cottages while I moved to Brook Cabin. Then in 1935, the year before we were married, we were threatened with losing the place by sale to someone else. So Evie bought the whole thing for $25,000. What an investment that was! When we were married, we moved into the 'big house' and I've been there ever since."

Roger makes a great point — and sometimes an almost ludicrous one — of the fact that even with three handsome pieces of real estate that his wife owned and that he for years enjoyed, he always remained very much his own spartan self.

"It was agreed that I would pay Evie each month only what I would have paid if I had been living alone. After that we never mentioned her money, or mine — which was not enough to mention anyway. She was wealthy, but lived simply; she had the children to look after and she hated household chores, so she always had a couple of servants and a nurse. I paid my monthly sum and she kept the accounts. I never knew how much she was worth and never asked. I did not want to know or to get involved in any financial matters. We did file a joint income tax return but when I signed, I always made a point of covering the figures with my hand so I wouldn't know how much she had."

With so few financial responsibilities and such comfortable living arrangements, Roger could continue to indulge in the luxury — to him — of taking an exceedingly low salary from the American Civil Liberties Union and of expecting the rest of the staff to do the same. Clearly this was advantageous to the organization's budget (if not to those of his harried staff members). Actually Roger's marriage and his new-found happiness with a wife who shared so many of his liberal and libertarian concerns was in every way a plus for him in the performance of his duties as director of the Union.

What I wondered aloud about, however, was whether his highly visible, conflict-ridden and ceaseless association with the United Fronts throughout the thirties had been in any way detrimental to his work at the ACLU.

At first he pooh-poohed the idea. "However emotionally involved

I was, I didn't invest much time away from my job. United Front meetings were at night or at lunch and calls on the chairman's time were not heavy. I did very little public speaking, but I called on my aptitude for organizing things to play the m.c. role, which I took to easily. Presiding over meetings required little preparation."

I said I was not thinking so much of the time he put in outside the office (which by then had moved to 100 Fifth Avenue) as I was of whether his activities had been at all corrosive to the ACLU's image.

"Looking back," he said, "I think that I and some of the other ACLU leaders made a mistake in getting so deeply involved in United Fronts led by Communists."

"Still, you always were involved with other organizations; a lot of them we haven't even talked about."

"Exactly. I was always active in one outside effort or another, but the problem, particularly with the United Fronts, was that the ACLU was confused with them since I was its chief spokesman. I sometimes think now that we would have been more effective and it would have been better for the cause if I had stuck to our single purpose, or if the Union had been directed by a lawyer with no leftist or political connections."

"But weren't most of those who came to the ACLU for help inclined to be people or organizations with leftist political connections?"

"Yes, of course they were. But first of all you must remember that those were very bitter years after the 1929 collapse. Unemployment, liquidation of farm property, general unrest in the country. All kinds of upsets occurred. The labor movement began again to strike for higher wages; the farmers for the first time demonstrated collectively against foreclosures.

"When Frank Roosevelt took over in 1933, the country was at the lowest point I've ever seen it. Nobody had any hope. There was a terrific depression of the spirit as well as the economy."

"And you at the ACLU had to respond to that situation?"

"Certainly, it was our duty. The unemployed began to be organized. We had to protect their rights to march, to hold meetings, to demonstrate."

"And I should think that inevitably at such a time of unrest there must have been even more infractions of civil liberties, particularly against radicals."

"There were. It was a terrible time for radicals. Terrible! And as you suggest, the ACLU was an organization that reacted to situations; it didn't create them. But the result was that the character of our clients always made us appear to be holding a leftist partisan view."

"So then after the Depression was over, after Roosevelt came in, did you deliberately begin to take the cases you did in defense of reactionaries?"

"Well, certainly we were accused of that, yes. Our critics charged that the only reason we were interested in the rights of Jehovah's Witnesses, or the Ku Klux Klan, or the German American Bund, or Gerald L. K. Smith and others on the extreme right was to give us a facade, a front to conceal the fact that we were really only interested in the left."

"And how did you answer your critics?" I asked, remembering that Roger himself had admitted much the same thing in his *Soviet Russia Today* article (which he now discredits), written just about the time these accusations were made.

"I answered that our critics couldn't understand the Voltairian doctrine that you hate what you're defending."

I said I wasn't sure I quite understood the Voltairian doctrine either.

"It's very simple. If the person you hate has no rights, then the person you like may have no rights either. And in order to defend the people you like, you have to defend the people you hate. Now take Gerald L. K. Smith, who was our pet reactionary. He was the epitome of bigotry, and the worst kind of bigotry because it was encloaked in Christian rectitude."

"Did he actually do anything? I mean did he have a profession?"

"I don't think he was a clergyman, although he acted like one. He edited a paper called *The Cross and the Flag* and those were the symbols of his life. He almost — but not quite — said that God had called him to his mission. However, he was a man of very practical dimensions. He had his paper and he had his organization. And when he hired a hall, he hired it to get his followers to come out and pay money."

"I can't remember what his purpose was; what did he do or say in the halls he hired?"

"Well, he was a professional anti-Semite and it was during his anti-Semitic campaign that he was denied the use of a hall — in Buffalo, I think it was. And we saw it in the newspaper and made a big stink and got the hall opened."

"You did this on your own — the ACLU did — without his asking you in the first place?"

"No, he didn't ask us first. But then when he saw that we were the only people who came to his defense as a matter of principle, he accepted us and would appeal to us all the time. He and Father Coughlin were the chief exponents of anti-Semitism whose rights we defended. We got injunctions in both cases and often, so they could secure halls in which to speak."

"To speak openly for anti-Semitism?"

"That's right."

"I'm trying to cling to that Voltairian doctrine," I said doubtfully, "so I guess you had to do it."

"We had to do it," Roger answered.

"Did you ever have to deal personally with Gerald L. K. Smith or Father Coughlin?"

"Never with Coughlin but with Smith all the time. I remember once he called me at Windy Gates and told me his latest troubles. I said I couldn't do anything for him from the Vineyard, but told him to go to the ACLU office in New York. He said, 'Oh I can't trust that office; you've got Jews in it.' I told him that they would be fair to him just the way we were all fair to him, but he said no, he would only deal with me personally. He accepted me. He even invited me to lunch with him at the Waldorf Astoria."

"And you went?"

"Sure I went, why not? His bodyguard was there — he was always afraid of being assassinated by Jews — and Mrs. Smith. I don't know if she was *the* Mrs. Smith or just *a* Mrs. Smith. But this was a strong man. He was anti-international in every way; he was anti-minority. I can't think of any form of bigotry he didn't have. But he liked me and accepted me as honest."

I suggested we move on, and with a view to working our way through the decade from right to left, I brought up the Henry Ford case, something of a star in the ACLU's firmament, since it was one of the few occasions in labor matters in which they defended the rights of management.

To understand the Ford case, it was necessary, Roger pointed out, to go back to the National Labor Relations Act passed early in Roosevelt's first term: an act that Roger and many of his colleagues on the ACLU Board had at first viewed with grave suspicion. "It took us quite a little while to accept the idea that the government should be a policeman for trade unions. But Roosevelt and his advisers had decided that the trade unions had been fought against long enough, that the unions were weak and employers were strong and the government better get in there and bolster the unions up."

"And you were afraid if the government helped the unions, they would try to control them?"

"Yes, we were wrong of course. To have the government regulate collective bargaining and not control it was something we couldn't conceive of in those early days. But it worked and we saw we were in error. And then pretty soon the employers came along and said, 'Look, here's this government machinery favoring the unions. Now how about us? Don't we have the right to free speech too?' And we said, 'No, you have no rights of free speech against unions now because the right to form a union is now a fundamental one under the National Labor Relations Act.' And the employers said, 'Well, can't we even talk?' And some of our Board members, most of them, certainly the ones who were pro-labor, said, 'No, you can't even talk,' because they held that any speech anywhere by an employer against a union was coercive and therefore banned. Dr. Harry Ward, our chairman, was of that opinion. But John Haynes Holmes, our vice chairman, was not, and that created a lot of contention on the Board."

"What line did you take?"

"I was on the side of Holmes."

"Because you were leaning over backward?"

"Maybe. It was a position that came naturally to me. But their argument, which I agreed with, was that if you're an employer you can tell your employees not to join a union: you can say that you'll do just as well for them as the union would. But what you can't do is say, if you join a union we'll fire you. And when Henry Ford challenged the order of the National Labor Relations Board forbidding employers to mention unions to their employees, we had to draw a line between his right to make a speech to his employees saying we advise you not to join the United Auto Workers' Union, and we hope if there's an election you won't vote to join, and his saying, if you join the UAW, we'll fire you."

As he often does in retrospect, Roger had somewhat simplified the issue that caused the controversy between Ward and Holmes, and also, at least partially, glossed over his own participation, casting himself as usual in a more conservative role than apparently he actually played.

In *The Pulse of Freedom,* a 1975 book written by six authors, each dealing with a decade in the history of the ACLU, Jerome S. Auerbach details the issue more precisely. The NLRB had charged Ford with high-pressure methods in his relations with his employees, with discriminatory firings, intimidation and physical assault. His anti-union campaign, the NLRB asserted, constituted a "direct address to fear of physical violence."

Considering these accusations, a labor committee of the ACLU, of which Roger Baldwin was a member, concluded that "When speech is thus implemented by force, by threats of discharge or violence, it is not the free speech about which the ACLU is concerned. Thus the ACLU's initial reaction, to which Roger was presumably party, was clearly anti-Ford and quite understandably so, since the championship of the rights of labor had always been their primary concern. In the Henry Ford case these rights were manifestly being threatened by the employer; hence the right of free speech of that employer was not the real issue.

But it *was* the real issue, argued John Haynes Holmes, when the findings of the labor committee were given to the entire ACLU Board. "Under the impact of our real sympathy for labor's cause," he wrote Harry Ward, "we are allowing ourselves to become mere advocates of the rights of labor to the denial of those rights as exercised by those who are against labor." Furthermore, he warned, he was reluctantly beginning to believe that "our enemies have good reason to charge us with . . . using the Civil Liberties principle as a means of fighting labor's battles and the cause of radicalism generally."

Clearly a nonpartisan compromise had to be sought and, as was frequently so in such cases, it fell to Roger to work out a solution that would be agreeable to the Holmes faction and to the Ward advocates (whom he today refers to as the fellow travelers). "What we came up with was this," he said. "Mr. Ford could go to the chamber of commerce and tell the businessmen that he was opposed to unions and he could be recorded in all the newspapers as having said so. But what he could *not* do was to put a notice on the bulletin board of his factories telling the workers not to join the UAW, because that would be threatening them that if they did join he'd fire them. It was a very fine distinction between free speech and coercion and the rest of our Board finally came around to it after quite a time. And then the Supreme Court upheld our concept of what employers could do and say."

"So you won the case."

"I wouldn't say *we* won it, but the case was won. As I remember it we came in only as an *amicus curiae*. But our participation and the position we took made headlines because we had been known to be opponents of Ford's fight against the unions and especially of the strong-arm tactics of his secret police."

Having come down on the side of the employer in the Ford case, Roger soon had another opportunity to resume his favorite bent-over-backward position, when he was asked by both parties in the fur industry to act as impartial chairman in their union-employer conflicts. The Fur Workers' Union was under strong Communist control; its president, Ben Gold, was a party member whom Roger knew and respected because the ACLU had already defended the rights of his union. He was, therefore, astounded that the employers would accept him as arbiter, so much so that he called the employers' lawyer, Emil K. Ellis, to make sure the employers knew what they were getting into. "I told him I was always pro-union, that I didn't object to a Communist leader, and asked him how did they think I could be impartial. They said they thought so because they knew me, knew my sympathies, but also knew I would do the fair and the right thing. So I took the job; it lasted about a year and it was an enlightening experience. I would visit shops, talk to employers, sometimes hold hearings of both sides and make adjustments. And I do think many of my decisions went against the unions. But Ben Gold was a good man; he held a firm hand on the union, but he was fair to the employers too, especially since many of them had risen from the bench to owning the shop. Both sides thanked me when I finished the job."

"Did you ever have any such direct contact with labor-management again?"

"One, yes. Once for a short time I was very much involved with the Cooks and Waiters' Union in New York. I forget exactly how it came about that the men who were organizing the union came to me because the restaurant bosses would not make collective bargaining agreements with them. They told me about conditions in the industry, and I said I wanted to see for myself, so I asked them to get me a job in the kitchen of one of the restaurants where I could work a few hours at night after the ACLU closed. And they did get me a job in a restaurant just south of Washington Square and pretty soon — I'm not sure of the sequence of events — the workers in that restaurant went on strike and so of course I found myself in the picket line with them. It was the only time I'd ever been in a picket line in my life.

"But then the head of the nightclub and restaurant owners was a fellow named Barney Gallant who had a very famous restaurant at University Place. And it so happened that Barney Gallant had once been a student of mine at Washington University in St. Louis. And when he heard I was helping the strikers, he moved in and got the strike settled very fast. So then the union boys came to me and said, 'We'd like to do something for you.' And I said there was nothing they could do — that I was just doing my duty in helping them get their civil rights. But they kept insisting they wanted to do something for me, so finally I said, 'All right, if you really want to, then send me a good French chef to teach me some good French cooking, because I'm just a camp cook and I want to know some of the tricks.' "

"Well" (Roger obviously relished this story), "the next thing I knew, this very elegant-looking gentleman turned up at the office. He had a white mustache, he wore gold-rimmed glasses, he spoke with a French accent, he had on spats and carried a cane. He said, 'The union sent me. I'm not working now and I will be glad to come to your house and show you some things about cooking.' I asked him where he had worked and he said he had been chef for Mr. Vincent Astor and also chef at the Sherry-Netherland. So I said, 'My God, I think you'd be much too grand for us,' but he said not to worry, he'd come to the house and bring all his implements.

"He told us what to order and then he'd come down to 11th Street at five o'clock and I'd watch him prepare for a seven o'clock dinner. It was all done with the most painstaking care. For a couple of weeks — it was two weeks, I think — Evie and I ate very well indeed. Then I said to him, 'Monsieur, I'd like to pay you.' And he said, 'Mr. Baldwin, you couldn't pay me. My last salary was twenty thousand dollars.' [This was in 1938.] But instead he asked me if I would pick out a good college for his twenty-year-old son and recommend him to it, which I did, and the boy got in."

"And can you now make crêpes, for example?"

"Yes, I can. In fact, I have a slight reputation for my crêpe suzettes. But as I once told Craig Claiborne when I was interviewed for the *New York Times,* I'm a camp cook with Cordon Bleu trimmings."

Reluctantly returning to soberer subjects, I asked Roger if he had had any dealings with the top men in the labor movement.

"Well, John L. Lewis and Philip Murray formed the CIO when the New Deal proposed to have government support for unionization."

"And were they friends of yours?"

"Philip Murray was, yes. But John Lewis wasn't anybody's friend. He was a power in his own right and he didn't team up with anybody. As far as I was concerned, he treated me as a sort of distinguished nuisance."

"That's what I wanted to ask you," I said. "But I couldn't have put it quite so neatly. Did any of the union leaders find your sort of do-gooding something of a bother?"

"I think they thought we were a bother, yes," Roger answered cheerfully. "Many of them thought so. These people had power; the ACLU didn't have any power. And we tried to horn in on their business because they were directly involved in civil liberties. All trade union organization was a civil liberties matter. But they figured they could do it themselves. They didn't need our help most of the time, although they did use us once in a while. But we put in our word because we represented a public point of view and we thought that view should be added to labor's own advocacy."

In addition to their defense of reactionaries and Communists, labor and management, the ACLU had other areas of activity that were less partisan. The issue of religious freedom, for example, occupied much of their time during the thirties and forties.

The religious sect with which the ACLU was longest associated was the Jehovah's Witnesses. Their case surfaced in 1936 when children belonging to the sect refused to salute the flag in school. The Jehovah's Witnesses children sat stolidly in their seats as the teachers tried to get them to stand and face the flag. Each refused, each saying the same words, as Roger recalls them: "God told us not to worship any image at all but His and our parents told us we cannot worship any earthly image and the flag is an earthly image."

That any child should have to go through a patriotic ritual to get a public education was, as Roger said, "a monstrous idea." The

ACLU brought suit and their defense of the rights of the Jehovah's Witnesses children lasted eight years. "We lost out all the way up," said Roger. "We lost out in the Supreme Court. Our friend Felix Frankfurter wrote the majority opinion. It was a very labored defense that said, in effect, that a country had a right to impose loyalty to that country on all its citizens and that public schools run at the expense of the taxpayer had to demonstrate that loyalty to the country's symbol — the flag."

"But what happened? Obviously that did not remain the law of the land."

"No, the court finally reversed itself. Harlan Stone, who had been one of the original dissenters, reversed, and then my only friend on the court, Frank Murphy — "

"Frankfurter was no longer your friend?"

"No, he wasn't," Roger said, truculently. "Not for a long time after that. But Murphy was the first to change his mind and that led to a re-argument and finally a reversal. Five to four, I think it was, with Frankfurter still sticking to his opinion, but at least the flag saluting was finally abolished. That would have been in about 1943, I guess."

But long before, before the case even reached the Supreme Court for the first time, the Jehovah's Witnesses, who had acted purely in accordance with their religious beliefs, had run afoul of the professional patriots.

By the end of the thirties when Hitler's continuing and alarmingly successful annexation of western Europe made America's intervention in the war seem inevitable, a wave of sentiment against all aliens and all nonconformists set in that threatened to destroy the freedoms so carefully nurtured during the decade. The refusal of the Jehovah's Witnesses to salute the flag met with mob violence. Other acts of nonconformity were "un-American." Aliens, no matter how loyal, were threatened with repressive treatment. The Nazi-Soviet pact only heightened this hysteria and made American citizens who were Communists or suspected Communists subject to flagrant abuse of their constitutional guarantees.

For Roger Baldwin the Nazi-Soviet pact was also a watershed that would soon lead to a bitter conflict within the American Civil Liberties Union and would seriously damage twenty years of harmony on its board of directors.

(16)

All Roads Lead to Elizabeth Gurley Flynn

THERE ARE MANY WHO BELIEVE that the ACLU has never fully recovered from the trauma of what has come to be referred to as the trial of Elizabeth Gurley Flynn. Actually it was not a trial in any legal sense, but rather a confrontation at which Miss Flynn, who had been a member of the ACLU's governing body since its inception, appeared before that Board to argue against the contention of some of its members that she was unfit to continue to serve because of her membership in the Communist party.

The meeting, which took place on Tuesday, May 7, 1940, at the City Club of New York on West 44th Street, began at eight o'clock in the evening and concluded at two-twenty in the morning when a tie vote pro and con Miss Flynn's continued participation on the Board was broken by the chairman, John Haynes Holmes, who voted against her, resulting in her expulsion.

Throughout this long meeting Roger uttered not a word. As executive director he was not officially a member of the Board and therefore could not properly speak or vote but his detractors and Miss Flynn's supporters generally considered him to have been the man who pulled the strings to bring about a decision that they believed tarnished the reputation of the Civil Liberties Union.

It was not the first time that the ACLU Board had faced a basic ideological disagreement, but previously, as for instance in the Ford case, they had managed — often aided by Roger's acknowledged gifts as a conciliator — to resolve their differences. This time, however, the emotional climate was so intense that opposing forces became and remained irreconcilable.

Most of the Board members were liberals who had been stirred by Marxist idealism and who believed, in varying degrees, that the Soviets were going to generate a new, revolutionary and a just society. Some who had been most fervent in their convictions or hopes were therefore the most disillusioned by the Nazi-Soviet pact.

Thus Roger's vehement reaction to the pact, which, he said, "threw idealism out the window," was shared by others — perhaps most notably by John Haynes Holmes and Morris Ernst — and led the Board to issue on February 5, 1940, a so-called purge resolution of which Roger was the acknowledged author. Although Roger claimed (then and now) that the resolution was simply a statement of an unwritten policy that had always existed, the document was, to say the least, an incongruous one to come from the board of directors of the American Civil Liberties Union; inconsistent and contradictory in the view of many, destructive to the entire concept of civil liberties in the opinion of the extremists.

"The Board of Directors and the National Committee of the American Civil Liberties Union . . . hold it inappropriate," the statement read in part, "for any person to serve on the governing committees of the Union or its staff, who is a member of any political organization which supports totalitarian dictatorship in any country, or who by his public declarations indicates his support of such a principle . . .

"Within this category we include organizations in the United States supporting the totalitarian governments of the Soviet Union and of the Fascist and Nazi countries (such as the Communist Party, the German-American Bund and others) . . ."

This latter, of course, was patent nonsense, as Miss Flynn was quick to point out in her answer to the purge resolution written for the *Daily Worker:* "The Nazi-fascist stuff in the resolution is just window dressing," she said, "as there are no fascists or Nazis on the Board. Its inclusion adds insult to injury."

A further clarifying statement, released by the ACLU to the press on the same day, pointed out that while no member of the Communist party was ever elected or appointed to any position of responsibility in the Union, "two members of the National Committee joined the Communist Party some years after their election and the Board did not think it necessary to disassociate them on the grounds of their political opinion.

"One of them, William Z. Foster, elected when he was an organizer for the A. F. of L. in 1920, served some years and resigned in disagreement on a matter of policy. The other, Elizabeth Gurley Flynn, one of the original incorporators of the Union, did not join the Communist Party until fifteen years later. She has since served on the Board of Directors and is the only member of the Communist Party on the Board.

"The occasion for raising this issue at this time is the increasing tension which has resulted everywhere from the direction of the Communist international movement since the Soviet-Nazi pact. The abandonment of the struggle against Fascism and the other changes in the Communist policy have raised sharp issues which were reflected in the attitudes of members of our Board of Directors . . ."

The vociferous opposition on the Board against the purge resolution was led by Corliss Lamont, Osmond Fraenkel, A. K. Isserman and others. Most importantly, Dr. Henry Ward, a charter member and chairman of the Board, had resigned with a public statement a few weeks after the issuance of the resolution.

The nub of Dr. Ward's argument and that of like-minded members of the Board was that loyalty to the Bill of Rights was the sole criterion on which membership in the ACLU governing body had always been based; issues outside the United States had always been rigidly excluded. "What constitutes 'totalitarian dictatorship' in different countries is a question of political opinion on which there is strong difference," said Ward. Thus, excluding those who made "public declaration in support of totalitarian dictatorship" was "censorship of the opinions of some by the opinions of others." And by penalizing those opinions the Union was "doing in its own sphere precisely what it had always opposed in law or administration."

Guilt by association and witch hunts were phrases flung at the ACLU Board. Seventeen prominent liberals cried out in an open letter that the purge resolution encouraged "the very tendencies it was intended to fight and would make the Civil Liberties Union a fellow traveler with the Dies Committee."

All this hue and cry, which took place weeks before the actual Flynn "trial," much exacerbated already strung-out emotions, the more so because Miss Flynn was an extremely likable, attractive and popular member of the liberal community.

"Elizabeth and I were very good friends," Roger said. "I was really fond of her." The feeling — at least after the purge resolution — was hardly mutual. In her hard-hitting *Daily Worker* article

(March 19, 1940) Miss Flynn wrote of Roger: "Mr. Baldwin's 'unwritten policy' is just so much sand thrown in the eyes of the public.
Not so long ago this breezy fellow-traveler boasted genially of the
broadmindedness of the Union. 'We even have Communists on our
board.' All is changed now. Dr. John Haynes Holmes says his conscience will not permit him to sit at the same board with a Communist. Mr. Baldwin says, 'Communists have no moral integrity.'
Well, I'll stake mine and any party member's against his any
time."

By the time the "trial" itself commenced, incredibly intense feelings had been generated; many still persist today. In fact, it often
struck me as I talked to various people about Roger, notably to
Corliss Lamont, Alan Reitman, Lucille Milner, and Osmond Fraenkel, that all roads seemed to lead to Elizabeth Gurley Flynn. Mr.
Lamont and Mrs. Milner were particularly bitter abut Roger's role in
the affair, both believing that he could have stopped the action
against her at any time he wanted had he not overreacted to the
Nazi-Soviet pact and as a result become infected by the prevailing
anti-Communist hysteria. Lamont went so far as to say that because
the ACLU took the lead by its purge resolution and firing of Miss
Flynn, other organizations followed in its anti-Communist path, thus
ultimately opening the floodgates for McCarthyism. Osmond
Fraenkel, taking a more moderate line, scoffed (if so mild a man can
in fact be said to scoff) at this viewpoint. However, he did feel the
purge resolution and its results were damaging to the ACLU and
were quite unnecessary to begin with.

Finally Lamont said unequivocally that he considered that all that
Roger Baldwin had ever done for civil liberties was negated by that
one dishonest action. I questioned the word "dishonest."
Misguided perhaps, but dishonest? Yes, Lamont insisted, the ma-
neuvering that led up to the purge resolution was downright dishonest.

More objective was Corliss Lamont's publication of the entire proceedings in his book *The Trial of Elizabeth Gurley Flynn by the American
Civil Liberties Union,* along with such pertinent appendices as the text
of the purge resolution and statement to the press, articles by Elizabeth Gurley Flynn in the *Daily Worker,* the constitution and bylaws
of the Communist party of America. Among all the carefully chosen documents, Dr. Harry Ward's letter of resignation and the open
letter from seventeen liberals seemed to me the most persuasive.

Thus my approach to Roger, even thirty-five years after the fact, was skeptical at best.

"How many liberals," I asked him, "did the ACLU lose as a result of the Flynn episode?"

"We lost a few," Roger said. "A couple of hundred."

"Did you feel badly about those you lost?"

"No, I think it was natural. If I felt the way they did, I would have quit too."

"Did you see any justification for the way they felt?"

"I think that people who said that Communists were still reliable friends of democracy were in error. And if they persisted in saying that even after the Nazi-Soviet pact, I was sorry for their illusion and sorry to lose them. But I couldn't go along with them because what they were saying practically was, 'You should keep Miss Flynn because you can still trust Communists to be democrats.' "

"Roger, weren't they really saying that loyalty to the Bill of Rights was the sole requirement imposed by the ACLU? Now was there anything in Miss Flynn's actions that indicated disloyalty to the Bill of Rights?"

"In her activities, no. Except that in her defense prior to the ACLU meeting at which she was ousted, she cited the Soviet Union as her primary loyalty. She said that was what she was committed to and she cited the Soviet Constitution."

"But," I asked, "did that really mean she couldn't work on civil liberties *in the United States?*"

"Not when she professed loyalty to a dictatorship. Elizabeth could not be consistent in saying 'I am supporting you, my friends in the Civil Liberties Union, and I am also supporting the dictators of the Soviet Union. I am doing both. I think the Soviet Union is correct in *denying* civil liberties to everybody. I think the Civil Liberties Union is correct in *extending* civil liberties to everybody. Now, Peggy, you know you can't do both things.' "

I asked why, if this were true, it had not always been true and therefore why the ACLU Board had not kicked Miss Flynn off two years earlier when she first joined the Communist party and came to them offering to resign from the Board. Roger said it was simply because they all liked her so much. "We said, 'Elizabeth, don't think of quitting. We all love you . . .' "

"Well then when the Nazi-Soviet pact happened, did you love her less?"

Unperturbed, Roger said, "After the Nazi-Soviet pact, we would have kicked God himself out."

"In other words you couldn't afford to like her anymore?"

"The inconsistency between what we believed and the Nazi-Soviet pact was so great that you couldn't tolerate anybody then who was a Communist. Because a Communist was no longer just a Communist after the pact. A Communist was an agent of the Soviet Union."

"Roger, I seem to remember a line you wrote well after the pact was signed — " I began shuffling through papers to find it while he watched me warily. "You wrote it when you resigned from the League for Peace and Democracy. You said then, 'I shall continue to work with Communists on specific issues of civil rights in the United States. The notion that the Communists are outside the pale of cooperation because of their adherence to Soviet foreign policy is so irrational as to be almost hysterical.' Now isn't what you did — your purge resolution and the firing of Miss Flynn — also so irrational as to be almost hysterical?"

"Certainly not," he pounced. "I'm talking about cooperation *outside* of an organization. The United Front, which is what I was referring to when I resigned from the League for Peace and Democracy, was *not* an organization. A Socialist can cooperate with a Communist in the United Front where people are working for a common end. But if you're Norman Thomas, you don't take Communists into the Socialist party."

"But the Socialist party and the ACLU are hardly the same thing."

"In this instance they are. You don't take Communists into the Socialist party; you don't take them into the ACLU. You must remember, Peggy, that Elizabeth Flynn *inside* the organization of the ACLU is an entirely different thing than Elizabeth Gurley Flynn representing the Communist party and working with us *outside* the ACLU in the United Front. She's not the same person. We didn't take nonbelievers into the family. We thought that everybody we elected was a believer — a true believer."

"But if she stopped being a true believer in your eyes, wouldn't that have happened at the time she joined the Communist party?"

"We should have fired her then," Roger conceded. "If we had been consistent, we should have thrown her out right then."

"You not only didn't throw her out," I rubbed it in, "you actually renominated her, knowing she had joined the party."

"We did, sure. That was our mistake. That was the error we made. Throwing her out in 1940 was not the error. The error was re-electing her. We should have recognized it at the time, but we had been working with Communists in the United Front and outside the ACLU so we didn't feel strongly about them. But the Nazi-Soviet pact made us feel strongly. The Communists were different people. They were supporting Hitler and we detested Hitler and all he stood for, and the Communists were in bed with him."

"If Miss Flynn had resigned — or if you hadn't reappointed her — would you have had the 1940 purge resolution at all?"

"Yes, I think we would have."

"Why?" I asked. "William Z. Foster had resigned; he was the only other party member. So wasn't the resolution written just to get Miss Flynn off?"

"No. The resolution spoke for itself. It just said this has always been our policy. We merely put into words what we had always done anyhow. We never elected any Communists. We tolerated one who got to be one. And the important thing to remember is that this is *still* the policy of the ACLU. The resolution on qualifications for leadership stood for twenty-seven years when it was changed — and I helped draft the new statement — in language, but not in principle."

"So then you still say it's impossible to believe in civil liberties and be a Communist?"

"Yes," said Roger.

"Flat statement?"

He nodded vigorously. "Flat statement."

"Well then," I pressed on, "do you say it's impossible to be a Communist sympathizer — not a card-carrying member — but a sympathizer and believe in civil liberties?"

"No, I don't say that's impossible."

"What distinction do you make?"

"Well, I make this distinction. A party member is committed to what the Communist International movement, or what Russia, does and the member apologizes for it and says you have to have dictatorship to get progress. That's what all Communists say; Chinese dictatorship or Yugoslav dictatorship or Russian dictatorship. It's a Marxist view. Marx was very clear in the 1848 Manifesto of the Communist party that dictatorship of the proletariat was the essential means to the triumph of the working class. And without a dictatorship it couldn't be done. And all party members accept that."

"And sympathizers?"

"Sympathizers might be very critical. I knew some sympathizers — fellow travelers — who would say, 'Well, it's the best we've got. The Communist party is the most militant, forthright and capable opposition we have. I think for Russia perhaps it's the only way they can solve their problems. So even if we don't like what the Soviet Union does, we go along with them.' "

I pointed out that he himself had certainly been a "fellow traveler" to that extent.

"Yes, I suppose I was," he said. "I accepted the fact that civil liberties were not suitable for Russia, but I certainly didn't approve of the dictatorship. And I knew so many people in the United Front who said just what I'm saying now. And yet they wouldn't dream of accepting Communist leadership when it took positions they couldn't agree with, like the Nazi-Soviet pact or, even worse, the invasion of Finland. Hundreds left after that."

"Then did those people switch back when Hitler invaded Russia and Russia became our ally again?"

"Yes, some people veered around and said, well, perhaps they weren't so bad after all."

"Did you veer around and come back at all?"

"No. Goodness knows how quickly they would switch it again some other way. They were unreliable allies."

"So your sympathies never really went back to the Communists?"

"No, not to this day. Of course if I were faced with a choice between fascism and communism, I would still take communism. I hope to God I would never be faced with that though."

"Is there no way that you could become more reconciled to the Soviet Union and to communism now?"

"Not unless they changed to allow some kind of democratic liberties. They don't allow any. They've kicked Mr. Solzhenitsyn out and they kicked out all my friends."

"But they weren't allowing any democratic liberties when you were in Russia either. And they were also kicking people out, or people like Emma Goldman were leaving in disgust, when you were writing *Liberty under the Soviets.*"

"That's true certainly. But the big difference was that Mr.

Trotsky was still there when I wrote that book and they were still tolerating."

This was Roger's standard justification for the often indulgent tone of *Liberty under the Soviets* and since he knew as well as I that it was not really a weighty one, I saw no reason to press him further. However, a few days earlier he had told me that he thought I was not being controversial enough with him on whatever we had been talking about, so, determined to give him no further cause for complaint, I handed him a copy of the letter from the seventeen liberals in Corliss Lamont's book and asked him to read it.

"What's this, what's this?" he asked, glaring at the book, and of course knowing perfectly well what it was.

I watched him while he read quickly through the letter with its blast of the purge resolution ("The phrasing is dangerous; its context is worse"), its well-reasoned argument that, after all, civil liberties within the Soviet Union were no different before the pact than after. "Could it be," the seventeen liberals asked, "that the majority of the Board of Directors of the Civil Liberties Union is taking sides in the developing European conflict? Is their real objection an objection to the position of the Soviet Union in that conflict? Has the question anything to do with the need for defending civil liberties in America?"

"All this letter says" (Roger shoved the book back at me), "is that you shouldn't pay any attention to what happens abroad. All you should do is to test whether people are loyal by their behavior to the Constitution and the Bill of Rights of the United States and to hell with anything else. And if they've got conflicting loyalties, and they think the Soviet Union is a superior system of government, you should pay no attention to it. And if the Nazis and the Communists get together, that's none of our business. That's what this letter says."

"It also says" (I picked up the book) "that 'the Civil Liberties Union has often found it necessary to mobilize public sentiment in order to defend civil liberties. Never before has it been necessary to mobilize public sentiment in order to defend civil liberties within the Civil Liberties Union.'"

Again the answer shot back. "Their argument was based on *public* policy and not on private organization policy. The ACLU is a private organization, founded to fight that kind of thing in public life.

And a private organization is like a church. You don't take nonbelievers into the church. We are a church; we have a creed and only
true believers should lead us."

"You keep saying 'true believers.' "

"Because Elizabeth would be a nonbeliever. Any Communist
would be. Because Communists accept dictatorship and that is a denial of civil liberties. Today that would be just as true. Communists
can't stay in the Communist party and dissent."

"Yes," I said. "I see that point. But it seems to me that five years
later you had changed your tune slightly, because five years later you
gave a Town Hall of the Air talk called 'Is Communism a Menace to
the American Way of Life?' in which you concluded that it was not.
You said that the real menace came from anti-Communists defending the status quo of the privileged."

"That's very true," Roger said blandly. "Anti-communism was
much more of a menace to civil liberties. Communism never affected our civil liberties very much. And the Communist party in
the United States was certainly never strong enough to be a menace
at any time or in any way. The only menace was the people who
believed in a Communist dictatorship, which is a denial of civil liberties. They did not belong with us in a leadership position."

"On your Board, you mean?"

"On our Board. We didn't care about membership in the ACLU.
We just didn't want people to be directing the organization who
didn't believe wholeheartedly in what it stood for. But the Communists were never any menace," he repeated. "We defended them all
the time. We still defend them. We will always defend them.
Which is why in many places in this country the Civil Liberties
Union is thought of as a Communist organization."

I said, "You know of course that many people suspect that the
purpose of the purge resolution was to improve your image so the
ACLU would no longer be thought of as a Communist organization."

"No," he said. "We didn't do it for that purpose."

"But you were aware that it would probably help?"

"Yes, I think it did help. We could always say we have no Communists in the leadership of the ACLU and by express resolution we
do not invite them to serve. But it doesn't convince people. They
think that civil liberties in themselves are leftist concepts because you
are defending minorities."

"That's very true," I said. But then, knowing I still had one or two hard questions to put to him, I added, "By the way, are you finding this conversation controversial enough?"

"Fine, fine," he beamed. "I believe in a real cross-examination."

"All right then, the Dies Committee — "

"What about the Dies Committee?" His tone was sharp.

"Well, there is a suggestion in Corliss Lamont's book — and he also told me the same thing when I interviewed him — that Arthur Garfield Hays and Morris Ernst had met with Martin Dies in Washington and made a deal that if the ACLU Board purged itself of Communists, the Dies Committee would give it a clean bill of health."

"That myth has been exploded so many times," Roger said emphatically. "It was exploded immediately after it happened. It's right in the minutes of the Board meeting the next week that there was no truth in it."

"Are you saying that Mr. Hays and Mr. Ernst did not see Dies?"

"No, I'm saying that they did see him. They went to Washington, as the record shows, at the instruction of the Board to try to get a hearing for the ACLU. But we never did get it. The Dies Committee never heard us."

"So there was no deal? The purge resolution had nothing at all to do with cozying up to the Dies Committee? There is no truth to that at all?"

"No truth at all! Absolutely none whatsoever! Corliss Lamont is very gullible. He'll believe anything he wants to believe. And he suspected some connection — but it was just a suspicion. All the evidence is to the contrary."

After a moment I said, "The atmosphere on the Board must have been really grim with all those suspicions and factions."

"It was terrible — terrible. The mutual tolerance we had always had gave way to mistrust. After the pact was signed in August, Elizabeth and the fellow travelers — about six or seven of them I guess — were waiting for the party line. So they were determined that we had to go on just as we were with no test of loyalty to our principles."

"What about Dr. Ward?"

"Oh, he was a strong partisan of no action, and of course nobody wanted to oppose the chairman. So the Board meetings were indecisive affairs, very tense and unhappy, with each group suspecting the other of trying to adopt some factional policy. As director I conceived myself as having responsibility for trying to hold the organization together. I would count votes before a meeting, based on who was coming, so I could decide what items to put on the agenda to avoid a fight. I would make up the agenda on the day of the meeting so that every last-minute proposal could be discussed. And most of those proposals were mine."

"Well that ties in with your detractors who say that you were the one who did all the work behind the scenes and pulled all the strings."

"That's the silliest idea in the world," Roger said vehemently. "These were strong-minded people; the evidence in that book on the expulsion of Elizabeth shows how strong-minded they were. I couldn't manipulate people like that."

"But you *did* manipulate them. You were the one who wrote the purge resolution."

"Yes, and the first draft I wrote was defeated."

"Never mind the first draft. The final draft was accepted because you were determined to see it through."

"Yes, I was. I was determined to see it through to a firm declaration of policy. I foresaw that it would probably result in a split and probably Elizabeth's expulsion, but it seemed to me the only way to save the organization from complete disruption."

"And then when Miss Flynn wouldn't resign, you were the one who fixed it so Dorothy Bromley would bring the charge against her because you thought it would look better to have a woman do it."

"Now wait a minute — wait a minute. Now you're talking about tactics. That's another matter entirely. How you handle the tactics within the organization is quite different from a matter of principle. I had to use what I could. And the main point about a tactic is not to use anybody to do anything they don't want to do."

"Who was Mrs. Bromley anyhow?"

"Dorothy Dunbar Bromley was a columnist for the Scripps-Howard newspapers and I didn't persuade her to do anything she didn't want to do." His tone suggested quite firmly that that was that.

Turning once more to the Lamont book, I leafed through quickly to find the actual charge that Mrs. Bromley had submitted. "I hereby formulate the following charge against Elizabeth Gurley Flynn," it read, "and ask that a hearing be held as to whether Miss Flynn be expelled on the basis of the charge that Elizabeth Gurley

Flynn is not entitled to retain directorship on the Board on the ground that she is a member of the Communist party."

Seeing those words in cold print, even after all that Roger had said to justify them and their implicit meaning, I still experienced a slightly chilling discomfort that such a resolution should have come before and been passed by the board of directors of the American Civil Liberties Union!

But nothing was to be gained by replowing the same ground. So instead I asked, "What about Elizabeth Flynn herself?"

"Oh Elizabeth," Roger spoke warmly. "Two hundred pounds of horse sense, Albert de Silver once said of her. She had great personality, great charm."

"How did you first come to know her?"

"In my St. Louis days, when I was much interested in the IWW boys, the name Elizabeth Gurley Flynn became familiar in the strike news. I kept seeing stories about the girl leader, Irish and beautiful, along with Carlo Tresca, the Italian anarchist."

"Wasn't Tresca the one who was murdered?"

"Yes, shot in the dark."

"And you spoke at his memorial service?"

"I don't remember. I probably did. I certainly would have. I would have done anything for Carlo. He was a great guy. But that was much later — long after Elizabeth died and he was living with Margaret de Silver, Albert's widow. Anyhow, after the war when I was looking for some working-class allies to join the first ACLU Board, I found Elizabeth in New York in the Workers' Defense League. Her interests were exactly what the ACLU proposed to defend, so we elected her to the first Board. She was an active and a faithful member. We became good friends socially, and all through those twenty years we had no differences of any consequence. And in fact, even in the three months that led up to the Board meeting [Roger never referred to it as a trial] my relations with Elizabeth were the same as ever."

Considering what Miss Flynn had to say in the *Daily Worker* about the "breezy fellow" whose integrity she questioned, I found that hard to believe and said so.

"It's true," he answered. "If you want to know, I myself took her to the Board meeting in a taxi."

I refrained from saying that I found that even harder to believe. But indeed, for anyone who knows Roger, there could be no greater warrant of his regard for Miss Flynn than that he should have spent money on a *taxi* to transport her.

"And did you ever see her again?"

"No, I never did. We exchanged some letters, we phoned on one or two occasions. There were no ill feelings. Just a sense of regret that such decisions had to be made and that they were more important than friendship."

Two weeks after the trial Roger spoke at the memorial service of another woman whose friendship, despite the many strains upon it, he had managed to retain.

Emma Goldman died on May 14, 1940, one week after the expulsion of Elizabeth Gurley Flynn, an action of which, one must assume, she would have approved.* Indeed she had continued to excoriate Roger in her letters for his naiveté about Russia, his "indefiniteness" about Russia ("very characteristic in you") for a number of years. Then Roger reviewed her book *Living My Life* for the *Survey Magazine*. "A rare and dynamic document," he called it, "vivid and nakedly honest, it reveals a great personality."

At once the "quality" of his writing, the "clarity" of his style and manner caused Emma Goldman to see him in quite another light. "Never before have I read anything of yours so splendidly done," she wrote him. "I always felt you to be a reformer, sincere in improving conditions, patching up as it were, but nothing fundamental. I was happy to see that the sacred fire of revolt is in your soul — " but then she felt compelled to add, "even if you have rarely shown it in your actions."

At the memorial meeting held May 31, 1940, at Town Hall in New York tributes were paid to Miss Goldman by Roger, by Norman Thomas, John Haynes Holmes, and by the sane male anarchist, Harry Kelly, among others. "It was the last chapter of a long and very fruitful friendship," Roger wrote to a friend to whom he sent the program of the memorial. "I think I owe more to E.G. than to anybody for the essential direction of such philosophy and social relations as I have. She opened up a world of thought and ideals at a time I needed something more searching than sociology and social work. And I have never strayed far from the moorings I put down then."

* On June 21st, 1976, it was announced that the ACLU Board had repealed the 1940 expulsion of Elizabeth Gurley Flynn.

(17)

Boxing the Compass

COMPARED TO ROGER'S TIRELESS AND EFFECTIVE fomenting that brought forth the Civil Liberties Bureau in World War I, his activities in World War II seemed very pale; indeed one pacifist group was reported to have said of the ACLU that it was "born in World War I and died in World War II."

Roger, of course, does not accept this untimely epitaph, and with very good reason. He does, however, agree that his own attitude toward the Second World War was very different — also perhaps for very good reasons. Pearl Harbor, the first attack by a foreign country on the United States, made this a defensive war; fierce hatred and fear of Hitler in Europe nullified opposition to hostilities and unified national purpose. Therefore, few of the tensions between opponents and advocates of the war, so pervasive in 1918, surfaced in 1942.

Nonetheless there were countless conscientious objectors, many of whom accused Roger of backsliding from his uncompromising World War I stand. "They expected support of their *positions*," Roger said in his Oral History, "while the Union was committed only to support of their *rights*. Where their moral positions — and I'd concede morality to any objector, whatever his stand — went beyond legal aid, we declined to support them. The absolutists were especially critical, yet there was nothing we could do to aid a man who refused all service except to give him our blessings on his way to prison."

In other aspects, the ACLU position after Pearl Harbor was also somewhat muted, largely because there seemed to be no real suppression of rights. According to Lucille Milner, secretary of the Union, "There was not a case of mob violence or vigilantism reported to the Civil Liberties Union; no spy hunting; no demand to jail or suppress anyone. Our representatives in the leading cities reported that there was very little interference with any of our civil rights as a result of the war. Public discussion of war issues was free but 'discreet' . . . Spy hunting was left to the proper authorities rather than to loyalty leagues and neighbors."

There is considerable question, however, how those "proper authorities" handled the matter of spy-hunting and how the Union, accustomed as it was to the tactics of professional patriots, responded to the methods of the government. Probably the most undeniable misuse of civil liberties by the United States resulted from Roosevelt's order, shortly after Pearl Harbor, that allowed the army to establish military zones anywhere in the country and then to remove from these zones any persons considered dangerous to national security.

The outcome, claimed a military necessity, was that 112,000 Japanese-Americans, two-thirds of whom were American citizens, were evacuated from their homes and sent to detention camps. Although the ACLU ultimately termed this "the worst single wholesale violation of civil rights of American citizens in our history," there are many who consider that the Union reacted far too mildly and too slowly to this blatant suppression. Among these is Dwight Macdonald who, in his 1953 *New Yorker* profile "In Defense of Everybody," makes it clear that he doesn't think much of Roger's apparent lassitude on this critical issue. Roger doesn't think much of Dwight Macdonald either, but he admits, reluctantly, that he can be counted on to be factually if not interpretively correct. "Dwight Macdonald is a good civil libertarian," Roger conceded, "but he didn't think I was one."

"No, he didn't. And he called your reaction to the Japanese internment 'feeble and confused.' "

"That wasn't my fault," Roger said, instantly defensive. "I take no responsibility for that. That was because our West Coast branches wouldn't go along with us."

"On the contrary," I said, "Macdonald implies they went further than you did. He says, 'The two Union affiliates in California after initial hesitation took a much firmer stand than the parent body.' And he adds that they carried two cases up to the Supreme Court!"

"We took a case up to the Supreme Court too; not from San Francisco but from Seattle, a case called Gordon-Hirabayashi. We took that up from the national office, so the question of whether we were weak compared to the California branches is a matter of opinion."

"Perhaps. But it's not a matter of opinion that, as he says, it was eleven days after the President's order that you made your first statement in which you criticized the order briefly and then went on to say that the ACLU had not the slightest intention of interfering with any necessary moves to protect the West Coast area. You added, 'We recognize this as the first and essential consideration.' "

"Well maybe I did say that, yes. But I remember there was a submarine — a Japanese submarine that did shell the California coast and scared the life out of them."

Ignoring this diversionary tactic, I pressed on with Dwight Macdonald's attack on him. "Three weeks later, he says, you got around to making a fuller statement, in which you said you considered the order open to grave question on constitutional grounds and expressed the hope that there would be 'an effort to reconcile, as far as possible, civil rights with military necessity.' And he says that those two statements represented the sum total of your public activity on behalf of the Nisei during the crucial early months of the evacuation. His argument is that if you had acted sooner you might have helped."

"I don't agree. I don't agree that we could have helped because it was only the army that was for the evacuation and they persuaded Frank Roosevelt that there was a danger on the West Coast. But the navy was against it, the air force was against it, Roosevelt's attorney general was against it, and even J. Edgar Hoover was against it. And if none of them could do any good, we certainly couldn't have."

"Still, I've known you to fight hopeless battles before. And I would have thought this would have been one of your biggest fights, because it was such a terrible thing our government was doing."

"Terrible thing. Terrible, yes, sure. But, well — perhaps in wartime it's very difficult to say that national security shouldn't be the first consideration. After all, you have to win a war. You can't lose it."

Although "national security," particularly in wartime, had not taken on the falsely sacrosanct overtones in 1942 that it came to have in the Nixon regime, I was nonetheless surprised to hear Roger invoke it. And many on the ACLU Board, although not a majority, felt that, in any case, national security could not justify any abrogation of civil liberties.

Once again the Board split into two factions with Whitney North Seymour, a conservative lawyer, leading the faction that put the war effort ahead of civil liberties and Norman Thomas leading the minority that took the opposite stand. As usual Roger was called upon to forge a compromise, in which he said, "The Union will not participate — except where fundamentals of due process are denied — in cases where, after investigation, there are grounds for belief that the defendant is cooperating with . . . the enemy."

Dwight Macdonald quotes Roger as saying about that statement, "I hated to write that one, and I'm ashamed of it now."

"Were you really ashamed of it?" I asked him.

"Well, that's pretty strong language."

"Yes, but it's your language that Macdonald is quoting."

"All right, then I suppose I said that to him. I don't remember. As I think of it now, I only remember that the compromise worked. It kept us together. We would have flown apart if we hadn't adopted something of the sort. But," he added, "I don't like compromises anyway."

"Oh come on now, Roger. Compromises are your stock in trade, aren't they?"

"They may be, but I still don't like them. I don't like to have to sit down and draft statements that are going to please both sides. I had to do it, of course, to hold the organization together, but when I was speaking for myself I never compromised."

"In the United Fronts?"

"Same thing. I was always holding the organization together."

"Yes, that's true."

"But" (he became suddenly quite bellicose), "I'd like to see the evidence that I ever compromised on principle. Occasionally I compromised on method. I am not and never have been dogmatic about what's right and wrong. I know judgments must be relative and that two rights are as likely to conflict as a right and a wrong. But on the whole, I think the ACLU over its fifty-five years has been about as consistent as the enormous pressures on it permitted. Just think of the unprecedented world events: almost continuous wars — hot and cold — revolution, collapse of the economy, the stronger role of government and the rise of minorities to equal rights. We played a part in all these experiences. And certainly we achieved recognition of our good faith in World War Two. If we hadn't, I certainly never would have been invited by General MacArthur to go to Japan."

It is impossible to overestimate the important part that General MacArthur played in the political life of Roger Baldwin. Equally it is difficult to understand how an army general — especially this army general — could conceivably have found such favor in the eyes of an acknowledged pacifist. But Roger relishes this inconsistency and is fond of saying how he has "boxed the compass" from Emma Goldman to Douglas MacArthur.

On January 9, 1947, Roger received a letter from the War Department saying that they had been requested by General MacArthur's headquarters in Japan to determine whether he would be available to "proceed to Japan and Korea for a sixty- or ninety-day period to consult with appropriate members of the Supreme Commander's staff on civil liberties." If he were available to accept this important assignment and interested in "rendering invaluable assistance to the success of our country's policies in the Far East," would he please fill in the enclosed copies of Standard Form 57, Application for Federal Employment, and return them at the "earliest possible date."

This letter came to Roger out of the blue. However, his involvement with problems of civil liberties in Japan had begun fifteen months earlier when on October 5, 1945, he had written to an old friend, the Baroness Ishimoto — a leading feminist whom he had known through Margaret Sanger — expressing his concern for the distress of the Japanese people at the end of the war and suggesting that the ACLU might be of help in influencing American policy on civil liberties.

His letter was promptly answered; by then the baroness had divorced the baron and was remarried to a Mr. Kanju Kato, a Japanese labor leader, whom, as it happened, Roger had also once met in New York. "We are both interested in establishing a unit of civil liberties in Japan," wrote Mrs. Kato. "Both Mr. Kato and I think this is the thing to be done here as the democratization of Japan is starting."

Roger at once set the wheels in motion; he got in touch with a young friend of his, John Orton (he had first met him at an Eleanor Roosevelt conference at Hyde Park), who was stationed at Supreme Commander Allied Powers (SCAP) Headquarters, and asked him to look into the civil liberties situation and also to get in touch with the Katos. Orton wrote back promptly and encouragingly, "The people are slowly feeling their way into the new freedom of expression and action," he said. Roger then wrote Mrs. Kato saying that Johnnie Orton had confirmed her feelings that an organization "working for the principles of democracy without partisanship of any kind would be useful in Japan." He understood that funds would be required to get such a movement going and he was confident that internationally minded people would contribute; if Mrs. Kato would please let him know how much money she needed to start off, he would see what he could do to raise it.

All this, of course, was simply a matter of Roger's doing his job, spreading the gospel where it obviously needed spreading. The notion that he himself would be personally involved in civil liberties in Japan, let alone civil liberties as practiced by the supreme commander of the occupying forces, never entered his mind. He was therefore "thunderstruck" when he received his letter from the War Department.

He may actually have been just a little embarrassed at the time that the ACLU should have become so eminently respectable that the army would invite its director to accept such a position, and even more so that the director's own record as a conscientious objector and fellow traveler would fit him for such an invitation. Actually, he says, his first thought was that someone had slipped up in checking his background and that of course General MacArthur himself knew nothing of the request made in his name.

The ACLU Board, Roger stated in his Oral History, was "overwhelmed with delight at the compliment. I was more discreet," he continues. "The conviction grew on me that, although this was not a time when excitement over communism was high, it might be high enough to raise an outcry over my United Front associations in the thirties."

Accordingly, Roger paid a call on J. Parnell Thomas, a man who was certainly not a friend and who for precisely that reason could be counted on to be the chief outcrier if there was to be one. Congressman Thomas, the chairman of the House Un-American Activities Committee, strongly advised Roger not to go to Japan at government expense, but to go as a private citizen at his own (or rather the ACLU's) expense. Roger was very much of the same mind himself and the Union Board readily agreed. The army, however, was dubious; no person had yet gone to Japan as a private citizen, and in order for Roger to go in that capacity, General MacArthur himself would have to approve. Boldly Roger suggested that MacArthur be queried and to everyone's surprise the general cabled Washington on March 4, 1947, saying that Mr. Baldwin could come on his own terms.

Roger was elated. He immediately put out a spate of memos and press releases on his projected service to civil liberties in Japan. He proposed to have meetings with lawyers, labor leaders, educators, political party leaders; he suggested the possibility of delivering some lectures on his own on such topics as "What Chance for World Democracy," "The United Nations and Human Rights," "The Prospects for Race Equality," "Democracy vs. Communism," in order to test reaction, particularly among students. He wanted to study problems of control of the press, freedom of speech, trade union relations to government and business, protection of minority rights, women's rights. His overall aim was to help build up an international democracy; his effort to reach "the native forces interested in international cooperation" was, he said, the first to be permitted since the war. His mission was therefore unique. So too was his status.

Although he still retained the original letter of invitation from the War Department that was to be his sole authority for being in Japan, he could not be regarded as an agent of the United States speaking for his government. Rather he felt he was to be looked upon as an individual speaking for "fraternal organizations" such as the International League for the Rights of Man, the World Federation of the United Nations Association and, of course, the ACLU, from all of which he carried flattering letters of introduction (including the one from the ACLU that he wrote himself).

Still there was also a certain ambiguity in being, as he put it, on nobody's payroll and under nobody's control. To Johnnie Orton, Roger wrote, saying, "I reckon you are my personal ambassador at the court of MacArthur." After telling him that he would be coming by boat, arriving in Yokohama on the *General Gordon* on April 12, he noted that, private citizen or not, everything he wanted to do depended on MacArthur, whom he hoped to meet shortly after his arrival. Meanwhile would Orton please find out exactly who at SCAP had asked for him to come in the first place so that he could "confer with that section at once and act as if I were coming for that service alone." Further he asked his young friend (who was also a friend of Evelyn's) to find where he could get bed and meals ("You know me, any old place will do"), to arrange for an interpreter, "preferably a Nisei who knows the USA and whose viewpoint would be close to mine." Meanwhile, until further notice he would use Orton's section at SCAP (Statistical Reports Section) as his address. "It is sure fortunate," he concluded, "I have you to lean on, or I should be quite lost without definite contact at GHQ."

As it turned out, Roger did not in the least need Orton to lean on; in fact he tends today rather to belittle the idea that he ever even *thought* he would need him. Still he admits that on the boat going to Yokohama he continued to feel somewhat uneasy about having nothing really "laid on" for him in Tokyo. Then one day he met a delightful fellow passenger, a Japanese lady who, as it turned out, was a Protestant minister and one of the few people who had been permitted to leave Japan during the occupation.

"She was a lovely lady," Roger recalled. "What was her name now? I can't remember, but she had lectured in the United States on the Japanese; sort of a messenger of peace she was, and on the boat she said to me, 'Don't worry about where you'll stay in Japan. My friends will put you up and you can work from there. We can get you transportation and see that you get around.' So I was greatly relieved and I certainly expected to do that.

"But when the boat docked in Yokohama I was called from my cabin to the purser's office and there was a colonel from General MacArthur's office [in the Oral History he was a major] and he said to me, 'General MacArthur presents his compliments and invites you to be his guest at the Imperial Hotel. He has put a car and driver at your disposal for the entire time you are here.' That was my welcome to Japan. I said good-by to Mrs. whatever-her-name-was, thanked her very much and told her I was going to be taken care of otherwise."

"And never saw her again?"

"Of course I saw her again," Roger answered indignantly. "She was a good friend of mine all the time I was in Japan."

"All right," I prompted, sorry to have interrupted him, "you had a car and driver — "

"With VIP on the windshield."

"You were put up free at the Imperial Hotel?"

"Except for meals which were twenty-five cents apiece."

"Roger, you must have been in heaven."

"Oh I was, but that wasn't all. I had an office in the Radio Tokyo Building with the Civil Information and Education Section, headed by a Colonel Don Nugent, an old Japan hand who was a very kindly and cooperative fellow but a bit mouselike; he worshiped Mac-Arthur."

"And how soon did you meet the great man?" I asked.

"The very next day after my arrival I was invited for lunch. It was a Sunday, I remember. I was driven to the American Embassy, which was where the MacArthurs lived. Mrs. MacArthur was there, so was Colonel Nugent, but the general hadn't come back from his office yet. After a bit he came striding in, kissed his wife, then came over to me and said, 'Mr. Baldwin, we've been waiting for you for a long time. I'm very glad you're here at last.' He was very cordial, very cheerful, very unmilitary — a very charming gentleman. As we went in to lunch I remember he put his arm around my shoulder."

Roger looked at me quizzically. "I know," he said agreeably. "You disliked his vanity and his pomposity and I don't blame you. But those qualities didn't show in private."

I asked him to tell me what did show in private.

"Well, I realized from that very first luncheon that he saw things the way we did. He couldn't have been more completely of our persuasion."

"A true believer?"

"Yes, exactly. That's what he was. But even before I met him, I had been very impressed with his speech on the *Missouri* at the time of the Japanese surrender. It was a very magnanimous speech you know; it was not the speech of a conqueror talking to a defeated nation, but the speech of a man who respected the enemy and regretted the war. It was a pacifist speech. But what I wondered about was his actual policy, if he was really carrying out the delicate concern for the feelings of a defeated people that he had shown in his speech."

"And you decided he was."

"What he said to me that first day was, 'I want you to see everybody, go everywhere; every door is open to you. I want you to tell me what you think is wrong about the Occupation policies in regard to the democratic purposes that we're trying to instill in the Japanese people. See what they'll do to respond to this kind of appeal, try to form whatever organizations are necessary. And tell me what we can do better.'

"You know," Roger added, seeing me continue to look skeptical although perhaps a bit less so, "there were many others like me who reacted the way I did to General MacArthur. For instance, a friend of mine, Mark Starr, who was educational director of the ILGWU, had been there before I was to try to start some educational work among the trade unions. He was an old socialist and certainly no admirer of the military and he had an interview with MacArthur and was just as impressed as I was. And then Walter Gellhorn, who was on our ACLU Board and is a professor of law at Columbia and very much of a libertarian, spent a sabbatical year in Japan and he looked very favorably on what MacArthur had accomplished."

I asked Roger how often he had seen the general while he was there.

"I should say five or six times in three months. I didn't see him of course unless I thought there was something he ought to do or know about."

"What sort of thing would you bring to his attention?"

"Well, censorship for one thing."

"What sort of censorship?"

"Censorship of the press. They had to have it, you know; but it was handled very subtly. It was done by briefings and not by actually cutting things out of the newspapers. An Occupation official met the press every morning at nine and told them what they should emphasize and what they should leave out."

I said that didn't sound like much of a civil liberties policy.

"It wasn't civil liberties at all. That's why I complained to MacArthur about it."

"You complained and then what happened?"

"Oh I think he modified it a good deal. Of course the general said you have to have some censorship. Under the Occupation there are some of our policies that we can't let them criticize because that would make it too difficult for us to carry them out. But I was surprised that the things they told the press to emphasize were always in the right direction."

"How about the things they told them *not* to emphasize or to leave out?"

"Also in the right direction. For instance they would say we don't want any favorable mention of such and such an organization which had been very militaristic. We don't want any mention at all of organizations that were responsible for bringing the military to power because the Occupation policy is to get rid of them. Well, you know I couldn't take exception to that."

"Perhaps not, but some of the journalists could, I should have thought."

"No, the Japanese were very obedient. I don't think they ever violated Occupation policy."

"Was there any other sort of censorship?"

"Yes, unfortunately there was. They opened mail. They had a spot check on certain letters and they had Japanese interpreters there to translate those letters and see what the Japanese were saying to each other about the Occupation. I saw that happening with my own eyes in the Osaka post office."

"And of course you reported that to General MacArthur."

"I did. I said, this is all wrong. People aren't going to write things in letters that are subversive or critical of the Occupation. So I don't think you ought to interfere with the Japanese personal correspondence. You can't get much out of it."

It did not surprise me that Roger would disapprove of anyone opening anyone else's mail. Still I could not help noticing that it was not so much the principle that he appeared, by his own account, to object to, but the fact that the practice would not yield any useful information. After a moment's reflection on this point, I asked what the general had said about mail censorship.

"He denied it existed. He said he had given strict orders that mail was not to be tampered with. But I told him what I'd seen at the Osaka post office and he said he'd look into it, and the next time we met he said, 'You're right, Mr. Baldwin. Even my own mail was opened. I found a letter that had been opened and resealed and I put a stop to the whole system.' "

Seeing that I was not greatly moved by this account, Roger tried again. "There were other things we talked about too. I remember one day saying to him, 'General, why are you participating in sin?' Naturally he asked me what I meant and I said, 'All these American

GI's are living with Japanese girls and having babies and you won't let them marry. Or if they do marry, you send the GI's home and won't let their wives go with them." But what else could he do, he asked. He couldn't let the Japanese wives go back to the United States because the Oriental Exclusion Act prevented it. So I said to him, 'Why don't you get Congress to change the law?' And that's exactly what he did. He got the 'Brides' Act' passed."

I said I was surprised that the general hadn't thought of that relatively obvious solution himself.

"Well, he didn't think of a lot of things," Roger answered. "He said he had me over there to think for him."

"It sounds to me as if he needed you quite a lot."

"He thought so."

"Well now, what about your other contacts. All those other people you were going to meet with."

"Oh I met with them all right. I started off working mostly through bar associations because they were the ones who had first formed any kind of a civil liberties organization. I met with them repeatedly and I saw everyone else in Tokyo from the attorney general to the prime minister."

"And out of all that the Japanese Civil Liberties Union was formed?"

"Yes, it was, but apart from the JCLU and, I think, even more important under the circumstances, was the governmental system set up to monitor civil liberties. The whole program was in the charge of the attorney general and they had an attorney general in every single one of the forty-nine prefectures in Japan; six thousand private citizens volunteered to act as civil rights commissioners, as they were called, to report any civil liberties or civil rights violations. Now that's a better system than ours, but the Japanese are so teachable that it really isn't surprising that once they got the notion, they did much better with it than any other country has done."

Roger also formed a United Nations Association in Japan, and started a branch of the Japanese American Citizens' League, an organization that had its headquarters in Salt Lake City. His major preoccupation in this connection was to try to help the over 5,000 Nisei who had been caught in Japan at the outbreak of the war and who had as a result lost their American citizenship and were fighting to regain their right to return to the United States.

Characteristically Roger's social life was very full. He had become friendly with Mrs. Elizabeth Vining, a Philadelphia Quaker who was a Bryn Mawr graduate, author of numerous children's books and tutor to the Crown Prince. She was a charming "widow lady" who had been adopted by the imperial family, so all doors were open to her and she swung a number of them open to Roger as well. Of course he had many contacts of his own among the Japanese through Mrs. Kato and John Orton, and he also soon joined the Tokyo Harvard Club where he found a very cordial atmosphere between Japanese and Americans.

Almost the only constraint he felt during his three months in Japan was among the Occupation personnel — not of course General MacArthur — but some of his underlings, military men who seemed to Roger to take the attitude that his being there was "a lot of damn foolishness and what is this fellow Baldwin doing around here anyhow trying to make us all behave like civilians."

Various of Roger's Japanese friends, among them George Togesako, the editor of the English-language *Nippon Times,* were eager for him to have an interview with Emperor Hirohito. Roger claims to have been somewhat reluctant at the idea of such a meeting since emperors are hardly the meat of democratic civil libertarians, but when General MacArthur gave his warm approval the audience was arranged.

Roger went to the Imperial Palace armed with a box of candy for the Emperor and some "new style pencils" for the Emperor's children. The meeting, which was widely reported in the United States, went well. After a predictably stiff opening, Hirohito expressed great faith in the United Nations and in the possibility of creating an ordered world without war. He spoke with approval of Occupation policies and hoped that the forces would stay in Japan until their job was completed. In every way Roger found this essentially shy little man to be "very responsive to liberal and democratic ideas."

At the end of their forty-minute talk, Roger presented the box of candy and the pencils for the children, remarking as he did so that the Emperor's three youngest children were the same ages as his three. (Roger always refers to and considers his stepsons, Roger and Carl, as his own.) The two gentlemen then exchanged a few fatherly pleasantries about their children and Roger was ushered out. The following day a chamberlain from the palace arrived at Roger's

hotel bearing three "exquisite pieces of art metal" as a token of esteem from the Emperor's three children to Roger's three.

"Of course you must remember," Roger said, returning to his favorite theme, "that it was entirely thanks to General MacArthur that
the Emperor was allowed to remain. The general realized right
from the start that he had to have the Emperor to rely on. The Emperor was the supreme head of the state and the Japanese would do
what he told them to."

"Wasn't MacArthur afraid that the Emperor would interfere with
his own mastery?"

"Sure he was, but he still knew he had to depend on him. He
said, 'I can't work without the Emperor. If you destroy him, you destroy my authority.' "

"Exactly who did he say that to?"

"Oh, there was a lot of opposition to keeping the Emperor, in
Congress particularly. The fact is that the war could have ended
sooner if the United States and the Allies had been reasonable and
guaranteed to the Japanese that they could keep their Emperor.
But we weren't making any promises to the Japanese. It was really
only the great prestige of MacArthur that did it. I'm sure the opposition would have prevailed if he hadn't taken such a fervent
stand in favor of keeping the Emperor. But he was always so respectful of the Japanese and their institutions. He never tried to interfere with them except in terms of liberalizing them and democra-
tizing them and stopping the restrictions. Of course" — he broke
off for a moment — "of course, I have to say that MacArthur approved of trying war criminals."

"You didn't approve?"

"Well, it's hard to say. In Japan it wasn't like the German trials in
Nuremberg, which I also went to, and which were based on the
theory of making aggressive war. The Japanese indictments were
not based on any such generality. They were based on specific acts."

"So you disapproved less in Tokyo than in Nuremberg."

"I think," Roger said finally, "that for the victors to try the van-
quished is a very bad business. And that's what happened in
Nuremberg; and that's also what happened in Tokyo."

Thus, since MacArthur, as victor, had approved trying the van-
quished, this was as close as I ever heard Roger come to an unfavor-
able word on the general. In fact it struck me that Roger's insistence

on going to Japan as a private citizen rather than as a War Department employee, so that he would be free to criticize what he saw, was, as it turned out, an unnecessary precaution.

Still, it is only fair to report that in his Oral History, which was recorded in January 1954, Roger did make a less than idolatrous statement. Someone had called MacArthur a Dr. Jekyll and Mr. Hyde and Roger conceded that he had met only Dr. Jekyll. "Mr. Hyde came out later," he said. "I was distressed by MacArthur's fall from grace — my grace — a year later when he banned all strikes against the government and collective bargaining in government unions. I deplored his getting tough with the Communists and so driving them underground. I applauded my friends in the labor section who resigned in protest. I was stunned and disgusted with the general's political ambition to run for the presidency, influenced doubtless by flattery and false prophets who had been too long away from the American scene."

"However," Roger concluded in his Oral History, "I have never qualified my admiration for what I saw of his role in 1947." And when Roger returned to the States from Japan in 1947, he came back with the zeal of a missionary, to glorify "the historic miracle" created by his new-found hero. Indeed, the various articles he wrote on the subject were as extreme, in the opposite direction, as his piece in *Soviet Russia Today* had been eighteen years earlier.

In one called "Shogun and Emperor," for example, he expressed amazement at the extent of skepticism that greeted his frequent and enthusiastic estimates of MacArthur. "The general is engaged in a crusade," he wrote. "A crusade for democracy . . . For the first time in history an autocratic military machine is succeeding in establishing practices of democracy in a land dominated for centuries by feudal lords, despots and family oligarchies. The evidence of success on the political and psychological fronts is overwhelming.

"I know little of the general's past in relation to his understanding of democracy," he continued, "but I do not hesitate to say that today he is one of the few men I have met in public life with an almost missionary spirit of promoting it. On every point we discussed I found him at once sensitive to the highest concepts of our democratic ideals. That covers not only political and social democracy but economic too — the issues of trade union rights, monopolies, special privilege in any form. He not only thinks in democratic terms but feels deeply and with assured conviction of their value. His attitude is that of a man with a profound sense of religion in his human relationships. Some of his associates call it 'mystical.' It is, in the sense of an abused word, 'spiritual' . . .

"But what my skeptical critics ask is how a general never known to be a liberal can so change his outlook, and can it be genuine when he is so warmly supported in the United States by some of the most unreconstructed Tories in our national politics."

Then, in a canny little jab, Roger concluded, "I cannot explain so readily why the Tories think he is their man. I don't know any Tories well enough to ask."

(18)

Keeper of the American Conscience

"Except for Franklin Roosevelt," I said to Roger one day, "we have talked very little about the Presidents and not at all about their attitudes toward civil liberties."

"Yes," said Roger, "and that's the sort of question you should have asked me before."

"I'm asking it right now. Specifically, will you tell me about your relations with the White House over the years and about how they varied from President to President?"

"Well, let me say first that the ACLU's relation as an organization to the presidency was quite remote. We did not have people — friends — on the White House staff that we could go to and make representations for civil liberties matters except, of course, in the Roosevelt administration and in the Truman administration, and, yes, we did in the Eisenhower and the Kennedy, and in the Johnson administration too for that matter."

"In other words, the Presidents on whose staffs you did not have friends were Hoover — "

"Oh but we had one on Hoover's staff," Roger broke in, "Albert Lasker, a member of his sub-Cabinet, was a fairly good friend of ours and we could go to him on matters."

"In other words," I tried again, "the President — singular — on whose staff you did not have a friend was Nixon."

"Certainly not," said Roger indignantly. "I don't think that our people ever knew one person in the Nixon White House."

Having thus established Roger's "remote" connection with the White House, I asked if we could go back a little further to the beginnings of the ACLU and to President Wilson.

"When Wilson came to the City Club in St. Louis as a candidate he impressed me as an exciting crusader for reforms. In fact I was quite a Wilson fan until he went to war. Then the Civil Liberties Bureau had a direct approach to him through Nevin Sayre, who was the brother of his son-in-law. I used it some, but to not much result. John Nevin Sayre, by the way, was the head of the Fellowship of Reconciliation."

"Of which you were also a member."

"Yes, I was a member way back in 1915 when it was a very, very Christian association because Sayre was very, very Christian. Too Christian; the Fellowship suffered for it. Now they have rabbis and Buddhists and anybody who believes in nonviolence. But when I joined, you practically had to be an evangelical moralist to be in; but they accepted me because, for some reason, they regarded me as a Christian."

"Which, after all, you are."

"Oh well, only as a Unitarian, and that's the mildest kind of Christian."

"But you still stuck to the Fellowship?"

"All the time. In fact I'm still a member. It's the one pacifist association that I have consistently maintained, but less on a Christian than a humanitarian basis. So" (he changed his tone briskly), "that takes care of our contact with Wilson. Now Harding — Harding we approached through Norman Thomas, of all people, who came from his home town of Marion, Ohio. We used Norman to help us get amnesty for war offenders with some success. Then Coolidge was approachable through Harlan Stone, his great attorney general, who was our good friend and whom we used quite effectively. But Coolidge usually acted to avoid a fuss rather than to assert a principle. Hoover we've already touched on; he was not really our man. Roosevelt, on the other hand, was so much our man there's no use mentioning him. Everyone in the White House was our friend in those days. It was almost the same with Truman where our access was also very good through David Niles, who was the President's contact with liberals and do-gooders. It was to Niles that I sent my views of MacArthur's role in Japan and Niles expressed to me Truman's appreciation."

"And when Truman fired MacArthur, whose side were you on then?"

"Oh, on Truman's, of course. The general tried to put himself above Truman and you can't do that to the President. Besides, I think Truman was a very good President — the best we've had since Roosevelt. He was a crusader, an honest fellow, a very simple kind man. We haven't really had a good President since. Certainly not Eisenhower. We had little contact with him in the ACLU, although he did have a fellow named Max Rabb, who was secretary of the Cabinet, I believe. We could go to him and he would present our positions to the President. But Eisenhower never did much about them."

"So that brings us to Kennedy."

"Well, Jack Kennedy was really one of us in spirit. And he had some very smart boys around him who knew what was going on. Let me see, who did we use there? I guess Bill vanden Heuvel who worked for Robert and Ted was our man. And the only time I ever got invited to the White House was by Kennedy."

"Not by Roosevelt?"

"Oh, I might have been invited to some conferences and receptions where there were a lot of people, but I never got what you might call a personal invitation until Jack Kennedy asked me to come to a luncheon for Tito, where I met the assorted big shots and shook the proper hands.

"Lyndon Johnson had a professor from Princeton — I forget his name — who became disillusioned with the Vietnam policy and quit.* And then John Roche who was hell-bent for Vietnam replaced him. I don't remember if it was through him or someone else that we had access to that administration. I don't even know who induced Johnson to send me a fulsome letter of congratulation on my eightieth birthday, but it was a surprise.

"Nixon I had met once when he was a congressman and someone arranged a debate between us about the House Un-American Activities Committee. It was quite an amicable affair and Nixon said he'd like to see me again, but he had different feelings later when he declined to send a message to the American Jewish Committee dinner where I was being honored. As I said, I never met him after he became President and never wanted to. And I have yet to know Mr. Ford."

"What it boils down to, then, is that the ACLU's golden era was during the Roosevelt administration."

"No question about it. The office was stacked with our friends

* Eric Goldman.

and supporters. Frank Roosevelt was very much aware of civil rights and civil liberties and the kind of staff he picked was too. People like Harold Ickes, Frances Perkins and Harry Hopkins. And all sorts of others; the attorney general, the head of the Indian Service, the chief counsel of the Post Office Department who passed on all matters of censorship, the head of the Federal Communications Commission and the SEC — name them, they were our friends."

"So did you take advantage of that welcome mat to press for more civil liberties?"

"I did, certainly. I should say I went to Washington far oftener with dozens of projects that I wanted our many friends to push."

"Can you give me an example?"

"Well, censorship was an example, although as it happened — or rather *when* it happened — that was not specifically one of our projects, but rather a project of a liberal senator from New Mexico named Bronson Cutting. He led the first fight in the Senate over the U.S. Customs Bureau control on importing so-called objectionable books. *Lady Chatterley's Lover* was the case in point. Cutting, who was a very literate fellow, introduced a bill that had the effect of making the importer of a suspect book liable only for confiscation of the material rather than for jail or a fine, which had previously been the penalty. It was a new idea that proceedings should be against the material, not the importer — in other words, not against a man but a book.

"Cutting was opposed by Senator Smoot, a Mormon gentleman, and a high official of the Latter-Day Saints in Utah. Smoots objected loudly, and he read long passages from *Lady Chatterley's Lover* on the floor of the Senate to prove his point that the content was so dirty that the Customs Bureau should not only bar the book but prosecute the importers. Apparently he read at such length that Cutting won the day by suggesting that Smoot was more interested in reading the material than he was in censoring it.

"The bill passed and we cheered from the sidelines, although our very liberal chairman, John Haynes Holmes, said, 'I've never seen a book that I thought should be barred from public circulation until I read *Lady Chatterley's Lover.*' And I asked him what was the matter with it? He said, 'Well it's those four-letter words,' and I said, 'But you know all of them, don't you?' And he answered, 'Yes, I know them, but I don't want to see them in print.' "

"But before *Lady Chatterley's Lover* you had had other obscenity cases, hadn't you?"

"Oh yes, sure. Lots of them. Morris Ernst handled most of them for us" — he chuckled — "Morris had rather a predisposition toward sex as a constitutional freedom. But of course in addition to censorship of imported books by the Customs Bureau, our own Post Office Department also refused to allow certain United States editions to be mailed. The two services usually worked together and the list of 'objectionable' titles was enormous — over a thousand of them.

"One of the early ones we handled in the thirties, before the Cutting bill became law, was Marie Stopes's *Married Love*. We went to court on that one to force the Customs Bureau to allow the book to be imported from England and the case was very famous because it was called *The United States* versus *Married Love*.

"Then we had James Joyce's *Ulysses* that we finally got imported in 1933 because we had that very good Judge John Woolsey who read the book and decided it was all right."

"How about you? Did you read these books to see if they were all right?"

"I didn't read *Ulysses,* no. That is, I read enough of it to decide it was perfectly harmless, but I thought it was a boring book because it was the life of one man for one day. Anyway I had made up my mind long before the case was brought that no serious book that was published by anybody in any language should be censored. I remember as a boy hearing about the *Memoirs of Fanny Hill* and, like other boys, I hoped to hear of somebody who had a copy. But I never did. It must have been fifty years later that it was freely circulated after the Supreme Court gave up trying to figure out its obscenity. I read it then and found it a dirty book in excellent good taste and I enjoyed it. I suspect the Supreme Court judges did too; each of them wrote a separate opinion after careful reading."

"If you yourself were instinctively against censorship, Roger, was this true of all the other members of your Board?"

"Well, we all may have had the instinct, but our problem was that we were always trying to make distinctions and that was very difficult. We tried it with obscenity. For a long time we accepted the idea that if the work had any redeeming social value — that was the exact language — its obscenity could be overlooked. But then finally we decided that that standard couldn't be interpreted. What did we really mean by 'redeeming social values'?"

"And how did you judge them?"

"Exactly. We couldn't make up our minds; so we finally gave up and said we aren't defining obscenity. And then the Supreme Court gave up too; they said you had to leave obscenity judgments to local community standards. But the ACLU objected to that as well, because we said how can you distribute *Playboy* on the basis of local community standards. It's a national publication. And if it's a dirty paper in San Francisco, it's also a dirty paper in New York."

"And in Boston. Wasn't 'banned in Boston' almost a commonplace?"

"Oh my goodness yes. For years Boston resisted all our attempts to get rid of its censorship of books, magazines and plays that they claimed were indecent. They had the famous Watch and Ward Society, the guardian of morals, that I used to hear about and make fun of when I was a boy. And Boston was the only city to have an official censor, actually called a censor, who was appointed by the mayor."

"Did you feel any sort of special responsibility for your home town?"

"In one way I did, yes, but in another way, I guess because I'd escaped from it, I felt a certain condescension toward its provincial pretensions. So I think maybe I took a sort of personal delight in baiting the censor with test cases."

One such case revolved around Lillian Smith's *Strange Fruit,* a novel published in 1944 about a love affair between a mulatto and a white Southerner. So "shocking" was this tragic story that the Boston and Cambridge police threatened to arrest anyone who either bought or sold it. Clearly this was a made-to-order setup for the ACLU. They responded by asking writer, teacher and wit Bernard DeVoto, ever a popular figure around Cambridge, publicly to buy *Strange Fruit* from a bookseller at Barnes and Noble. Both DeVoto and the bookseller were arrested; the Union appealed and the resulting publicity made the state legislators a bit more cautious about allowing the police unlimited powers of censorship.

Strange Fruit paved the way for another significant judicial decision when, thanks to the Union's efforts, *Forever Amber* was *unbanned* by a Boston judge, with the notable comment that "It acts like a soporific rather than an aphrodisiac. While conducive to sleep, it is not conducive to sleep with a member of the opposite sex." *

One of the earliest Boston censorship incidents that Roger remembered involved H. L. Mencken, Arthur Garfield Hays and the Reverend J. Franklin Chase, the secretary of the Watch and Ward Society. The case at issue revolved around a harmless little story called "Hatrack" by Herbert Asbury, which concerned a small-town prostitute who longed for respectability. Mencken had published this so-called sinful story in the April 1926 issue of the *American Mercury,* of which he was editor, and the Reverend Chase had promptly banned it, threatening legal action against anyone who publicly sold that issue of the magazine. Accordingly Mencken and Hays journeyed to Boston where, by pre-arrangement, they stationed themselves prominently on the Boston Common, prepared to sell the issue to the Reverend Chase himself. Chase duly appeared, handed Mencken a silver dollar (which, it is reported, Mencken bit to see if it was real), received the forbidden magazine and at once had Mencken arrested by the Boston Vice Squad. A brief trial followed; the judge dismissed the charges against Mencken on the merits of the case, but the editor's triumph was short-lived. The April edition of the *American Mercury* was barred from the mails by the United States Post Office Department.†

Over the years the ACLU tried, not always with success, to free from censorship such publications as *The Sex Side of Life* (a pamphlet by Mary Ware Dennet), *An American Tragedy, Lysistrata, Nudist* magazine, the Czechoslovakian film *Ecstasy,* and the plays *Waiting for Lefty, Within the Gates, The Children's Hour, Tobacco Road.*

"Of course in time the whole absurd system broke up," said Roger. "Obscenity took on a different character; the courts tried to define it and the more they tried, the more vague it became and the more tolerated. I don't remember when the censor was officially abolished in Boston, or when the last prosecutor anywhere stopped notifying distributors of the dangers they ran, but it was a long time ago. Boston is like the rest now; full of pornography and as indifferent to it as, say, Las Vegas. It was a good long fight for the

---

* Quoted in Dwight Macdonald's "In Defense of Everybody," *The New Yorker,* July 11, 1953.

† By an odd coincidence Bernard DeVoto was also involved, although peripherally, in the 1926 Hatrack case. Still a beginning writer at the time, he had sold to Mencken a story called "Sex and the Co-ed," which was scheduled to appear in the upcoming May issue of the *American Mercury.* Unable to risk having his magazine banned for the second straight month, Mencken was forced to withdraw DeVoto's story.

ACLU and, as a matter of fact, I think we all enjoyed it. There were no human casualties.

"We don't recognize obscenity at all in the Union now. We used to talk some of hard-core obscenity but again we found it impossible to define. Some said we would 'know it if we saw it,' but considering what you see on any big city newsstand today, I doubt that. There seem to be no prudes left among us."

"Is that better, do you think?"

"I think the *freedom* is better, even with its abuses, and I dislike setting up judges of propriety. We've had too many bans and I was glad when their day was done."

"But," I asked, "coming into the fifties, you couldn't say that bans on political dissent were ended, could you?"

"No, unfortunately not. Of course we didn't have official censors against political dissent, but for years we've had laws making crimes out of certain *advocacies* — laws that were first aimed at alleged sabotage of the IWW and then at the political *theory* of communism. The ACLU fought those laws and their concept — first the Sedition Acts, which were passed during World War I, and then, in 1938, the Smith Act, which is still on the books today with the blessings of the Supreme Court."

The Smith Act, which was the first federal sedition statute to be passed in peacetime, authorized the use of wiretaps against subversives, tolerated loyalty oaths and other constraints against government employees. The same year it became law, the Dies Committee came into being, theoretically to protect Americans from the menace of forces hostile to democracy, which, practically translated, meant Communists.

Roger has pointed out that the Dies Committee was the fourth un-American committee he had known in his public career, the others being the Senate Committee of 1920 headed by Senator Overman of North Carolina, the Committee of the House in 1931 headed by Hamilton Fish and the House Committee of 1935 headed by John W. McCormack of Massachusetts. All started out to investigate un-Americanism; all wound up, as Roger put it in a 1939 speech, in a "blaze of publicity with reckless charges of Communism directed indiscriminately against all sorts of individuals and organizations. Not one produced a single fruit except turmoil."

The Dies Committee, he said in that same speech, was "worse than its predecessor committees which had at least stuck closer to the facts and avoided political intrigue and bias, bad as their records were for unsupported evidence and loose conclusions." But the Dies Committee, he suggested bitterly, "proceeded on the premise that any organization in which a single Communist can be found to occupy any sort of position is tainted by Moscow. One drop of red, according to the statesman from Texas, will color any outfit however patriotic or American it may otherwise be."

To a considerable extent the Dies Committee was aided by the FBI (although J. Edgar Hoover and Martin Dies were rivals, and thus enemies), and in 1942 Roger wrote an article, commissioned by the *New Republic,* also condemning, although in more measured terms, the FBI's activities against Communists. While he conceded that FBI agents, who were all lawyers and therefore should know the rules of evidence, did avoid trespassing on the civil rights of individuals, he denounced them for following the lead of the Dies Committee in concentrating all their investigations on Communists, while totally ignoring the existence of Fascists even during a time of war against fascism.

Curiously, since the article was relatively low-keyed, Roger had a change of heart and decided to withdraw it from publication in the *New Republic.* In a note attached to the typescript he explained that an interview with Mr. Hoover had convinced him that Hoover had "largely changed his views on the dangers from labor and the left. He is violently anti-Dies and against all the witch-hunting for Reds."

Today Roger confirms his shifting views of J. Edgar Hoover. "At first he was very cautious about maintaining the principle of civil liberties. I think he wanted to appear as a law enforcement officer who defended the Constitution and people's rights under it. So I'm afraid it took me a long time to come to the conclusion that he was really a menace."

"Do you think Hoover changed, or that you were too generous about him in the first place?"

"Oh I think he changed a great deal. I think he changed when he found that scaring people about Reds was the most profitable thing he could do to get more money out of Congress. He was the protector of our country, and the country would be obligated to J. Edgar Hoover for saving it from the Communists."

"Then I should think you would have been in constant conflict with him."

ROGER BALDWIN

"As a matter of fact we weren't. I think on several occasions Mr. Hoover either wrote or said that the FBI wasn't interested in the ACLU and that we weren't suspect."

"Surely you don't look on that as a good recommendation?"

"Certainly not," Roger said.

"Do you think he thought better of you because you got rid of Elizabeth Gurley Flynn?"

"Oh no. The dealings I had with him were long before that time. I don't think I ever saw him after."

"But you *did* think he was a menace," I persisted.

"Yes, I just *said* that. I think in the end he turned his agency into a political police force. But the FBI wasn't the only problem. In fact I would say that the regular uniformed police probably presented the greatest single difficulty to civil liberties. Police departments are, on the whole, corrupt institutions. Not so much the commissioners with whom we had some good relations in New York, but the regular foot patrolmen — they're the trouble.

"And of course the laws and the government functionaries were not by any means the only tools that were used to control political dissent. In addition there was a regular army of 'defenders of the faith,' professional patriots who were bent only on preserving the status quo. In fact from the time the ACLU started, the fears arising from the Russian Revolution and from the tiny Communist party in the United States aroused the authorities to act on the slightest evidence. And that led the public to suspect Communists among all sorts of liberals, dissenters and foreigners."

"Still," I asked, "that fear wasn't constant from 1920 on, was it? There seem to have been certain periods of hysteria and then some times of quieter tolerance."

"Of course. The waves of excitement and repression rose and fell with the presumed dangers."

"Presumed, not 'clear and present'?"

"Presumed. It was not what the Communists did that was the danger; it was what they made us do to ourselves. Arthur Garfield Hays was the one who said that. Fighting communism made us witch hunters. This country became full of intolerant zealots, ready to outlaw any person or group suspected of espousing the hated doctrine of communism. And that of course led to guilt by association."

"And Senator Joseph McCarthy."
"And Senator Joseph McCarthy."

We were both silent for a moment, letting our thoughts drift back to that dreadful time in the 1950's when McCarthyism ran rampant. Although it seemed endless, it lasted mercifully for only four years, from 1950 when Joseph McCarthy stood up in Wheeling, West Virginia, and waved a paper allegedly containing a list of 204 members of the State Department who were Communists, until 1954 when the Senate passed a resolution censuring him.

Roger recalled it as a chaotic period of "hot peace or cold war" in which we all confronted extreme expressions of our fears of war and of Soviet infiltration. McCarthy in his opinion was the worst demagogue we had known, even though he only perfected what others like Dies and Parnell Thomas had started. Writing in 1953, Roger commented on the remarkable fact that we, as the world's strongest democracy, were the most fearful of communism. No other country seemed so "hypnotized" about communism; there was, for example no "un-French Activities Committee." No other country had loyalty oaths, or tests of patriotism; none had guilt by association that led to the sacrifice of thousands of innocent people who lost their jobs, their friends and their reputations.

"Did the ACLU represent many of those who were victims of McCarthyism?" I asked.

"The ACLU did the best it could. But there was very little we were able to do. We had a terribly futile feeling about stemming that tide. It was too strong. We could only hope that the passion would run its course and that, as happened so many times in history, people with power like McCarthy would abuse it so far that they would destroy themselves, as McCarthy finally did."

"Did you personally have any dealings with McCarthy?"

"Well, you won't think this is a very good reflection on my liberal standing, but the fact is, I had no contacts whatsoever with McCarthy personally. I wasn't on any lists and neither for that matter was the ACLU. So he never touched me."

"Why do you think you escaped?"

"I think because of my connections with General MacArthur. MacArthur had endorsed me and that made me so respectable that McCarthy didn't dare touch me."

In point of fact, it was not strictly true that McCarthy did not touch Roger. While he never directly attacked him as a subversive (as, for example, he did Judge Dorothy Kenyon who was Evelyn Preston's great friend and a prominent member of the ACLU Board), McCarthy did manage to read into the *Congressional Record* on May 26, 1953, a "report on Roger Baldwin," which he had received from the House Un-American Activities Committee and which detailed Roger's extensive involvement with the United Front and referred to him also as a draft dodger.

"Another reason why he may have left us alone," Roger suggested, "was that the ACLU policy might have been a little too conciliatory during the McCarthy period. Perhaps it was a mistake to try to tell them how good we were and to assure them that we had no Communist sympathies. Maybe it got us somewhere, but I was never satisfied that it was a good policy."

"Then why did you follow it?"

"I didn't," Roger said, a slight note of triumph creeping into his voice. "It was my *successor* who encouraged this line."

I stared at him.

"You seem to have forgotten that by the time Joe McCarthy started his Red-baiting, I had retired as director of the ACLU."

Familiar as I was with the chronology of Roger's public life, I had indeed overlooked the date of his retirement — November of 1949 — just a few months before his sixty-sixth birthday. As I took this in now, I responded with a sense of dismay to the stunning realization that we were coming to the end of Roger's active association with the organization he had created and which for thirty years had borne his unmistakable stamp. "The ACLU *is* Roger Baldwin."

"Had you always had it in mind to retire at sixty-five?" I asked him.

"Yes, I had. All the other organizations I was connected with had sixty-five as a retirement age and I thought that was just about right."

"But you could have stayed on longer at the ACLU?"

"Oh I could have, yes," Roger said airily, "but I wanted to set a good example."

There are faint suggestions in some quarters — none explicitly stated — that while Roger certainly could have stayed on longer if he had wanted to, the Board of the ACLU was not all that sorry to have him "set an example." And the reasons why his retirement may have been regarded as fortuitous were probably two-fold. Certainly the Board had never fully recovered from the Elizabeth Gurley Flynn schism and some members had not forgiven Roger for his part in that drama.

But, perhaps, more important was an ideological difference as to what direction the ACLU should take in the future. Roger had always held the Union on a very tight rein. Believing firmly (and frequently stating) that "bigger was not better," he preferred to depend on a small elite group at the center to make and implement intellectual and policy decisions. Others on the Board, however, felt the time was due, if not past due, for expansion, for more affiliates and for a genuine national grass-roots organization.*

So there are those who feel that Roger had to, as one friend put it, "pull himself up by his britches" to find a new outlet for his energies and talents after 1950. If this is so, Roger gives not the slightest hint of any such struggle. On the contrary, he says that by the time he quit he was relieved to get out of the job. "I was awfully fed up with it."

I said I found that hard to believe, but he insisted that because he had by then had a taste of international affairs, the "American scene" didn't seem so important to him.

Surely, I suggested, he had had quite a few tastes of international affairs before. But I supposed that the difference was perhaps the big bite he had had of Japan and General Douglas MacArthur.

He had also had quite a bite of Korea, he pointed out, when he stopped there on his way home from Japan, and even more so of Germany, where he'd gone a year after his trip to Japan and in a more or less similar capacity, at the request of General Lucius Clay. Certainly these assignments in 1947 and 1948 were absorbing and exciting to Roger. In fact, it is worth noting that in the typescript of his Oral History, which runs to some eight hundred pages, over four hundred pages concern his active service with the Occupation forces of Japan, Korea and Germany.

Still, when he claims so vociferously, as he has done on more than one occasion, that the years after his retirement as director of the

---

* At the time of Roger's retirement the ACLU had a budget of $75,000 for 9,000 members. By 1970 the total budget was between four and five million dollars for 250,000 members; there were forty-nine statewide affiliates and four hundred subchapters, as opposed to fifteen or twenty such groups in Roger's day.

ACLU gave him more satisfaction than any of the previous years, one is justified in suspecting that he perhaps protests too much.

Of course he did not by any means cut himself adrift from the Union. "For a long time after I quit, I was chairman of the National Committee, until that whole structure changed. They insisted that I have my name on the door and have a private office and a secretary. I was called 'International Advisor,' so I handled a lot of correspondence there — for instance, in regard to international affairs in Puerto Rico and the Virgin Islands where I did a great deal of work on civil rights."

"And you didn't breathe down your successor's neck?"

"Well, I went to the office at least two or three times a week, but I got along very well with my immediate successor, Pat Malin. He had been a professor of economics at Swarthmore; he was an old young friend whom I'd known since he was a student. He and I maintained our happy relations for the ten years he served us. He left to take a better job as president of Robert College in Istanbul and unhappily died a few years later. I didn't get along quite so well with his successor, who was the only lawyer-director we had and who was only with us about four years. But his successor, the present director, Aryeh Neier, is much the best of our directors. In fact I think he's better than I was."

"In what way?"

"I think he's a more careful administrator. He makes fewer mistakes than I did."

"Roger, somehow we've never discussed your mistakes. Offhand, can you tell me what a few of them were?"

"You mean at the ACLU?"

"Yes."

"Well — " he thought a moment. "All right, I'll give you an example: Prohibition. The ACLU never got involved in the massive violation of due process, the search and seizures and all the other violations that were connected with that. We thought the Volstead Act was none of our business since it didn't touch on democratic liberties. We were wrong. We should have read the Bill of Rights."

"Does anything else come to mind?"

"Perhaps we were at times too pro–trade union, and we sometimes looked more pro-left or pro-Communist than the evidence justified. We should have been more sensitive to our 'image,' as we say nowadays. Then, too, the record will show a lot of foolish statements and motions by somebody or other connected with the ACLU, like, for instance, taking 'In God We Trust' off coins or postage or denying Congress its chaplains. Or even, in my view, the error the Board made in arguing in the Supreme Court for taxation of church property. Then I made my own errors and blunders, I guess. I was probably wrong in holding down the expansion and budget of the Union. I was also too much of a man of action to be studious, even to be careful. I had too many outside activities like the United Fronts, which gave me a reputation as a free-wheeler inclined to the left. It would have been better if I had stuck to the ACLU alone, the way Aryeh Neier does. He has no attachments outside; he wouldn't have got into the United Fronts; he's much less impulsive than I am."

"And do you get on well with him?"

"Oh I do, yes. Of course there's quite an age difference, and I often have the impression when I talk with him that he is holding me off out of fear that I am going to criticize him."

"And have you ever criticized him?"

"Not directly, no. And," he grinned, "hardly ever indirectly. But I'm on the National Advisory Council these days and the National has a right to attend Board meetings but not to vote. So I attend. And I speak out too."

"I'll bet you do."

"I speak when I'm asked to, and," he chuckled, "also when I'm not asked to. If I see them going off the line, I intervene right away. I regard myself as responsible for keeping them to the true faith and quite often when they start to go away from the true faith, I bring them back."

Obviously then Roger has in the years since his retirement paid close (and, by his own admission, sometimes irritatingly close) attention to what was going on at the ACLU offices. He has not hesitated to put in his own oar, but when he retired as director the days when it was *his* oar that really pulled the boat were over. And that inevitable fact was marked in 1949 by great ceremonials honoring Roger.

John Haynes Holmes, as chairman of the board of directors, thoughtfully and lovingly orchestrated Roger's retirement. The press release in which he announced it carefully stated that Mr. Baldwin "does not intend to retire but will henceforth devote his extraordinary energies to specialized work in the field of international civil rights."

Before this news was made public, Mr. Holmes had undertaken the monumental task of writing to hundreds of Roger's friends and associates, inviting each to contribute a letter about Roger Baldwin to mark this occasion. The four hundred responses that are bound in two magnificent red leather volumes include tributes from lawyers, men of God, senators, publishers, generals, journalists, pacifists, labor leaders, playwrights, cabinet members, doctors, novelists, reformers, historians, Supreme Court justices, lady friends past and present, international figures, painters, poets, teachers, governors, and, leading the list, the President of the United States. (According to Ida Netzer, Roger's long-time secretary at the ACLU, Roger's first question on learning that such a volume was in progress was, "Is there a letter from General MacArthur?" Fortunately there was.)

The letters are for the most part sensitive and often heartfelt outpourings of appreciation, affection and high regard. Some among them are notable, both for their authorship and for their felicity of expression.

"I am afraid many of us have been prone to assign to him, and to him alone, the tremendous role of keeper of the American conscience," wrote Max Lerner. "Having cleared our own consciences thus, we have been willing to let Roger carry on for us."

Reflecting the same theme, Justice William O. Douglas wrote (in a handwritten note), "On many occasions Roger Baldwin has awakened the conscience of America to some wrong being done to a human being. Again and again he rallied the force of public opinion in the cause of personal liberty."

From India Roger's old friend Eduard Lindeman wrote of having recently chanced upon a picture of Mahatma Gandhi "and there, behold, stood Roger at Gandhi's side, smiling in the impish way he has of letting you know he was having a good time supporting an unpopular cause."

Corliss Lamont, while openly conceding their serious differences, chose to concentrate on Roger's deep appreciation of "the beauties and wonders of external nature, his expert knowledge of birds and trees and other aspects of the nonhuman world. If anyone could teach civil liberties to the animal kingdom," he concluded, "Roger would be the man."

Many others touched on the naturalist motif. John K. Jessup described Roger as "a man with one foot caught in the Constitution and the other in the woods of America." Mrs. Van Wyck Brooks recalled a hot summer afternoon on Martha's Vineyard when Roger had led her up a steep ladder to the barn loft at Windy Gates to see a massive white owl sitting on a beam beside her owlets. "Wisdom and industry confronting wisdom and industry, I thought, as Roger and the bird faced one another."

Incredulity and dismay at how the ACLU would survive without him was perhaps the dominant note struck. "Isn't the American Civil Liberties Union truly the length and shadow of Roger Baldwin?" asked Mrs. Evarts Graham.

"You could no more retire from the fight for liberties than Joe Stalin could install a chapter of the ACLU in the Kremlin," wrote Robert Gessner.

And, said Laura Z. Hobson, "the only time you ever struck a serious blow at civil liberties in this country was when you decided to retire from the ACLU. How could you?"

From his chambers in the Supreme Court came a gentle letter (also handwritten) from Justice Felix Frankfurter. "It was a joy for me to be one of your comrades-in-arms in many a struggle and for many years until I came down here. Since then you and I have had different functions in the service of our democratic society. But I can say, as did Carlyle to his friend John Stirling, 'and so we parted agreeing in all things except opinion.' I salute your past as a sure promise of your future."

The indefatigable John Haynes Holmes, with his eye on that future, also announced the formation of the Roger N. Baldwin Foundation for the Advancement of Civil Liberties. The proposed foundation's initial project was to be an annual lectureship on civil liberties to be given at Harvard, and followed, it was hoped, by a series of lectures also given annually at southern universities. To ensure a "firm beginning," twenty-five thousand dollars was to be raised by friends and admirers of Roger Baldwin. Official announcement of the foundation was to be made at a dinner honoring Roger at the Waldorf Astoria on February 22, 1950.

Roger's response to all this fanfare was anything but gracious. He complained to John Haynes Holmes that he hated testimonial dinners, which he always found "dull and typed." Since he had always avoided such honorary occasions, he had "little stomach" for being the cause of one himself.

As to the foundation, he questioned the value of university lectures on civil liberties and proposed to use the funds for scholarships for young people aspiring to be specialists in the field — especially the field of international civil liberties.

So uncooperative and at times churlish was his behavior that John Holmes was obliged to write him a scolding letter about his attitude toward the whole affair. "Frankly, I doubt if you have the right to embarrass and trouble your friends on the Board in their desire to offer greetings and gratitude to you on your retirement from the work of a lifetime now gone. And not only the Directors, but a great company of friends everywhere who want to praise you! You owe to these a fitting chance to express their inmost feelings . . . Least of all, should you, with exaggerated humility, frustrate and defeat this spontaneous desire to pay tribute to you. I myself feel embarrassed and hurt that my labors on your behalf in this proposed dinner are being met by your refusal of cooperation which threatens to spoil everything I have done."

Cannily Holmes then pointed out that Roger not only owed his friends and comrades the chance of a fitting farewell but that the ACLU needed and indeed welcomed the opportunity the dinner afforded to advertise their efforts. "Your name presents a magic influence which we can use productively in the Union's interest. I ask you, is it right thus to ban this dinner which holds through you such benefit for the cause which you have served so long and well?"

Roger's prompt reply expressed his genuine distress that his good friend John Holmes should have had to write him such a letter. He said that if there could be a slight shift in emphasis and mood, a lighter, quasi-humorous approach to the planned celebrations, he would be "not unwilling to take gracefully" what others wanted to say of his public work.

He went on to explain: "One of my reasons for feeling a bit out of tune with the preparations is that I am not in any real sense retired or retiring yet. Maybe some five or six years from now when I may feel the years slowing me down. What I feel now is only a great relief from administrative duties to carry on an even more active schedule on my own time. That seems hardly the occasion for the usual celebration of a man's past.

"John Dewey waited until he was ninety. I could wait, too!"

(19)

Citizen of the World

ON MARCH 4, 1975, I SAW A STORY in the *New York Times* headlined, "80 Americans Appeal to India to Restore Fundamental Rights." Knowing without question that Roger's name would have to be among the eighty, I looked to see what sort of attention he had received. He was mentioned twice. In the body of the story, among the ten or so most prominent signers, he was identified as Roger N. Baldwin of the American Civil Liberties Union; in the small-type listing of all the signatories he was Roger N. Baldwin, Honorary President, International League for the Rights of Man.

This name tag dichotomy points up what Roger has come to refer to in his conversations with me as "The Problem of the Last Twenty-five Years." By that he does not mean that *he* has had any problem with 1950 to 1975; on the contrary, he continues to view this period as the most exhilarating of his life. But some of his constituency, it seems, has often failed to recognize the significance of these years and continues to connect his name only with the ACLU.

"Apparently I have no other distinction in the press," he grumbles. "No matter what I do, I never seem to be known by any other label."

Knowing that I myself continually labeled him that way (and would do so on the title page of this book), I tried to make amends. "The fact is, Roger, you really haven't talked at all about the International League for the Rights of Man."

"That's because you haven't asked me."

"All right, tell me now. How old is the League and when did you first become connected with it?"

"Well, the first time I had anything to do with it was when I went to France in 1927 and met a lot of the people who were in the French League for the Rights of Man. The ACLU had already had some fraternal relations with it because it was the most active and oldest group in the field abroad. It started in 1902 with the Dreyfus case. The Dreyfus case was the first — at least I don't remember any earlier one in modern times — to dramatize the need for a citizen organization to watch and protect people from the government. The French Fédération des Droits de l'Homme really came out of Émile Zola. It was his crusade that started it."

"Did you continue your association with the League from 1927 on?"

"Not really, no. I went to Europe again in 1929 and '31 and '35 — mostly short trips — but by then I was involved with the United Fronts and that seemed to me more important at the time than what the French League was doing. So I didn't have much to do with the League until 1942 when the operation moved to New York. What happened then was that a group of distinguished French refugees — top people from the Sorbonne, many of them were — came to the United States and set up an American branch of the International League for the Rights of Man, which was incorporated in the state of New York."

Shortly thereafter Roger was invited to join the directing board, and did so. Prominent among the governing body were such personages as Henri Bonnet, later the French ambassador to the United States, Henri Laugier, then a professor at the University of Montreal and later the assistant secretary general of the United Nations, and Gastano Salvemini, a professor at Harvard. The governance, aside from Roger and one other director, was entirely French; indeed all the meetings were conducted in French. Although they maintained an office at 70 Fifth Avenue, issued a few pamphlets, and raised a little money from foreigners and Americans, there was not a great deal that such a small group could do in the middle of the war, cut off as they were from all connections abroad.

But as the war drew to a close the League began to assume new importance. The United Nations came into being and, from its inception, was committed to the acceptance of Nongovernmental Organizations (NGOs). Clearly an international league that had throughout the century been concerned with civil liberties and the rights of man was an especially desirable organization, particularly since its machinery was already set up and operating in New York. Accordingly in 1946 the International League for the Rights of Man was one of the first NGOs to be recognized by the UN. At this point Roger was asked to become chairman of the board and after some initial hesitation he accepted.

The record here is a bit fuzzy. Roger says that when the war ended and the French members started returning to France, the secretary of the League, a French woman lawyer whose name he has forgotten, came to him and said, in effect, that the time for French leadership had passed. "She wanted me to take over," Roger recalled, "In fact she said to me, *"Je veux le pousser dans vos mains."*

However, this wish to push their brain child into American hands does not seem to have been warmly accepted by the French progenitor organization in Paris, which regarded the New York International League for the Rights of Man as a usurper, and declined from 1946 on to maintain formal relations with it. Even today there is no French affiliate, although there is a Swiss Ligue des Droits des Hommes.

Although it is quite clear that no self-interest moved Roger to become involved with the ILRM, it did turn out that the League suited his purposes very well, as he indeed suited theirs. If his mission to Japan (and the one to Germany a year later) had been the principal stimulus for his move to the international phase of civil liberties, the League for the Rights of Man was the instrument that made that transition possible. For the League opened the door for him to the United Nations, which had from its beginnings greatly excited Roger. "Maybe if it hadn't been right there on my doorstep I wouldn't have felt that way," Roger admitted, "but because it was, I started haunting the place. The UN doesn't interest some people — maybe it doesn't interest you — because no decisions are made there. Nobody has any power. But it's a fascinating place just the same. It's the town meeting of the world. It's the only place where everybody comes. Everybody!"

Being Roger, of course, he already knew a large number of those Everybodies — the delegates and the personalities in the Secretariat. But what the ILRM provided for him was a genuine reason, not just to haunt the UN but to be part of the action. As chairman of the board of the League, he represented an important Nongovernmental Organization that was, in fact, he says, the only such organization devoted exclusively to the principle of human rights. In the NGO lounge he found a new and compatible home among many dedicated volunteers.

"I was a volunteer and so were all the people on our various committees who did the work."

"What sort of work did you actually do?"

"Lobbying."

Here perhaps was the crux, I thought. At the UN, Roger lobbied to influence; at the ACLU he had acted to achieve. But certainly I dared not suggest this (to me) vital distinction. Instead I asked what exactly his lobbying had consisted of.

"Daily contacts with fellow NGOs, auditing meetings, talking with delegates and the Secretariat personnel, most of whom were Americans in top posts, attending special commissions on human rights and colonialism and women, submitting our views in writing when we had anything to offer, as I did on every reasonable and even some unreasonable occasions. Of course we ran afoul of the Russians right away and stayed so simply because NGOs don't exist where governments control everything."

"Did you personally attend the General Assemblies?"

"I wouldn't have missed them for the world. They were just wonderful shows. Everybody came, the Pope, Queen Elizabeth, all our Presidents, Castro, Khrushchev, de Gaulle, all the British P.M.'s, Nehru. The UN intention was to include every sovereign state, but power politics blocked that idea until the happy day, I remember, when I sat in the Security Council and watched our ambassador Henry Cabot Lodge break the dam to get Japan in. After that anybody could get in and everybody did too. Now there are one hundred and forty countries and they're all equal, however unequal their size and importance; that has heartened me as the only way to organize the world. All in, none out — all with a voice — a parliament of men, at least in form, even if without power.

"I also traveled a great deal. To Europe — Geneva mostly — for meetings. In fact, much of the sense of participation I've had in these later years has come from travel. I visited every country I could where I had a purpose. My around-the-world trip in 1959 was arranged in part by the UN. Then I made trips to Africa, to the Near East, the Middle East, Latin America, Japan again — "

"You say you went wherever you had a purpose. What was your purpose in all these countries?"

"To see at first hand the struggles for freedom and equality that were, after all, the two moral principles that had dominated my whole public outlook. And also to urge a commitment to internationalism and to lobby for whatever our League had decided should be our positions on the issues."

"On the issue of human rights — I may have my dates wrong — but hadn't the Declaration of Human Rights already been adopted by the time you started working actively at the UN?"

"By 1950 it had, yes. It was adopted in Paris in July 1948, the summer I was in Germany. And for quite a while afterward we were all very hopeful that the platform laid down in Paris would soon be followed by some sort of international bill of rights with a court or agency to intervene against violations. We thought eventually a world court would even render decisions the way the United States Supreme Court does. I myself was very devoted to this line of thought."

"And Mrs. Roosevelt?"

"Well, Mrs. Roosevelt, of course, was the chairman of the Human Rights Commission. She was the most respected voice in the world for human rights; I followed her leadership with confidence. She was very earnest and for a long time she never lost her faith, nor did I lose mine, that this was a new world in which human rights could thrive and that the declaration laid down in Paris would soon be followed by some international authority to protect those rights.

"But we had not counted on the passions of the cold war or the pressures of the colonial people to become independent. Naturally people were absorbed with such problems as getting Africa and Asia free of European control. So human rights never really went very far beyond the remarkable set of principles which were embodied in the 1948 declaration. Even today they still stand mainly as guides and goals for the development of world law in a future era."

"Were you never disillusioned about the UN?"

"Of course I was, on that score particularly; Mrs. Roosevelt was too. As the debates in the Human Rights Commission grew more sterile and repetitive and full of cold war rhetoric, we both became somewhat disillusioned and bored with the sessions."

"Were you and Mrs. Roosevelt good friends?"

"I wouldn't exactly say good friends, simply because I think I always was a little in awe of Mrs. Roosevelt. But I had known her for a long time and she had been one of my inspirations even before she blossomed out after her husband's death. I remember one summer during the New Deal days, she invited me to be a discussion leader at a student conference she held at her summer home in New Brunswick. I was happy to take part under her guidance and in such a homey atmosphere. She would sit around in the evenings knitting and chatting with the students; Joe Lash was one who became her great personal friend and later her biographer. We were all her guests and she was the very unpretentious hostess. Mrs. Roosevelt had that quality that I have noted in other great people — a complete unawareness of position and reputation coupled with intense concentration on the person or affair at hand, as if the only thing that counted was the present moment and the person present.

"But on the somewhat more personal side, I used to see Mrs. Roosevelt because she was a great friend of Geraldine Thompson, who was my wife's aunt. And Mrs. Thompson used to invite Evelyn and me to lunch with Mrs. Roosevelt fairly often, maybe a half a dozen times over the years, at the Cosmopolitan Club where genteel ladies gathered for the more serious things of life. There were always other family members or friends and Mrs. Roosevelt usually held the stage — modestly. She was often quite frank about her role at the UN. She used to say that the General Assembly was such a good place to take a nap. And she often did just that."

"But the Human Rights Declaration wasn't your only concern, was it?"

"By no means. I was much preoccupied with the freedom from foreign rule of millions in Asia and Africa. That was what really gave me the satisfaction."

Certainly, Roger says he always took heart in the "nationalism of independent states, the creation by the UN of a third world of powers, the end of white supremacy over the darker majority of mankind, the vast improvement in the status of women, and the sovereign equality of all nations whatever their size." Above all, he found promise in the mere fact of the UN's existence as a collective enterprise, one that every nation wanted to get into and none wanted to get out of.

But his overall view was not always so optimistic. In a 1970 article he spoke with bitterness of "a world divided by fear of war and by the madness of an increasing arms race between the great powers." He decried the "chaos of a world dominated by the terror of nuclear arms and the ugly realities of power politics." He disparaged the "air of unreality" about the UN human rights efforts. "Injustices, crying to heaven for redress, persecutions, repressions, executions are never officially noticed by the UN." And in one unusually discouraged appraisal, he spoke of the "deterioration of the United Nations" and referred to himself as an "unhappy observer."

But today, he admits, "my outlook is sometimes extreme enough for me to be called a Pollyanna."

Today he believes that the UN has "laid the cornerstone for salvaging the world's problems," that the evils that made life so tragic for so many are going to be overcome. "I get excited," he says, "when I think about the end of empires and when I think about equality among people and about the end of wars. Because all my life I've been working on little pieces of those problems and now I'm able to see the end of it."

"Do I understand you to say you see the end of wars?"

"That's right," he said. "Wars are finished. All over."

"Well, I must say, *that's* a banner headline."

"Wars are finished because they're suicidal and there can be no victor. Every war in history was one somebody thought they could win. But nobody thinks they can win a war now. There may be some cruel conflicts like in Northern Ireland or Cyprus, but no real global wars. The world is small now — oh, don't misunderstand me — I think it's in terrible shape these days, but it's been growing better and better. That's why I've felt so encouraged during the last twenty-five years. Because even though I didn't do much to help it along, I was there at the United Nations when all this was happening.

"Just think of the international agencies — the public and the private ones — that have tied the world together. Agencies for education, for labor, for trade, for air travel — all regulated internationally. Think of the new environmental agency that was formed in Sweden a few years ago. I was there in Stockholm for that — I was eighty-eight years old at the time — and it was enormously encouraging. For the first time we began to consider how to protect ourselves from the evils in our own environment. For the first time in our world's history we've begun to have a real global concept. The airplane and the radio have made it possible to treat the world as a single unit.

"And pretty soon we're going to have money regulated internationally and then we're going to end inflation. It's really a very simple matter. Nations will give up their currencies, and we'll have a world bank with an international currency that everyone accepts."

"Do you mean you actually think the framework exists today to make a global currency?"

"That's what I'm saying, yes. And I'll go even further. I'll go so far as to say that nations themselves are downright silly. I think dividing people up in geographical units and drawing lines around them and putting an army on the border to protect them is ridiculous."

"So you also see a possibility of giving up nations?"

"Sure. Nations will end because we won't have any more wars to defend them."

"Well, even accepting that premise, what kind of national ethos would we have then?"

"The same kind we have now. People will still feel they belong where they are. The changing world order isn't going to affect the way people feel about Boston, for instance. They'll still go right on calling Boston 'The Hub' and still think they're at the center of everything. But anyway, states and countries and geographic localities will still exist, but they'll exist for purely sentimental, administrative purposes, not for defense purposes."

"What about language?" I asked, feeling that Roger was beginning to extemporize rather freely now.

"Oh we'll have two languages," he said airily. "Everyone will learn their own and one other universal one. Like Latin. Way up until the Middle Ages, Latin was the common language of all educated people. We'd have to find something else. Something very simple."

"Roger, it seems to me — "

"I know, I know, it seems to you that this is a bad time for optimists. But even so, I'm still holding out. I like to think that we're moving in the direction of becoming citizens of the world at heart, even if we stick to our flags and our guns for a little longer."

What it also seemed to me was that this vision of an ideal future, this optimism, was the mark of the man. Surely the usual tendency with advancing years is to look back and think wistfully of the good old days. Roger Baldwin, at ninety-two, looks ahead and thinks brightly of good new days.

(20)

A Contradictory Fellow
with a Simple Purpose

"I HOPE YOU'RE MANAGING TO FIT all the material in place," Roger
wrote me one day, "and to make a convincing picture of a contradictory fellow with a simple purpose."

"I hope so too," I said to him on the phone that evening. "But I've
still got quite a lot of material to fit in. You know, you're a hard
man to end a book about."

He chuckled. "That's because I keep going on and on. By the
way," he added, "you're not forgetting that you're supposed to be
the Greek chorus. Are you sure you're putting in your own commentaries all along?"

Roger had repeatedly expressed that concern and I thought I understood his reasoning. The views of the Greek chorus were ones
he could justifiably disavow if those interpretations were at variance
with his own.

"If you think I'm a damned liar, I hope you'll say so."

"I think you're a contradictory fellow with a simple purpose."

He laughed. "After all, you know me now from more perspectives than anyone else."

From the perspectives of his three children — his daughter and
his two stepsons? Perhaps I have at least an inkling. From all three
I get a picture of a generally happy and lively family life, of a pat-
tern of activity strictly but willingly adhered to: five days a week in
New York at Bleeker Gardens and at City and Country School;
Friday to Monday at Dellbrook; summers on Martha's Vineyard.

Within the framework of this ritual, Evelyn emerges as the strong parent, the one who made the decisions and who at all times directed the course of the children's lives. Roger (or Bunkle, as the boys have always called him), somewhat remote in his father role, was more the companion, most particularly the weekend companion, taking them with zest and enthusiasm on bird walks, canoe trips, an early morning swim, exploring a new pond, hiking in the woods — always, with Roger leading the troops, it was an "adventure," and always exciting.

Roger, Carl and Helen share numerous views of their father. Each agrees, for example, that he and Evelyn really never did quarrel and, in fact, Helen rather resents this, claiming that as a result she herself never learned to fight very well. (Informed of this response, her father said he thought she had acquired a pretty good idea of how it was done.) Each of his children laughs at Roger's ceaseless caution about money, his one "city suit," his stubborn unwillingness to take taxis. (Helen laughs, but also worries about his insistence on taking the subway home alone late at night.) Each smiles at Roger's fondness for the "best people," despite his lifelong concern for the underdog.

I myself often had opportunities to observe and enjoy Roger's duality on this score, the most notable time being when he came bouncing into my house in Cambridge one summer's day straight from Maine where he had just been celebrating the eighty-fifth birthday of his old friend Clarence Dillon, a vintage millionaire and founder of the banking house of Dillon Reed. (He is also the father of C. Douglas Dillon, who served Kennedy as secretary of the treasury.)

Euphoria is the only word that can be used to describe Roger's infinite pleasure at having spent the weekend with what he referred to as the "topnotch rich of the country," an elite company that included Rockefellers, Aldriches and Mrs. Marshall Field. "They don't care what they spend," Roger exulted. "Everything was laid on. Everything! The only time I was better treated was by the army. The army really lays it on for VIPs."

"So here we have the pacifist who loves to have it laid on by the army," I said, "and the defender of the poor who loves to have it laid on by the rich." Roger chortled appreciatively. "But go on. Tell me more about the Dillon household."

"Well, the butler, of course, unpacked my suitcase."

"And, of course, nothing much was in it," I suggested.

"No, that's right. Nothing much."

"But you did take your dinner jacket for the party, didn't you?"

"No," Roger said firmly, "I did not."

"You own a dinner jacket, don't you?"

"Yes, but I did not take it with me. I had on this suit [his gray flannel city suit] and I said to the butler, 'Get me one of Mr. Dillon's black bow ties and we'll fake it.' So he did. He sponged and pressed my suit, and I wore a black bow tie and no one knew the difference."

Such was Roger's act of defiance, the one gesture he made to show that he was not really being taken in by the rich and the powerful. His gray flannel suit with a black bow tie was his badge of fealty to the deserving poor.

When I mentioned this episode to Carl Baldwin, he laughed at yet another example of Roger's strong sense of "Who People Are and Where People Come From." This predilection, he said, even caused Roger to regard the success of the Beatles with bewilderment. "How could they be so famous?" he kept asking. "They're just four kids from *Liverpool*."

Over and above the views that his three children hold in common about their father, each summons up many different aspects of life with Roger Baldwin. Helen recalls "endless strays," many of them ex-cons, wandering in and out of their various houses and always being jovially received by her father. With less enthusiasm, she remembers how Roger used to drown cats (the one member of the animal kingdom he hates) because they were molesting the birds (which he, of course, loves).

Carl has a certain sense that as a family they were somehow rootless. Rarely did they go to Boston or see the Baldwin relatives there; they never saw the Preston relations, and, in fact, neither he nor his brother ever saw their natural father, Steve Raushenbush, until they were both young men. So, Carl recalls, "we were surrounded with beautiful things, with nature, great books, good ideas, art and music, but still there was a feeling of not knowing exactly who we were in terms of actual people."

For the boys, even taking the name Baldwin was haphazard. At City and Country School, because Raushenbush was a difficult name to spell — or even to remember — they were called the Bush boys, even by their teachers. Moving on to high school, they — or rather Roger, who was the older — felt he could not properly register as

Roger Bush. It therefore seemed more logical simply to become Roger Baldwin. Carl then followed suit.

Young Roger had perhaps the most difficult adolescence of the three, for he had the misfortune in this particular family of being less verbal and of being something of an All-American boy. He was a star basketball player, but, of course, Roger and Evelyn could not conceivably have gone to an event so mindless as a basketball game in a high-school gymnasium, so they never once saw him play. Nor did they ever go to see him — although for different reasons — when he was a soldier, stationed at Fort Dix.

Furthermore Roger sensed a certain "depersonalization" in his family's relationships. His father was not what he calls a "back porcher," spinning tales, but rather a raconteur who went directly to the "logical core" of what he was saying. And always, it seemed to him, his parents talked about issues and not people.

As an example he remembers seeing a letter from the Meiklejohns inviting the Baldwins for a weekend. The letter ended by saying how much the Meiklejohns looked forward to seeing them and suggested "this time let's not talk about civil liberties. We want to hear about Roger and Evie instead."

"Well," said young Roger, "I thought to myself, good luck to the Meiklejohns, but I think they're going to have a hard time accomplishing that."

Of the three Baldwin progeny, Helen is the one most directed toward the public problems and liberal concerns to which Roger has devoted his life. As such she is also the most critical of his inconsistencies and of instances when his egalitarianism falls short of her exacting mark. On one occasion he sent her from Puerto Rico, where he was as usual spending the winter, a recent newspaper story about him. Attached to the clipping was a note in which he had commented, "Not a bad job considering the interviewer was an Italian woman from New York." Helen, who is married to an Italian, is a feminist and lives in New York, did not take kindly to the fact that, as she puts it, "the great civil libertarian could manage to slur three minorities in one sentence." Roger, for his part, was so contrite and eager to make amends (as he always is, where Helen is concerned) that he spent the money to phone her from San Juan, full of apologies.

Sometimes Helen also finds in her father an inexplicable lack of reality. When she traveled around the world with him in 1959 she acted as his secretary, and in that capacity she read a letter that Roger had written to Madeleine Doty, whom they were going to see in Geneva. In it he suggested that he thought it best that in front of Helen they not mention their previous relationship. Helen by then was twenty-one years old and had just graduated from Radcliffe. She had known about Madeleine Doty since she was first old enough to look her father up in *Who's Who*. But because Roger himself had never told her about his previous marriage, he assumed his grown daughter knew nothing about it.

However, it should also be noted that in this very private family where people did not talk to each other about other people, Helen did not mention to her father, even after she met Madeleine Doty, that she knew who she was. In fact it was I who told him. "Had it not occurred to you," I asked him, "that Helen would have looked you up in *Who's Who?*"

"No," Roger said, and, as if it answered the entire question, added, "We never had any copies of *Who's Who* lying around the house."

In his own comments about his family's communication habits, Roger says, "I don't ever remember asking Helen or the boys about their likes and dislikes of people. We weren't inclined to discuss that. Evie and I didn't either. We just let appearances speak for themselves. You see, we found that if you promulgate your feelings about people, you can get into trouble. If you keep silent, you don't. And we kept silent."

It is not surprising that such restraint would also make open expressions of emotion difficult.

Roger recalls Evelyn's final illness in 1963. Helen, at the time, was living in Rome. Evelyn was in the hospital, but Roger had not realized how ill she was and had not sent for Helen to come home. Then, one Saturday morning, he had a phone call from the doctor summoning him to the hospital. "When I got there," Roger recalls, "the boys — Carl and Roger — were already there, so I knew something was terribly wrong. The doctor then told us that he'd asked us to come because he had sad news for us. Evelyn was not going to get well. She had cancer. It was a matter of a few weeks or a few months. I remember that neither one of the boys said a word. I know they felt very deeply about their mother but they just — well, somehow they couldn't react to it.

"Helen was different. I phoned her in Rome and told her to

come home, and she was only back a week before her mother died. She was very restrained, of course, but she was able to show how much she was moved by Evie's illness. She was so devoted to her mother and she's so much like her in every way."

"Did Evelyn know the truth herself?"

"No. The morning before she died, Helen and I went in to see her and she said she was feeling quite down with all the radium therapy she was taking. Still she didn't know it was cancer — she called it something different, or the doctor called it something else, I guess. But the next morning, Sunday it was, she called me up and said, 'Oh Bunkle, I'm feeling so low.' And I cheered her up by saying, 'Sweetheart, the doctors say you have to be low before the turn comes. First you sink to a low with this radium therapy and then you turn and you begin to get better.' And thank goodness she believed me. The nurse says she never said anything to indicate she knew the truth before she died that night."

After a moment he added, "But one thing she did say to me a few days before. She said, 'Bunkle, we've got such a nice family and that's such a comfort to me.' "

"And to you too, I'm sure," I said.

"Yes, my family's all right. It's a wonderful family. Seventy per cent of Helen is Evie. She tends to be shy the way her mother was and she conceals it as her mother did under an exterior that may seem a little forbidding at first. Helen's a very positive character. I think sometimes she probably thinks I'm a little stupid. And I wouldn't dream of displeasing her or making any suggestions to her that I didn't think I had a right to make. She might not tell me to mind my business, but she'd make it very clear just the same."

I said I expected that was true of most of our relations with our grown children.

"Well, she's a great girl, but I'm careful with her. An extraordinary girl, and I love her."

Helen, for her part, has created a continuity for her father which, because she is so much her mother's daughter, follows not only in regime but in spirit the life he had with Evelyn. She has absorbed Roger into her own family — her artist husband and her two little girls — maintaining the pattern of weekends at Dellbrook, summers at Windy Gates. Except for the four months he spends each winter in Puerto Rico (and the month or so in summer visiting family, friends and the likes of the Dillons), Roger lives all the time with Helen, who now owns 242 West 11th Street, having bought from her brothers their share of the property. As he did with her mother, Roger pays Helen for his share of the expenses. The house is elegant but worn, cluttered but spacious with its high ceilings and long windows giving onto the hollow block that is Bleeker Gardens.

The basement kitchen is cozy, if untidy. Newspapers, letters and toys are shoved off the table as, with apparent unconcern, excellent meals miraculously appear, prepared mostly by Helen but with Roger often adding his own brand of "camp cooking with a Cordon Bleu touch." Helen is at once brisk, forbearing, irritated and affectionate toward her father. Roger is very much himself — cheerful, demanding, opinionated and tolerant. The rapport between them is evident. Helen treats him like a parent who is sometimes bothersome but never like an *old* parent who is tedious.

In point of fact it is almost impossible for anyone to treat Roger like the ninety-two-year-old man that he is. With his extraordinary ability to "relate" (a word he would hate) to all ages, he himself often seems quite ageless.

Because he is so perennial, I suggested that it might be appropriate to talk a little about a few of today's problems that we had not yet touched on.

"Fine," he said cheerfully. "I always like a contemporary approach."

"All right. Let me try you on one or two questions. For instance, both your wives were feminists. You have always been concerned with the rights of women. What then is your view of today's Women's Liberation Movement?"

"If it's going to accomplish equality I'm all for it."

"Don't you think it will?"

"No, I don't think equality will come about at all as long as we have a society in which men handle the money and women spend it. We'll only have real equality when women have a legal right to an equal share of their husband's income. Men should pay their wives for the work they do at home."

"You say a legal right. Does that mean you think the Equal Rights Amendment will accomplish this?"

"I think it will get rid of the discrimination in favor of men which the law now makes on the assumption that the man is the earning partner and the head of the household."

"Wasn't there a time when the Equal Rights Amendment was looked on almost as a joke — the 'little old ladies in tennis shoes.' "

"Yes, of course. The bill was twenty-five years before the House."

"Then all of a sudden the liberals got behind it."

"Yes, and we at the ACLU did too. We reversed ourselves. We used to take the attitude that the best way to effect equality was to deal with specific issues like equal pay for equal work. In other words not to legislate in general but to legislate in particular. But now we've come around to thinking that the constitutional amendment is worth fighting and fighting hard for."

"Fair enough," I said, and then moving on, I asked, "Now what are your views about today's art?"

"There my answer is very simple," he snapped. "I don't like it. I don't like modern art, or modern music or modern literature. I don't like any of that kind of novelty."

"You amaze me," I said. "I never thought I'd hear Roger Nash Baldwin say anything so uncharacteristic as, 'I don't like novelty.' "

"I'm a classicist," he said stubbornly. "Norman Thomas once said he'd leave modern art to his grandchildren and I feel the same way."

"But have you tried to like it or understand it?"

"Yes, of course I've tried."

"How?"

"I've looked at it. And it offends me. I like my art to be representational. Oh I don't mean picture–post card stuff — though I think that's pretty too. But it has to be more than imitation. Van Gogh is one of my favorites; he had wonderful perceptions. And I love Chinese and Japanese art too; that's representational but it intensifies things."

"What about music?"

"I've listened to the music and I can't bear it. All that dissonance gets me."

"Who have you listened to?"

"Well Honegger and people like that. I tell you I would even have some trouble with Richard Strauss though. I belong to the old school. Brahms, Bach, Beethoven."

"Mozart?"

"Mozart and Wagner. I was a great fan of Wagner. He was my favorite for a long time."

"And does that same attitude apply to architecture?"

"Oh yes — *yes* — if anything that's worse. Just dreadful. The new Boston skyline irritates me beyond end."

"Is it just the high-rises you object to?"

"No. I think most so-called functional architecture takes little or no account of beauty. I don't see any relationship between space and line in modern architecture."

"You're a classicist, Roger, which means you have a high regard for balance and symmetry and order."

"Yes, those are the principles I admire."

"But those are not the principles that govern your life, are they?"

"No they are not," he said, his tone clearly suggesting that that was that.

"All right," I said. "I'll put modern art in your inconsistency column. Now, the Vietnam war? Of course you were against it since you're against all wars."

"Yes, of course I was. But this was different. Because a civil liberties issue arose with the Vietnam war that did not arise with the Korean war or with World Wars One and Two. In the first place it was not constitutionally fought; legally it was not a war but it was a kind of police action. That was number one. And number two was that being unconstitutional and not having the support of any congressional declaration of war, and dividing the country as it did and creating the tremendous opposition that it did there was a civil liberties issue involved. We civil libertarians said you can't use the draft to fight that kind of war; we said, you can't take boys and put them in an unconstitutional war; you can't force them to serve when what you're doing is illegal. And so we made a civil liberties issue out of the Vietnam war and opposed it *as such.*"

"Then you were sympathetic to the young people who demonstrated against the war in the sixties?"

"Yes I was. I thought they were right."

"And how do you respond in general to the young today? Do you, for instance, also have a sympathy for the counter-culture movement?"

"I hope so. I think I have an understanding of it."

"Would you say you had an identification with today's young? I ask that because you have always laid such stress on not sticking to the status quo."

"This is different, however. I cannot identify with the counter-culture young people because they are only negative. They resist values of society like moneymaking, profiteering and getting ahead of the next fellow. They discard all competitive standards. But then they don't offer anything instead."

"And the communes that have grown out of the counter culture?"

"Same thing. They offer no substitutes. In fact they're growing more and more conventional. The young people today are lonely and many of them feel rejected by their families and they need a sense of community, but really they're not trying to be anything except a group that lives together and works within the framework of our capitalist society. They don't challenge the institution of capitalism. They live off of it."

"I seem to remember that you were once very interested in that early commune, Brook Farm, weren't you?"

"Yes, I was. I wrote a paper on Brook Farm for my summer school course in 1906. It was the earliest experiment of that kind that I knew of — almost a hundred years ago. I used to hear my parents talk about it. Brook Farm was also a counter culture of sorts, based on high thinking and simple living. But their support also came from the outside, so they didn't have any more of an alternative to the capitalist system than the young people do today."

"Suppose you were twenty years old today. Do you think you would be one of them, living in a commune?"

"No, no, no." He sounded horrified. "I most certainly would not. You must remember, I have always lived inside the system. And I have always been a pretty staunch adherent of the values I was raised with. I never challenged the capitalist system as such."

"Now, Roger, I can't let you get away with saying that. You may not like to be reminded of it, but you did say — and write — 'Communism is the goal.' "

He was not in the least abashed. "Whatever ideas I had about socialism or anarchism or communism were all for the future," he said matter-of-factly. "They were not for now. I lived within the system and worked in it. I always hoped it would change and maybe change in the direction of those ideas I had. I may have challenged the morals of capitalism but I never challenged its existence or its practicability. It works. And you must remember the ACLU has lived and still lives off the capitalistic system. Even today my income — which is my pension from the ACLU — depends on people having the profits of the capitalist system."

"I wonder if you had heard someone in the 1920's saying what you are saying right now, what would you have thought."

"The question you're really asking is whether I've changed or whether the situation has changed. And I tell you that events — the events of history that I've lived through in the past fifty years — have changed the situation altogether. And I say that today I have the very same values I had in the 1920's."

"But don't you consider that you perhaps have pulled away a little from the radical views you held in the past?"

"Not at all. I'm just as radical as ever in the sense that underlying all this socialism and communism and anarchism — labels that people put on movements and ideas — lies one single thought: that mankind has got to learn to get along with each other. I would do anything that I could to get rid of greed and power. And I think you have to take very radical measures to get rid of something that has dominated the lives of people for centuries. The Christian ethic of love is the best way I know, even if it hasn't worked for two thousand years. People believe you can't turn the other cheek and get anywhere, you can't love your neighbor and get anyplace. But those are still the right doctrines and I call them the most radical doctrines of all."

I nodded, aware that there was considerable justification in what he was saying. Certainly he had always held instinctively to the Yankee and Unitarian values that were his heritage. And yet over and over again he had been willing to take contrary views and to put himself in an exposed position where he had indeed been buffeted by the currents of history.

"I'll give you an example of how things have changed," he went on, now warming to a lighter aspect of his theme. "The other day, right here in Boston I saw a young lady walking down the street in nothing but a bikini — a bikini, mind you. And with her was a terrible-looking fellow with a hairy chest and he had on nothing but bathing trunks and a pair of sneakers. Well, I'll tell you, I'd have arrested the pair of them in a minute for walking down Commonwealth Avenue that way."

"Well, if you had arrested them, Roger, then they could have gone to the ACLU and got freed."

He grinned. "Fortunately, they could have, yes."

I asked him for his reactions to the morals of today's young. Did he object to everyone sleeping with everyone else. No, emphatically, he did not object, his only reservation being that he thought boys and girls living together in the same college dormitory was a mistake. "You go to college to learn something. You don't go to college to make love."

"But can't you do both?"

"I don't think you can do very much of both and still do either very well."

"Speaking of youth," I began —

"I thought we were speaking of sex," Roger picked me up alertly.

"We were. Would you rather go on talking about that?"

"No, I'm afraid not, not at my age. Except maybe to say that I'm reminded of what Justice Holmes said on the subject at ninety."

"Which was?"

" 'Oh to be seventy.' But go on. You were going to ask me something more about youth."

"As a matter of fact, I wasn't. I was going to ask you about the secret of old age."

"Now that's quite a question."

"Would you care to take a shot at answering it?"

"Sure I would. And first I'd have to say that my health has been my best asset in that department. I've had a few illnesses that were serious enough to bring me to death's door, but happily that door was locked each time I knocked. The most recent was when I had pneumonia not so long ago. I was pretty sick, but I got over the physical problems quite easily. I was still a little weak and tired but my real problem was that I seemed to have lost my sense of commitment. For a while there I didn't give a damn whether school kept or not. But then finally I woke up one day and decided — well, now I think school *should* keep."

"So that's one ingredient?"

"Yes, commitment, and never being bored. You know, Peggy, I wake up every morning and know it's going to be interesting. I'm not really Dr. Pangloss, although I may sound like him at times, but it's not just that I keep thinking that all is for the best in this best of all possible worlds, but that I think every day is an adventure. I've never had to ask myself what to do next, because my itch is always for action. I remember an old aunt of mine who was just as chipper and lively at eighty as she was as a youngster. And when I asked her what *her* secret was, she said, 'Oh, I just get ahold of some unpopular cause and hang on.' "

I looked at this man with whom I had spent so many hours. Wrinkled yes, and increasingly deaf and sometimes a little slow to rise from a chair, but otherwise without physical or mental impairment. And I thought how that "itch for action" of his had manifested itself for the better part of this century, and in how many ways that we had not even talked about: his deep concern for the statehood of Puerto Rico and for the problems of the Virgin Islands, for example; in his twelve-year participation as a member of the visiting committee in economics at Harvard University; in his lifelong — and often contentious — association with the Audubon Society.

And I thought of the causes, popular and unpopular, that he had not only "got ahold of," but nurtured. How many organizations — again, many that we had not ever discussed — had he endowed not only with his good name but with his conviction, his talents and his energies. He was an organizer, an operator, and in some eyes a manipulator; for all his undoubted dedication, perhaps never truly a *driven* man, but always a driving man.

"In the long run, Roger, wouldn't you have to say your enduring cause has really been the ACLU?"

"Of course, of course. No question about it. And for a very simple reason."

"Because it was yours. You invented it?"

"No, that's not the reason. Not at all. The reason is because no fight for civil liberties ever stays won. So I always had to stick with it. I could never quit."

"Suppose, instead, you had had a cause that came to a neat ending?"

"Then I'd have had to find another cause — without an ending. After all, I'm a crusader and crusaders don't stop."

"Have you ever once said to yourself, 'After all, I'm ninety-two years old. I've done my part?' "

"No never. I've said to myself, 'I'm ninety-two years old and I've reached the biblical age when men are supposed to be finished.' "

"And what have you answered yourself?"

"That I feel no more finished now than I did when I started."

Note on the Sources

Index

Note on the Sources

All the Roger Baldwin quotations, unless otherwise attributed, derive from my extensive series of interviews with him and from his written memoranda in response to my general and specific questions.

All documents (letters, speeches, press releases and clippings, published and unpublished articles) unless otherwise identified are in the Roger Baldwin Papers at the Firestone Library of Princeton University. The letters and excerpts from his diary that appear in Chapters 1 and 2 are from Roger Baldwin's own memorabilia.

The Madeleine Doty material is in the Sophia Smith Collection at Smith College, except for the letter quoted in Chapter 15, which is in the Roger Baldwin Papers at Princeton.

Each of the several quotations taken from Roger Baldwin's Oral History — a part of the Oral History Collection at Columbia University — is acknowledged in the text, as are all the secondary sources.

Index

Addams, Jane, 45, 69, 71, 72, 104, 128, 152; and AUAM, 66–67, 120; description of, 52–53
Alcott Family, 4
Ali, Shaukat, 145
Alsberg, Henry, 140
American Civil Liberties Union, 54, 62, 125, 155, 198, 241–243, 262, 288–289, 291; attitudes of board toward National Labor Relations Act, 193–194, 217–218; censorship cases, 256–260; composition of first board of directors, 126–137, 253; defends reactionaries, 215–216; and Elizabeth Gurley Flynn, 223–236; and E.R.A., 285–286; Ford case, 216–219; founded, 124; Jehovah's Witnesses case, 221–222; and McCarthyism, 263–264; office set-up, 156–157; Paterson, N.J. case, 159–163; reaction to World War II and internment of Japanese-Americans, 237–241; relations with U.S. Presidents, 253–256; Roger Baldwin's retirement from, 264–270; role of, in late 1920s, 174; Scopes case, 163–168; statement of purpose, 128; test cases, 157–158; and the United Front, 213–214; ACLU (mentioned), 138–140, 168–169, 180, 205, 208, 271
American Federation of Labor (A. F. of L.), 119, 224
American Fund for Public Service, 148–150. *See also* Garland, Charles
American Mercury, 259, 259n
American Union Against Militarism (AUAM), 66, 74, 129; after outbreak of World War I, 69–72; conflict over Bureau of Conscientious Objectors, 72–73; genesis of, 67–68
Amnesty International, 140
Anti-evolution act (Tennessee), 164
Asbury, Herbert, 259

Associated Silk Workers, 159–160
Association for Improving the Condition of the Poor (AICP), 46
Astor, Vincent, 220
Atkins, Zoë, 31, 59, 62
Atlantic Monthly, 156
Audubon Society, 291
Auerbach, Jerome S., 218

Bailey, Forest, 174
Baker, Harvey H., 36
Baker, Newton D., 70, 75
Balch, Emily, 68, 70, 73, 152
Balch, Mrs., 22
Baldwin, Belle (aunt), 42, 207
Baldwin, Carl (stepson), 206, 249; recollections of Roger Baldwin, 279–283
Baldwin, Deborah (sister) (Mrs. Roger Thomas), 2, 23–26
Baldwin, Frances (sister-in-law), 115
Baldwin, Frank Fenno (father), 1, 7, 12–13, 22, 39, 191; joins family in Europe, 24; letters to Roger Baldwin in jail, 106–107; relations with Roger Baldwin, 20–21; separates from wife, 26–27
Baldwin, Helen (daughter) (Mrs. P. Mannoni), 13, 207, 212, 249; makes home for Roger Baldwin, 212, 284–285; Roger Baldwin's feelings for, 284; recollections of Roger Baldwin, 279–284
Baldwin, Herbert (brother), 2, 15, 23–26, 56, 109, 115, 181
Baldwin, Lucy Nash (mother), 1, 23–27, 115; attitudes of, 7, 12, 13; letters from Roger Baldwin to, 176, 183, 185–186; writes Madeline Doty about Roger Baldwin, 121
Baldwin, Margaret (sister), 2, 23–26
Baldwin, Robert (brother), 2–3, 6, 15, 23–26, 109, 115
Baldwin, Roger:
    birth of, 1; family background,

Rabb, Max, 255
Ramapo River, 212
Rankin, Jeannette, 127
Rappelyea, G. W., 164
Rauh, Ida, 89
Rauschenbush, Steve, 206, 210, 281
Redding, Louis, 162–163
Reed, John, 111
Reedy, William Marion, 60, 61, 62;
  editor, *Reedy's Mirror,* 31
Reissig, Herman, 202n, 203
Reitman, Alan, 226
Remick, Jack, 28
Revolutionary Pamphlets, 65
Rice, Sedgwick, 76
Roach, John, 255
Rome, 25
Roosevelt, Eleanor, 241, 275–276
Roosevelt, Franklin D., 134, 193–194,
  214–215, 238–239; and civil liber-
  ties, 253, 254–256
Roosevelt, Theodore, 16, 49
Rosenwald, Julius, 53
Royce, Josiah, 16
Russia. *See* USSR
Russian Reconstruction Farms, 183
Russian Revolution, 124, 183, 262
Ryan, (Monsignor), 158
Ryman, Charlotte M., 9–12, 23–24

Sacco, Dante, 170
Sacco, Nicola, 169–171
Sacco, Rose, 170
Sacco-Vanzetti case, 168–172
St. Louis, Mo., 27–28, 48, 55; clubs in,
  56, 59–60; city club, 49, 63, 253;
  description of, 30–32; new charter
  for, 47–48; race relations in, 50–51
St. Louis Post Dispatch, 31, 48, 65
Salvemini, Gastano, 272
Sanger, Margaret, 54–55, 241
Santayana, 16
Sayre, John Nevin, 131, 254
Schneiderman, Rose, 127
Schubert, Fritz, 181–182
Scituate, Mass., 1
Scopes case, 163–168
Scopes, John Thomas, 164–167
Scudder, Vida, 135
Sears, Francis P., Jr., 14
Sedition Acts, 260
Self-Culture Hall (settlement house),
  27–28, 30, 32, 36, 60
Seymour, Whitney North, 240
Shaler, Nathaniel S., 16
Shaukat, Ali, 145
Sherry Netherlands, 220

"Shogun and Emperor," 251
Siberia, 180–181
Simmons, H. Austin, 112
Sinclair, Upton, 170–171
Singh, J. J., 148
Single Tax. *See* George, Henry
Simpson, William, 123
Skvirsky, Boris, 186
Smedley, Agnes, 144–145, 148
Smith, Gerald L. K., 215–216
Smith, Luther E., 48
Smith Act, 260
Smoot, Reed, 256
Snyder, Alan, 115
Socialist Labor party, 100, 193
Socialist party, 109–111, 132, 140,
  197–200, 228
Solzhenitsyn, Alexander, 230
Soviet Russia Today, 190–192, 190n,
  215, 251
Soviet Union. *See* USSR
Spanish Loyalists, 202–203
Spanish Refugee Relief Campaign,
  202–204, 205
Stanford, Mary, 136
Starr, Mark, 246
Stedman, Seymour, 133
Steffens, Lincoln, 16, 44–45
Stephens, Doris, 89
Stevenson, Archie, 83–85
Stix, Charles, 48
Stokes, Anson Phelps, 78, 136
Stokes, Graham Phelps, 136
Stokes, Helen Phelps, 74–75, 128,
  136
Stokes, Rose Pastor, 78, 91, 136
Stoltz, Otto (Toto), 37–39, 77–78, 98,
  119, 135; death of, 206–209
Stone, Harlan, 222, 254
Stopes, Marie, 257
Strange Fruit (Lillian Smith), 258
Strong, Anna Louise, 42–43, 107
Sunderland, J. T., 145
Supreme Commander Allied Powers
  (SCAP) Headquarters, 241, 243–
  244
Supreme Court, U.S., 130, 164–167,
  194, 219, 238, 260, 267; Jehovah's
  Witnesses decision, 222; and ob-
  scenity, 257–258
Survey Magazine, 67, 236

Taft, William Howard, 49
Taylor, Graham, 53
Tennessee Supreme Court, 167
Thirty Years Later (Harvard Class of
  1905 Report), 192, 193